Russian

Political

Thought

Russian
Political
Thought

A Concise History

S. V. Utechin

FREDERICK A. PRAEGER, *Publisher*

New York · London

FREDERICK A. PRAEGER, PUBLISHER
64 UNIVERSITY PLACE, NEW YORK 3, N.Y., U.S.A.
77–79 CHARLOTTE STREET, LONDON W. 1, ENGLAND

Published in the United States of America in 1964 by
Frederick A. Praeger, Inc., Publisher

This book is Number 140 in the series of
Praeger Publications in Russian History and World Communism

Manufactured in the United States of America

CONTENTS

Preface

THIS brief survey of the history of Russian political thought is primarily intended for students of politics rather than of Russian history, and no more than a very elementary knowledge of the latter on the part of the reader is assumed (nor is any familiarity with the Russian language). It may also perhaps be of use to those who have not made politics their special field of study yet are interested in present-day Russian political thought and would like to know more about its historical roots. I am well aware of the shortcomings of this work, and the only excuse for its appearance is the complete absence of English-language textbooks on the subject.

The problem of transliteration of Russian names has been solved by a compromise between the requirements of strict scholarship and those of convenience for the reader unfamiliar with Russian. The system adopted is basically the British Standard one, except that "y" has been used instead of "ii" in surname endings, and in cases where there is a traditional English spelling this has been retained (e.g., Tolstoy, Zinoviev).

In recording my gratitude to people who have helped me in the by no means easy task of producing this book, I must first mention my wife, Patricia Utechin, who has cooperated with me at all stages. I have greatly benefited from discussions with and advice from many friends and colleagues, and I owe an especial debt to those among them who have been kind enough to read the whole book, or parts of it, in proof: Dr. J. L. Fennell, Mr. D. J. Footman, Mr. Max Hayward, Mr. A. F. Kerensky, Professor D. Obolensky, and Professor L. B. Schapiro; many mistakes have been eliminated thanks to their vigilance, but they cannot be held responsible for any remaining errors of fact or judgment. Thanks are also due to the London School of Economics and Political Science and to St. Antony's College for enabling me to devote a considerable part of my time and energy to work on this book, and to the staffs of the Bodleian Library, the British Library of Political and Economic Science, the British Museum, and the library of St. Antony's College for unfailing efficiency and charm in meeting what were sometimes very out of the way requests; I should especially like to note my good fortune in being able to make use of the Russian Loan Collection of St. Antony's College, which contains much of the source material used. I should like to acknowledge the kindness of the editors and/or publishers of the following books and journals for allowing me to make use of passages from previous writings of mine: *Everyman's Concise Encyclopaedia of Russia* (J. M. Dent & Sons, London; E. P. Dutton & Co., New York); *Revisionism,* ed. by Leopold Labedz (George Allen & Unwin, London; Frederick A. Praeger, New York); *St. Antony's Papers* (Chatto & Windus, Ltd., London); *Soviet Studies* (Basil Blackwell, Oxford); *The Twentieth Century;* and Pantheon Books, for permission to quote from their edition of *Doctor Zhivago* by Boris Pasternak. Finally, no author could ask for a more patient and encouraging publisher than Mr. Frederick Praeger or a more sympathetic and tactful editor than Mrs. Jean Steinberg.

S. V. UTECHIN

St. Antony's College, Oxford
July, 1963

INTRODUCTION

POLITICAL thought is concerned with the ways in which people live together in society and in particular with the structure and functioning of public authority. There are different ways of thinking about these matters. One can analyze the meaning of such concepts as "individual," "society," "private," "public," "authority," "state," "government," "law," etc., or think of how people ought to live with each other and how public authority ought to be constructed and ought to function—these are the approaches of political philosophy. One may try to establish how in fact people live together and authority functions in particular societies—this is the approach of political science. Finally, one may be concerned with one's own participation in political life —and this is the art of politics. In order to acquire a good idea of the political thought of a people in the course of its history it is obviously desirable to study the results of all three approaches: the speculations of that country's political philosophers, the findings of its political scientists, and the activities of its politicians.

The main source of our knowledge of what other people have thought are their own utterances on the subject that have in one form or another been recorded. This would be an easy source if people had a perfect understanding of their own minds and were always able and determined to tell others "the truth, the whole truth, and nothing but the truth." Unfortunately, self-deception and inability or unwillingness to convey one's thoughts correctly are by no means uncommon. The question of self-deception can hardly arise with *bona fide* philosophers and political scientists, and they may be absolved from the suspicion of deliberate deception of others. But for a variety of external reasons (censorship, for example), they may not be able to express themselves as frankly or fully as they might wish, and in such cases the student must try to reconstruct the full meaning for himself. The case of practical politicians is far more complicated: they may easily misunderstand their own motives and intentions, they may be incapable of conveying them clearly or be prevented by external circumstances from doing so, or they may wish to deceive. They may even choose not to say anything at all, but simply to act, so that their thinking has to be deduced from their activities. The difficulties for the student are further increased when, as has often happened, a person combines two, or even all three, approaches to political thought. When, for example, a political philosopher produces a study of political behavior, the question arises of the extent to which a piece of writing that purports to be a study of what is, is in fact designed to convey the author's ideas of what ought to be. Similarly, a politician concerned with achieving a practical effect may choose as his means a medium which appears to be a philosophical treatise or a scientific study. And in so doing he may want to mislead the public about the nature of the work, or, on the contrary, want them to realize its true nature of political appeal or command but to pretend that they accept it at its face value. The same applies, *mutatis mutandis,* to the actions of politicians. As a result of all these complications, the sources that the student of political thought has to deal with fall into three categories, according to what they were intended to be: (1) genuine, that is, words or actions which are what they appear to be; (2) genuinely deceptive, that is, those which are not what they appear to be but were meant to be taken for what they appear to be; and (3) apparently deceptive, that is, those that are not what they appear to be and were not intended to be taken as such.

The relative importance in a given period or for a particular trend of political thought of one or another of the three approaches—philosophical, scientific, or practical—and of one or another category of sources may and does in fact differ. It is therefore understandable that a general survey of the history of political thought in a particular country may look somewhat uneven and untidy. Political life is untidy, and an attempt to present its reflection in political thought as a streamlined process would be made at the expense of reality; conversely, the very unevenness and diversity of the material presented may help to convey a feeling of the manifold ways in which people have thought about political matters.

If I attempt to write a historical survey of Russian political thought, I must think that there is a reasonably clearly definable body of thought that can be described as Russian. How is such a body of thought to be defined? Is it those thoughts that can be found only in Russia, and nowhere else? Such a definition would not be very helpful, since it would demand a scrutiny of the thought in every other country in the world in order to make up a list of thoughts that have occurred elsewhere and can therefore not be considered as Russian. But even if such an enterprise were feasible, it would hardly be worth while, for the residue of peculiarly "Russian" thoughts would probably be very small and would almost certainly be confined to minor points. The main problems of political life are by their very nature such that they are either universal or at least relevant for more than one people, and particular ways of approaching these problems are seldom confined to one country. It is more sensible to define Russian political thought as the sum total of what Russian people have in fact thought about political matters in the course of their history. Most of this Russia would share with some other countries, and for a better understanding both of the development of Russian thought itself and of its place in the political thought of mankind it is useful to put it into the context of a wider body of thought.

The question of what this larger whole should be has itself been one of the main preoccupations of Russian political thinkers, and it has received different answers. Before the eighteenth century, the obvious frame of reference was the Orthodox Christian thought, which essentially meant Byzantine thought. Rationalist thinkers of the eighteenth century in principle took the whole of humanity as their frame of reference, but since civilized humanity was identified with Europe, it was in practice European developments (exemplified by the more advanced Western Europe) in the context of which Russia was thought to be meaningful. This "Westernist" approach has on the whole been prevalent in Russian writings during the nineteenth and twentieth centuries, though there have also been several schools of thought that postulated essential differences between Russian and West European political thinking. According to the Slavophiles, Russians

had a spiritual make-up which was different from that of the
West Europeans and which they to some extent shared with other
Slavs. The Eurasian school advanced the view that Russia formed
a peculiar Eurasian cultural entity, neither European nor wholly
Asian, but nearer to Asia than to Europe. Both these schools considered political thought to be one of the main fields in which
the peculiarity of Russia expressed itself. The Communists, although generally following in the wake of Westernism, have
asserted that with the appearance of Leninism, Russian political
thought had overtaken West European and American thought.
Most foreign scholars have also adhered to one or another of these
Russian schools. A more balanced view has been suggested recently by Professor Dimitri Obolensky, who has argued—it seems
to me convincingly—that historically and culturally Russia belonged to Europe, within which it formed, together with those
Balkan countries where Orthodox Christianity has been the prevalent religion (Greece, Bulgaria, Serbia, and Rumania), a special
subdivision which he proposes to call Eastern Europe.* Common
to all countries belonging to this subdivision are the predominant
Byzantine influence before the eighteenth or nineteenth century
and the Westernization that followed it. The problem of finding
a larger whole to which Russian political thought can be related
thus solves itself fairly easily. Such a larger whole is the European
Christian and post-Christian thought. Since Russian thought during the last two and a half centuries has developed with unceasing
references to West European thinkers and trends, we merely have
to follow suit in dealing with this period. But comparisons with
West European thought are also meaningful when dealing with
earlier times, for, in the words of the late Sir Ernest Barker,
"Byzantine political thought . . . does not differ in kind (though
it may differ in detail and emphasis) from other forms and examples of political speculation,"† especially, one might add, from
the political thought of medieval Western Europe. The reasons

* Dimitri Obolensky, "Russia's Byzantine Heritage," *Oxford Slavonic Papers,* I, reprinted in Sidney Harcave (ed.), *Readings in Russian History* (New
York: Thomas Y. Crowell Company, 1962), I.

† Ernest Barker (ed. and trans.), *Social and Political Thought in Byzantium
from Justinian I to the Last Palaeologues. Passages from Byzantine writers
and documents* (London and New York: Oxford University Press, 1957), p.
vii.

for this similarity are clear. Political theory is variously described
as stemming from jurisprudence (Maitland*) or from the study of
history (Barker†). Now Byzantine law was Roman law, and the
same Roman law, codified in Byzantium, was to a considerable
extent effective in medieval Western Europe and in Russia. The
other component of medieval law was the customary law, whose
West European and Russian varieties do not differ greatly. As
for historical studies, what concerned medieval thinkers most—
both in Byzantium and Russia and in Western Europe—were
Biblical history and the history of the Macedonian and Roman
empires.

It is not surprising, therefore, that on the whole, Russian political thought is strikingly similar to that of Western Europe. Let
us take as an example one of the central notions of medieval
Western Europe, the notion of kingship: "Ideas inherited from
the Germanic kingship hovered about the king," writes a recent
authority.‡ "He was the leader of a people, especially in war.
His claim to authority was based at least partly on his people's
consent, as illustrated in the still-lingering rites of election. . . .
The idea that kingship rested on consent was fused with two
other ideas: the idea that certain families had an hereditary claim
to the kingship and the idea . . . that kingship rested on divine
institution. In a rather vague way, the king was felt to be a sort
of trustee under the common law for the common interests of his
people, who might appropriately depose him if he proved false
to his task." All these ideas may be found in medieval Russia.
The forms and methods of thought were also similar. Writing
about the West European theories of the ninth to thirteenth
centuries, Dunning thus described "the method characteristic of
all reasoning of these centuries": "A certain few precedents of
profane history were appealed to, but beyond this the Bible and
the teachings of the church fathers were held to be conclusive"§
—this description is equally applicable to medieval Russian writ-

* F. W. Maitland (trans.), O. Gierke's *Political Theories of the Middle Ages*
(London: Cambridge University Press, 1900), p. viii.

† Barker, *op. cit.*, p. 20.

‡ Ewart Lewis, *Medieval Political Ideas* (New York: Alfred A. Knopf, 1954),
I, 141.

§ William A. Dunning, *A History of Political Theories Ancient and Medieval* (New York: The Macmillan Company, 1930), p. 163.

ings. Going on to the fourteenth century, the same historian says that "in form and method the philosophical literature of the fourteenth century retains and intensifies the characteristics impressed upon it by the preceding scholastics. The dogmas of authority are cited and are refuted by opposing dogmas; all literature, sacred and profane, is ransacked for fables that can be exploited to sustain a cause."* Again, a student of Russian thought immediately recognizes a very familiar picture. Finally, the types of people whose thoughts are of particular interest to the student: Maitland wrote of Gierke's list of authorities, "In Dr. Gierke's list of medieval publicists, besides the divines and schoolmen, stand great popes, great lawyers, great reformers, men who were clothing concrete projects in abstract vesture, men who fashioned the facts as well as the theories of their time."† And Barker in his book on Byzantine thought: "I have drawn on legal documents and administrative records, as well as on literary works, in the selection of the passages here translated."‡ The same types of authors and kinds of texts are considered in this book.

All this does not mean that there are no significant features distinguishing Russian from West European thought. There are many, especially in medieval thought. Thus, ideas stemming from the papal claim to secular authority are almost absent in Russia. On the other hand, the idea widely held in nineteenth-century Russia of the social and political importance of the Russian village commune has no equivalent in modern West European thought. And the problems that arose from the eighteenth century onwards in connection with the cultural, political, and economic impact of Western Europe, so prominent in Russian thinking, have no real counterpart in the West; in this respect, Russian thinking may be studied as an early example of what takes place in an "underdeveloped" country that is undergoing the process of Westernization. Russian thought developed on the whole more slowly than the West European: whereas in Western Europe the fifteenth century was the last in which the general

* *Ibid.,* p. 220.
† Maitland, *op. cit.,* pp. vii–viii.
‡ Barker, *op. cit.,* p. viii.

lines of political philosophy were essentially medieval,* in Russia this kind of reasoning continued at least for another century. However, the time lag in the appearance of individual ideas was not uniform, and in a few cases the Russians even seem to have been ahead of Western Europe: e.g., strong national consciousness developed earlier in Russia than in the major West European countries, as did the idea of the sovereignty of the lay legislature in matters of Church organization. The legal profession has never been as developed in Russia as in Western Europe and the contribution of lawyers to political thought was comparatively small in the Middle Ages, though this deficiency was made up in the nineteenth century. But most of these are differences of detail and emphasis.

An attempt is made in this book to present a survey of the history of Russian political thought from the inception of the recorded Russian political tradition to the present day. The bulk of the book is devoted to the last two and a half centuries, while the first two chapters, dealing with medieval and Muscovite Russia respectively, have an introductory character: they are intended to give some conception of the stock of political ideas current in Russia before the beginning of her close contact with Western Europe. Similarities with thinking in the West, whether they can be identified as borrowing or not, are usually pointed out, both to put the Russian thought in perspective and to clarify it by comparing it with material that is likely to be better known to most readers. Within the limits imposed both by the size of the book and its purpose as an introduction to the subject, an attempt is made to show the diversity (both in form and substance) of political thinking in Russia rather than to concentrate on a few trends; such a concentration, besides not doing justice to the many Russian thinkers and streams of thought, would involve a greater risk of arbitrary selection; the wider one casts the net, the less likely is it that something of importance will be missed. This procedure has, of course, its obverse side—much of the material must be treated rather cursorily. Theories that have recently been extensively treated in English-language literature receive comparatively little attention, and vice versa. This may have

---

* Dunning, *op. cit.*, p. 280.

upset the kind of balance that a reader familiar with this literature might expect, but I believe that as a result such a reader will
gain in the breadth of his knowledge of Russian thought. Two
arbitrary decisions have been made, mainly for reasons of space,
concerning the scope of the book. Foreigners who were not themselves the products of Russian society and Russian education have
been omitted, even though they may have written in Russian;
secondly, political thought among the national minorities has
not been dealt with, except for instances where such thought was
concerned with general Russian problems rather than specifically
local ones—thus all separatist movements have been omitted,
while federalist tendencies have been included.

The material is arranged partly in chronological order, partly
by doctrines, and partly by political tendencies. Thus the chapter
on Muscovite Russia is singled out on the basis of chronology but
the sections within it by political tendencies; the chapters on
Slavophilism and Westernism are both singled out on the basis
of doctrine, but the sections of the former are also by doctrine
while those of the latter are by political tendency.

There is little that is original in this book. Although I have
read most of the writings I deal with, I have as a rule followed
the interpretations of these writings given by the accepted authorities. Only where the subject matter falls within my own
particular field of interest or where I have been unable to agree
with the accepted authorities is this not the case. The book as a
whole, however, is something of a novelty, since to my knowledge
no attempt has hitherto been made by one author to survey in
one small volume the whole history of Russian political thought.

Russian
Political
Thought

1. Medieval Russia

Public Authority in the Pre-Christian Era
(Ninth and Tenth Centuries)

THE OLDEST known written Russian source that sheds some light on contemporary Russian political thought—the text of a treaty concluded by the Kievan Prince Igor with Byzantium in 944—belongs to the middle of the tenth century. But the symbiosis of the Eastern Slav, Finnish, Turkic, and Norman ethnic and social elements, which was the earliest form of the medieval Russian nation, was a whole century older, and for that period we have to rely entirely upon such clues as are provided by the known facts of political practice and, to the extent to which practice had hardened into customary law, on the implications of that law. Our sources here, apart from archeological and linguistic evidence, are Byzantine and Arabic writers and, above all, the information derived from the oral tradition preserved in the oldest Russian chronicles.

The ninth and tenth centuries witnessed the last stages of a transition from tribal structure among the Eastern Slavs, with tribal princelings (the names of several such princelings are recorded from the fourth century onward) exercising some measure of authority, principally military, to a system that has been compared by an erudite and thoughtful scholar (the late P. B. Struve) to the structure of ancient Greece at the time of the Athenian hegemony. With tribal areas clearly defined, each tribe became more of a territorial than an ethnic unit. The main town of a tribal area, the residence of the prince with his retinue and of the wealthiest and most powerful families with their large households, became a kind of polis dominating the whole area, and the areas themselves began to be called by the names of their chief cities rather than by the tribal names of their inhabitants. Similarity with the Greek polis was not confined to the relation of the city with the surrounding countryside and the smaller towns there. The political situation in the city itself was determined by the relations between two authorities, each acting in its own right—the prince and the assembly of free citizens. The assembly (*veche*) was usually dominated by the upper stratum of the citizenry, the "major" people, distinguished by their wealth and the large number of their dependents both in the city and among the peasantry in the surrounding countryside.

Rather in the same way as a city dominated a particular area, a big and wealthy city with a powerful prince might establish its hegemony over a number of other cities. Political groupings larger than tribes had been known among the Eastern Slavs before the ninth century—they seem to have been in the nature of tribal alliances for military purposes under the leadership of a strong tribe. In the middle of the ninth century, the capital of the tribal area of the Slovenes, Novgorod, situated at the northern end of the international trade route from the Baltic Sea to Constantinople via the river Dnieper, acquired a predominant position among the northern Slav and the neighboring Finnish tribes. But by the end of the same century, Kiev, the capital of the most advanced of the southern tribes (the Polians), situated near the southern end of the Dnieper trade route, had become the foremost political center, "the mother of Russian cities" as Prince Oleg is said to have called it when, in 882, he transferred his residence from Novgorod to Kiev. The hegemony of Kiev lasted for almost three centuries, well beyond the chronological limits of the period we are concerned with now.

Prince Oleg was not an indigenous Slav tribal prince. He belonged to the clan of the Scandinavian *konung* Rurik who, according to the earliest Russian chronicle (dating probably from the end of the tenth century), accepted an invitation from the northern Slavs and Finns and established himself as a prince in Novgorod in 862. Members of Rurik's clan gradually replaced the Slav tribal princes in all the main cities of Russia. This process of take-over established an exclusive claim for Rurik's descendants to princely authority in the "Russian land," which was almost universally recognized as their exclusive right until the fourteenth century. Later the house of Rurikids ruled in Moscow as grand princes and czars until 1598.

The hegemony of Kiev and its princes* over the other Russian territories expressed itself in practice chiefly in collecting a yearly tribute from them and in military leadership. The treaties with Byzantium concluded by Oleg and Igor (in 911 and 944, respectively) are mainly concerned with the protection of Russo-Byzantine trade, showing that such protection was considered an important function of the Kievan princes. The treaties also contain valuable information on the internal political conditions in Russia. The Russian delegations that negotiated them included not only representatives of the princes themselves, but also personal representatives of a number of their relatives and of some of the magnates who did not belong to the princely family. Thus it seems that the magnates, who had their own retinues, were so strong and influential that they could successfully claim direct participation in conducting the foreign affairs of the country.

One more aspect of political practice in the tenth century deserves attention: religious policy. There were many Christians among the inhabitants of the chief cities, particularly Kiev, since at least the middle of the ninth century, and at first there was apparently no political or social discrimination against them. Thus some members of the Russian delegations to Byzantium were Christians, and upon the conclusion of the treaties they kissed the cross while their pagan colleagues swore before an image of Perun, the Slav equivalent of Zeus. Toward the end of the century, Prince Vladimir, apparently in an attempt to consolidate tribal cults into a kind of state religion, built a pantheon in Kiev with images of the various pagan gods. Christianity was excluded from this syncretic official cult, but the whole enterprise seems to have been a failure, and the same Prince Vladimir soon embraced Christianity and in 988 made it the state religion. According to the chronicles, the new faith was chosen by the

---

* "Prince" is the most common rendering in English of the Russian word *knyaz'*, which is derived from the Scandinavian *konung* (king). In contemporary West European sources, the title *knyaz'* was translated as *rex*. Conversely, the Russians sometimes translated "king" as *knyaz'* (the more usual Russian word for "king," *korol*, is a corruption of the name of Charlemagne).

prince after he had listened to missionaries who in turn extolled Judaism, Christianity in its Byzantine and Roman forms, and Islam. One of the reasons for rejecting Islam is said to have been its prohibition of the consumption of alcohol: "It is Russia's joy to drink," Prince Vladimir said, "we cannot do without it."

The decision in favor of Byzantine Christianity was reinforced by the impressions of the delegation which the prince, together with his retinue and the city elders, had sent to Constantinople: The delegates reported that they had been overwhelmed by the beauty of the Greek liturgy, that they had "not known whether they were on the earth or in heaven."

Political Thought of Christian Kiev
(Eleventh and Twelfth Centuries)

The establishment of Christianity in its Byzantine form decisively influenced Russian political thought from the eleventh until the end of the seventeenth centuries. Two features of Eastern Christianity were especially relevant for the attitudes of medieval Russian thinkers toward political problems. One was the much stronger stress than in the West upon the resurrection rather than upon the sufferings of Christ. "The powerful imagination of the Oriental, combined with the harmonious intellectual clarity of the Greek, allowed the Christian mystic of the East to foresee and anticipate mentally, in this life and on this earth, the ineffable bliss of the coming transfiguration. Through this, he became reconciled to real life; he looked beyond this life and viewed everything not in its present, earthly shape but in its future, transformed, celestial guise."* Another typical and most important feature, clearly connected with the first, was the renunciation by the Church of secular power. This basic attitude of the Church all but eliminated one of the main sources of political controversy and main impulses to political thinking characteristic of medieval Western Europe, and thus, incidentally, made the Russian intellectual tradition the poorer.

The main sources of theoretical inspiration were the Scriptures and the writings of the Fathers of the Church on the one hand,

* N. S. Trubetskoy, "Introduction to the History of Old Russian Literature," *Harvard Slavic Studies*, II, 1954, 95–96.

and the Byzantine political tradition on the other. The relevant texts of the Old Testament were known in Russia in the eleventh and twelfth centuries, but were not used by political writers until the seventeenth century. The teaching of the New Testament on the limitation of secular authority by the law of God was very well known, though its influence was on the whole general rather than specific; only occasionally does one find textual quotations in support of particular political views. As for the Church Fathers, knowledge of their writings in Russia was selective. The teachings of St. John Chrysostom on the institution of princely authority by God, and of Chrysostom and St. Basil the Great on the distinction between a true ruler and a tyrant were well known and very popular in medieval Russia, whereas St. Augustine's *City of God* was not translated until the 1520's. Byzantine governmental practices, law, and political writings provided obvious points of reference, and they were unanimous on one central problem of political theory: the source of the monarch's authority. He was regarded as God's lieutenant upon earth and derived his authority from the ceremony of anointment. But they were not unanimous on the other key problem, that of the limits of the monarch's authority. In Byzantine law and political theory, two standpoints were represented, that of the absolute power of the monarch and that of limitations placed upon his power by the law of God to which he was subject. The Russians were thus unable simply to follow the Byzantine example on this point. As for the citizens' assemblies, there was no lead in the Byzantine sources on how they should be regarded, except the negative one that there was no suggestion of any institutional limitation to the monarch's authority. On interstate relations, however, the Byzantine views were quite clear. There was, according to them, a definite hierarchy of states and their rulers, with the Roman (Byzantine) Christian Empire and its emperor at the apex, the place of each state in the hierarchy being determined by the emperor.

The available sources, which are quite numerous for the eleventh and twelfth centuries, show that the Russians approached the main problems of political theory with a considerable degree of independence and discrimination. The three most outstanding thinkers of this period were St. Vladimir—the Kievan prince who established Christianity as the state religion in 988 and was later canonized; Metropolitan Hilarion; and Prince Vladimir Monomakh. St. Vladimir expressed his idea of a Christian prince in his Church Statute, in which he stated that having consulted the Greek *Nomocanon* (a collection of canon and civil law) he had found that it was "not proper" for a prince to adjudicate over certain offences or to judge Church people, the jurisdiction in both cases properly belonging to the Church. We see here implemented Cicero's idea of justice as rendering to everyone what is his due. Compared to Byzantine law, St. Vladimir even extended the category of people who were to be under the jurisdiction of the Church. Another important aspect is that St. Vladimir recognized his power as being limited by superior norms not issued by him and which he had no authority to alter. Further on in the text of the Statute, he made the point that this limitation was to be binding on all his successors "forever." There was, however, a significant exemption from this basic rule: the limitation of his judicial power applied only in relation to his Christian subjects, there being by implication no such limitation as far as non-Christians were concerned. This somewhat resembles St. Augustine's idea that justice can only exist among a people who worship the true God. St. Vladimir's Statute remained the basis of all subsequent legislation on the judicial powers of the Church for many centuries (in matrimonial matters until 1917).

Metropolitan Hilarion was the first Russian to occupy the Kievan see—the usual practice of the patriarchs of Constantinople was to appoint Greeks. Hilarion's best known work, his *Sermon on Law and Grace,* dating from about 1040, which was much copied and quoted by medieval Russian writers, dealt with a wide range of problems. Starting from a contrast between two spiritual principles of social life—the law given by Moses and the grace brought by Christ, which he identified respectively with slavery and freedom—Hilarion proceeded to draw a picture of the historical development of humanity as a process of the replacement of law by grace and the gradual expansion of the realm of the latter as more and more countries became Christianized. An important aspect of this process was to him the passing of national exclusiveness, since "new wine" required "new skins." It was a matter of great pride that in extending the realm of grace God had not neglected Russia. Russia had deserved this, for even before it had embraced Christianity it had not been a poor and unknown country, but one known and heard about in all corners of the earth. The merit of Christianizing Russia belonged to its great *kagan** Vladimir (and by implication not to the Byzantines), whose feat Hilarion compared to those of the Apostles and of Constantine the Great. Somewhat inconsistently (it would seem to us now) for an advocate of replacing imposed law by received grace, Hilarion, in describing how the whole population of Russia had followed Vladimir in accepting the new faith, referred approvingly to the fact that even those who had not been so inclined had acquiesced because Vladimir's piety was combined with power. In describing Vladimir, Hilarion drew up his ideal of a prince: Vladimir had shepherded his land with justice, courage, and sense. The secular power should actively concern itself with the interests of the faith, respecting at the same time the directions of the Church authorities. A good prince, like Vladimir, was justified in "subjecting to himself all the surrounding countries," some peacefully but others, where necessary, by the sword. The *Sermon* finished with a prayer for Russia, that "as long as the world stands" she should be delivered both from temptation and from the hands of aliens—a prayer that for centuries was repeated in Russian churches at times of crisis.

Three points of outstanding interest emerge from Hilarion's *Sermon*. One is the similarity of his views on the duties of secular power and its relations with the Church to the views of such Western Fathers of the Church as St. Ambrose of Milan and St. Augustine, and the implied rejection of any caesaro-papist tendencies. Secondly, asserting the independence and glory of the Russian state, he by implication rejected the Byzantine claim of su-

---

* *Kagan* (the word is of Hebrew origin) was the title of the rulers of the Khazar state centered on the Lower Volga area. A number of the East Slav tribes had been tributaries of the Khazars in the ninth and tenth centuries, before the establishment of the Rurikids. Kiev had also paid tribute to the Khazars, and the use of the title *kagan* by Hilarion might have reflected the idea that the Kievan princes were the heirs to the authority of the Khazar *kagans*.

zeranity over Russia and consequently the idea of the universal Christian Roman Empire. And thirdly, we see in Hilarion's *Sermon* the beginning of that trend of thought which led to the idea of Holy Russia and to the doctrine of Moscow as the Third Rome.

The arrogance and intolerance of Metropolitan Hilarion toward those who did not share the true faith contrasted sharply with the humility and charity of his contemporary St. Theodosius, one of the founders of the famous Cave monastery in Kiev. Writing to one of the Kievan princes to warn him against close contacts with the Latins, Theodosius nevertheless urged him to "have mercy not only upon those of your own faith, but also those of alien faiths: If you see a man naked or hungry or suffering from winter or misfortune, whether he be a Jew, or a Saracen, or a Bulgarian, or a heretic, or a Latin, or some kind of a pagan—have mercy upon everyone and rescue them from misfortune if you can."

Vladimir Monomakh was a resourceful ruler who, in the late eleventh and early twelfth centuries, succeeded in restoring for a short time some kind of order in a country torn by princely feuds. He left, in his *Instruction* to his children and to "others who might hear it," a summary of his political views. A prince should trust God, be modest, generous, and just, especially to lowly and suffering people. He should be well educated and should continue to educate himself in mature age—here Monomakh gives the example of his father, who had learned five languages. A good prince should be active and industrious, should perform his duties himself, not relying upon officials. Monomakh is quite definite in his views on interprincely relations. Each prince should be content with what has fallen to him through inheritance and should not try to acquire other cities; diversity of fortune is God's will and in accordance with nature—no two human faces are identical, birds inhabit different lands and do not all try to settle in one. Princes are not equal, and the junior must respect the senior and obey him, while equals and juniors must be treated with love and protection. Those who derive inordinate pleasure from the exercise of power should be restrained by other princes. The personal feelings of the prince should not affect his conduct of public affairs—this is evident from Monomakh's letter (appended to the *Instruction*) addressed to a prince who had killed one of Monomakh's sons in battle. The tone of the *Instruction,* rather subdued and sad, contrasts sharply with the festive, triumphant note sounded in Hilarion's *Sermon,* and this is due not only to differences of temperament and occasion. The contrast reflects a profound change of public mood in Russia in the second half of the eleventh century, from the joy and confidence of a victorious, newly united, and Christianized country to the anxiety and uncertainty of a country suffering from internal disaffection, already splitting up into several semi-independent principalities and constantly harassed by a powerful enemy on the southern border, the nomadic Cumans.

Having dealt up to this point with individual thinkers of Christian Kiev, we must now turn to a different source, the chronicles. The eleventh and twelfth centuries were the classical period in the history of Russian chronicle-writing. A chronicle was usually the work of several scholars in succession, each of them incorporating the texts of his predecessors into his own. They were not only a record of historical events, but also of the views of historical personages and of the chroniclers themselves, who never hesitated to add their comment. Thanks to their great popularity and to the relatively stable core of their content (based on the Primary Chronicle compiled by the Kiev monk Nestor, an erudite and judicious scholar), the chronicles have for centuries influenced the political ideas and attitudes of the Russian reading public. Because of the manner of their compilation they were probably the most important single vehicle of the development of a tradition of Russian political thought until the polemical literature of the fifteenth century. Ideas given currency by the eleventh to early thirteenth century chronicles (before the Mongol conquest) add up to an impressive, though rather disjointed, doctrine of Russian Orthodox statehood.

This doctrine has been summarized as follows by the only modern historian to make a thorough study of it, M. V. Shakhmatov: Popular will is not a self-sufficient and final justification for authority; nor is popular will assumed automatically to be just; both the will and the power of the people must be justified by higher principles. Popular will and power must be limited by the necessity of having princely authority, by the prince's public subjective rights, by the obligation of love and obedience to the prince, by the obligation of all people to love and obedience toward each other, by the duty to refrain from committing injustice and sins, and by the responsibility of the people in the face of the punitive power of God and the princes. Force is and must be a component of the prince's power, but princely power must not be naked force—it must take into account the dictates of God's will and of righteousness. Power in general, and consequently the power of the Russian princes, is established by God, and each prince is appointed by God; even their acts issue from God's will. Law and justice should be firmly established in the Russian land, and in particular princes should only claim those seats to which they are entitled either by natural inheritance, by testament, by seniority, by appointment, or by election. The prince must be virtuous, he must love the people, serve them, and die in battle for them. Thus the idea of power put forward by the chroniclers included many elements, the most prominent among them being force, will, hierarchical priority, and moral leadership. The Russian land is a great and glorious country; the Russian people are a people chosen by God and loved by him, a new Israel. The Russian state must be one state, but three different theories were put forward by the chroniclers as to how this unity should be realized. One assumed that the prince of Kiev should be the sole ruler of Russia. A second, that several princes of the same clan should rule simultaneously in different parts of the country as their common inheritance, with the senior prince of the clan sitting in Kiev while junior princes occupied their respective family seats in other cities; the whole should be held together by the authority of the senior prince (the limits of which were differently defined by different chroniclers), by meetings of the princes, and by treaties between them. The third theory stood for a final break-up of the state into hereditary principalities with only a nominal unity.

The political theory of the chroniclers reflected fairly well the constitutional practice of the time. Beside the princes, there were three institutions exercising some public authority during the

Kievan period: citizens' assembly, magnates' council (*boyarskaya duma*), and convention (*snem*). Citizens' assemblies, though they had no fixed composition or rules of procedure, were generally recognized as expressing the will of the population of their cities, and they consistently cited popular will as a sufficient justification of political action. Assemblies of capital cities were usually successful in insisting that the establishment of a new prince was invalid unless he made a contract with the city promising to respect local customs and the rights of the citizens: a prince who broke the contract was likely to be deposed by the assembly. The magnates' council, in its composition and functions, was an exact equivalent of the *curia regis* of West European states. And in general, relations within the princely clan and between princes and their senior retainers were developing in Kievan Russia along lines similar to the feudal system of Western Europe. Conventions were meetings of princes accompanied by their retainers, sometimes with the participation of bishops and of senior officials of the capital city.

Finally, discussing the political thought of Christian Kiev, one cannot neglect its legal code, the *Russian Truth,* the earliest version of which dates from the middle of the eleventh century. It is mainly a codification of customary law, similar in its spirit and in its material norms to the *leges barbarorum* of Western Europe. Its chief interest for our purposes is that it reflected the attitudes of the time toward the different social classes. It fully recognized slavery, providing for compensation to the master in case of the murder of a slave. And a senior member of the princely retinue was protected by a double amount of *wergeld* or of compensation for injury, as compared to a simple freeman.

Novgorodian Republicanism
(Twelfth to Fifteenth Centuries)

The hegemony of Kiev in the political life of Russia lasted until the middle of the twelfth century. After that time, the individual principalities, based in most cases upon the old tribal areas and ruled by different branches of the Rurikid dynasty, acquired complete *de facto* sovereignty. The suzerainty of the Kievan grand princes became nominal and the title itself usually went either to the strongest prince or even to a protégé of his. Fragmentation of political authority engendered two opposite tendencies in political thought—the unitary, which continued the traditional theme of the unity of the Russian land and stressed the common interests and duties of the Russian princes, and the particularist, which laid the stress on the special features and particular interests of individual principalities.

A new institution began to develop toward the end of the twelfth century and at the beginning of the thirteenth. This was the council (*sobor*), a kind of enlarged magnates' council with the participation of clergy, junior retainers, and the common people. Only a few cases of the convocation of such councils before the Mongol conquest are known, but it is interesting to note that they were roughly contemporaneous with the beginnings of the *parlements* in France and of the English Parliament.

But perhaps the most important development in the field of political thought in the late twelfth–early thirteenth centuries was the victory of the republican principle in Novgorod. Throughout the Kievan period, the citizens' assemblies of the capital cities, including Kiev itself, claimed the right to invite and to depose princes, and these claims became particularly insistent in the twelfth century. Only in Novgorod, however, were the citizens able to secure full recognition of this right and to establish a republican form of government under which princes, appointed by the assembly, had scarcely any authority outside the strictly military field. They were subject to a number of stringent regulations in order to prevent attempts on their part to usurp wider powers. Thus they were not allowed to reside in the city of Novgorod or permitted to own land in Novgorodian territories. In the words of the Novgorodian chronicle, the Novgorodians "held their region as God had entrusted it to them, and as for the prince, they kept him according to their will." Thus, theoretically, it was a democracy established by God. The popular will, as expressed through the prevalent party in the assembly, was regarded as the sole source of secular power in the republic. The archbishops, who played an important part in the government of Novgorod, also came to be elected by the assembly. Considered in the light of Church history as a whole, this was a reversal to earlier practice, but in Russia it was an innovation born out of the republican spirit of Novgorod and anticipating the theory on Church government put forward by Marsilius of Padua nearly 200 years later. Proud of their liberties, the citizens called their republic Sovereign Great Novgorod. The parties in the assembly were not stable and usually formed themselves around one or another of the great patrician families of the city, who thus secured for themselves the majority of offices filled by election. But at times parties arose out of a division of opinion on a particular issue or out of different class interests; perhaps the most interesting instance of the latter occurred in 1258, when Mongol officials wished to carry out a census of the city population. According to the chronicle, the "black people" did not want to submit to the census, but the magnates ordered them to submit "because the magnates did good for themselves, but evil for the small people"; this passage can be considered as a direct reflection, rare in medieval political writings, of the views of the poor people.

Republican institutions prevailed in Novgorod throughout the period of its existence as an independent state until it was annexed by Muscovy in 1478. Novgorod's so-called "suburb" Pskov on the northwest frontier of Russia and the Novgorodian colony Vyatka in the northeast of European Russia were also city-republics until annexed by Muscovy in the late fifteenth–early sixteenth centuries. All these northern Russian republics paralleled the contemporaneous city-republics of northern Italy and Germany. After their fall, the republican tradition was taken up by the autonomous Cossack communities, which established themselves along the southern borders of Russia in the sixteenth century and were governed on republican lines until the early eighteenth century. The example of republican Novgorod was also one of the sources of inspiration of the eighteenth–early nineteenth-century Russian radicals.

The Mongol Suzerainty (*1240–1480*) and the Problem of Sovereignty

The conquest of most of Russia by the Mongols (or Tatars, as they were called by the Russians) and the period of Mongol domination that followed had considerable consequences for the de-

velopment of Russian political practices and thought. The impact was twofold. On the one hand, the Mongols facilitated the
process of political fragmentation. They left intact the majority
of the existing principalities, usually confirmed in office the princes
of the various local branches or sub-branches of the Rurikid dynasty, and recognized the claims of various principalities, such as
Vladimir (later Moscow), Galicia, Tver', and Nizhnii Novgorod,
to the status of grand principalities in place of the former single
Grand Principality of Kiev. The Russian grand princes were vassals
of the Khan of the Golden Horde, who in his turn was a vassal of
the Great Khan of Mongolia and China. The fact that a Russian
prince's tenure of office depended on his loyalty to the Khan gave
the whole structure of authority a feudal character. The Russians
translated the title "khan" as "czar,"* the term hitherto reserved
for the Byzantine emperor. On the other hand, the Mongol domination also furnished a strong centralizing impetus. The tribute
that the Mongols instituted was collected first by the Mongol tax-
collectors, and later by the Russian princes acting as agents of the
Mongols, on the basis of population counts, which had been unknown in Russia before. For the purposes of taxation and military conscription (the latter also not previously practiced in Russia), the country was divided into districts with approximately
equal numbers of inhabitants. Mongol troops (consisting partly of
Russian conscripts) stationed at key points throughout the country gave the Russians their first experience of a standing army.
The system of regular overland mail communications, established
by the Mongols for their own needs but manned by Russians, was
yet another centralizing administrative device. When the khans
left the collection of tribute and of internal customs duties to the
princes and made the Grand Prince of Moscow the chief tax-
collector, they greatly enhanced his power in relation to other
princes. Internal political conditions in individual principalities
also underwent significant changes. By the end of the 14th century, citizens' assemblies, which during the first decades after the
Mongol conquest had emerged as the main rallying points of anti-
Mongol sentiment, lost their character of independent political

* The Russian word *tsar'* is a corruption of Caesar (cf. the German
Kaiser).

authorities everywhere except in Polotsk, Smolensk, and the northern republics. However, they remained important as local government bodies and retained the right of petition. The council, a representative institution that had begun to develop in some of the principalities before the conquest, disappeared for three centuries. And it has been suggested that a number of typical features of Muscovite political thought and practice of the sixteenth and seventeenth centuries (the concept of the sovereign as the supreme owner of the whole territory of the state; compulsory service to the sovereign by the magnates, the gentry, and the townspeople; the servitude of the peasants; the importance attached by the magnates to the order of precedence) also evolved under the Mongol influence.

The judiciary was not directly affected by the Mongol conquest, but the indirect impact of Mongol domination was important. The death penalty and corporal punishment were introduced into the practice of Russian courts in the 14th century under Mongol influence. Torture as a means of investigation was also legalised, except in the republic of Pskov which distinguished itself in this respect both from the rest of Russia and from contemporary Western Europe.

There were also further developments in the field of Church and state relations, both in practice and in theory. The Mongols did not interfere in the religious life of Russia and, moreover, they exempted the Church from the otherwise universal tribute. This strengthened the Church in relation to secular power in Russian principalities. But the rise of strong princely power in Tver' and Moscow, and the Church's policy of active support for Moscow as the nucleus of national consolidation, led to a controversy in which the traditional view, held since the days of St. Vladimir and Metropolitan Hilarion, on the relations between the Church and the secular authorities was challenged. At the beginning of the fourteenth century, the monk Akindin, in an epistle to a grand prince of Tver', maintained that the prince had the supreme disciplinary power in relation to the Church hierarchy—a view similar to that of Akindin's contemporary in Western Europe, Marsilius of Padua. The opposite view, also distinct from the traditional, was represented in the middle of the century by Metropolitan Alexius, who put the dignity and authority of a bishop, and in particular of the head of the Russian Church, above those of a prince.

Important though these contrasting views on the relations between spiritual and temporal powers were, both in their own time and for future thought, another doctrine put forward by Akindin was even more significant. Justifying his view of a prince's power and duties in the Church, Akindin wrote: "In thine land, Lord Prince, thou art Emperor." He thus introduced into Russian thought the idea, first formulated by the English jurist Alanus three centuries earlier and vigorously upheld in Akindin's own time by Philip the Fair of France, that, within his domain, a king had the same authority as an emperor. This principle, which in Western Europe became the foundation of the concept of the sovereignty of national states, was destined to play the same role in Russia.

For the time being, however, the views on Russia's external sovereignty were conflicting. The Tatar yoke, as the Mongol suzerainty was called in Russia, was generally regarded as transitory, but there remained the more fundamental (from the theoretical point of view) problem of Russia's position in relation to the Byzantine Empire. The name of the emperor continued to be mentioned in Church services, but in 1393, Grand Prince Basil I of Moscow, annoyed with Byzantine interference in Russian Church affairs, forbade this practice, declaring "We have no emperor and do not want to know one." This drew a rebuke from the Patriarch of Constantinople, who in a long epistle restated the whole doctrine of the universal Christian empire and insisted on the duty of all Christians to obey the emperor. Grand Prince Basil II, the son of Basil I, accepted the Byzantine view, at least in principle, and called the emperor "holy autocrat of the whole universe."

Thus we see that political ideas current in medieval Russia were on the whole very similar to those of medieval Western Europe. The most important difference was the absence in Russia of ideas connected with the papal claim to secular authority. On the other hand, there was a strong national consciousness not paralleled in the major West European countries until the thirteenth century.

2. Muscovite Russia

THE BREAK-UP of the Mongol empire and the gradual weakening of the power of the Horde opened up a prospect of shaking off the Tatar yoke. After the middle of the fourteenth century, the leadership in the struggle for independence rested firmly in the hands of the grand princes of Moscow, and in their eyes it was one aspect of the more comprehensive task of establishing their own sovereignty over the whole of Russia. The idea of Russian unity had not been completely forgotten during the centuries of fragmentation and Mongol domination, and it was now revived in the form of the practical task of "gathering the Russian land" and symbolized in the title Grand Prince of Moscow and of All Russia. No specific theoretical justification for this Muscovite claim was advanced until 1471, when Metropolitan Philip, in an epistle to the Novgorodians (who, trying to avoid subjection to Moscow, were considering recognizing the suzerainty of the King of Poland and Grand Duke of Lithuania), argued that people should recognize as a power established by God that which had been so recognized by their ancestors—that is, in this case, the power of the Rurikid dynasty which was now ruling in Moscow.

The period of the late fifteenth–early sixteenth centuries was one of intensive political thought and argument in Russia, stimulated by events of great importance for contemporary Russians: the Florentine Union of the Eastern Churches with Rome, in 1439, and its rejection by the Russian Church; the fall of Constantinople, in 1453; the appearance in Russia of a protestant movement, the heresy of Judaizers, in the 1470's; the final reassertion of Russia's independence, symbolized in Grand Prince Ivan III's decision of 1480 to cease paying token tribute to the Khan of the Golden Horde; and Ivan's attempts to confiscate land belonging to monasteries.

Three distinct trends of political thought emerged in the course of these controversies, all of them in one way or another concerned with the nature and extent of the power of the Muscovite rulers. One was primarily interested in determining the place of the independent Muscovite state in world history, and this culminated in the elaboration of the doctrine of Moscow as the Third Rome. This doctrine, akin in its basic idea to the West European concept of *translatio imperii* from the Greeks to the Germans, was first stated by the Metropolitan Zosimas in 1492. In a charter giving the Pascal Canon for the beginning of the eighth millennium since the creation of the world, he briefly summarized the main historical events leading to his own time, ending with the statement that there was at present "the new Emperor Constantine of the new Constantinople—Moscow." This claim to the status of the imperial city for Moscow was extended by the Pskovian monk Philotheus who, in a number of epistles addressed to the grand princes, claimed for the whole of the "Russian land" the succession to the Roman Empire. The Greeks having fallen from Orthodoxy by accepting the Florentine Union, Russia was the only country to have preserved the Orthodox faith. The Greeks had been punished with the capture of Constantinople by the Turks, and the Grand Prince of Moscow was now the only sovereign Orthodox ruler. On him, therefore, fell the task of defending the true Christian faith and the corresponding dignity of the Roman Emperor. In Philotheus' famous phrase, two Romes had fallen (to heresy), but the third stood and there would never be a fourth. Thus the idea of a universal Christian empire, which had been rejected implicitly by Hilarion and Akindin and explicitly by the Grand Prince Basil I of Moscow, was now resuscitated and turned to Moscow's advantage. As often happens, the practice had in fact preceded the theory. The title "czar" had occasionally been applied in the past to particularly outstanding Russian princes, beginning with Vladimir Monomakh. Grand Prince Ivan III, who had married the niece of the last Byzantine emperor in 1472, began to call himself Czar after he had stopped paying the symbolic tribute to the Tatars in 1480, although his grandson Ivan the Terrible was the first monarch to be officially crowned as Czar (1547). In the absence of male heirs to the Byzantine throne, Ivan III's claim to the title was probably sound enough (it was recognized by Venice and, in the sixteenth century, by the Pope, the Patriarch of Constantinople, and the German Emperor), but neither Ivan himself nor his successors in the sixteenth century combined with it any territorial claims, and they rejected all suggestions by West European governments and by the Patriarch that Muscovy should join in the struggle against the Turks in order to take possession of her Byzantine heritage. But when Russia did take an active part in the wars against the Turks during the eighteenth and nineteenth centuries, the claim to Constantinople was advanced periodically. (It was also accepted as one of the war aims by Russia's allies in World War I.) The view that the Russian monarch was the protector of all Orthodox Christians took deep roots and played an important part in Russian foreign policy from the sixteenth to the nineteenth centuries.

The idea of Byzantine and Roman roots of the authority of the Muscovite rulers received official recognition in Moscow not in the form advocated by Philotheus, but in the shape of a fictitious genealogy that depicted Rurik, the founder of the Rurikid dynasty, as a descendant of a "relative" of Augustus, the first Roman emperor. This story was combined with another legend according to which the crown used by the Czars in the sixteenth and seventeenth centuries, usually called "Monomakh's crown," had been sent to the Kievan prince Vladimir Monomakh by a Byzantine emperor. False genealogies and historical legends of this type were, of course, common stock in trade of European political pamphleteers of the time; one need only recall the French story that depicted the Franks as descendants of the Trojans!

The other two main political theories of the late fifteenth–early sixteenth centuries were not so much concerned with the nature of the Muscovite state as with the limits of the power of its rulers. These two schools of thought emerged in the course of a fierce controversy about two practical problems: how to treat the "Judaizing" heretics, and whether the prince had the right to confiscate land belonging to monasteries. One of the contending parties is traditionally known as the Josephians, so called after its most outstanding representative, Abbot Joseph of Volok. Joseph, like Akindin before him, advocated active interference by the state in the affairs of the Church. But his argument was different: It pleases God, he said, if people obey and serve secular authorities (whether emperor, prince, or any other ruler), because these authorities are guardians of the people and take care of their interests. This sounds rather modern and utilitarian, but Joseph's argument was in fact akin to the medieval West European notion that a king was a kind of trustee for the common interests of the people. In matters of Church administration, the competence of the secular power, in Joseph's view, extended even as far as control over the adherence of monks to the rules of the monastery. But in the hotly debated question of monasterial land holdings, Joseph took up an uncompromising position against the prince's right to confiscate such land: The property of the Church and of monasteries was God's property, and a prince had no right to seize it. Joseph also justified Church property on social grounds—as a source of funds for the maintenance of people who could not provide for themselves. He also said that if monasteries were poor, people from good families would not take up monastic life—and then where would the Russian Church get her bishops? (Bishops in the Orthodox Church have to be monks.) These views prevailed at the Russian Church Council of 1503, although Ivan III had hoped to get a free hand in the matter. Joseph's views on the treatment of heretics were equally strong and uncompromising. In many letters and in the collection of his main theoretical works, known under the title *The Illuminator,* he argued, quoting the Scriptures and Byzantine precedents, that it was the prince's right and duty to see that heretics were condemned by a Church council and to have them executed. The demand that heretics should be burned had already been raised in 1490 by the Archbishop of Novgorod, Gennadius, who recommended the example of the King of Spain in "cleansing his land," but Joseph gave this demand a theoretical justification. If a prince had the right and the duty to punish common criminals, this applied *a fortiori* to offenders against the true faith, who were much more dangerous both to the Church and to the welfare of the state: Many a state had fallen after succumbing to heresy. Pity and mercy were out of place in dealing with heretics, for they could not be healed. Since heretics, according to Joseph, resorted to cunning and dissimulation, he recommended the use of the same methods against them, calling it "God-inspired wise perfidy." These passages in Joseph's writings were quoted favorably in the last years of Stalin's rule. In 1504, the Church Council adopted the Josephians' views on the punishment of heretics, and several prominent heretics were burned during the winter of 1504–5, the first cases in Russian history. Several more people were to be burned during the sixteenth and seventeenth centuries.

Joseph of Volok's insistence on princely jurisdiction over heretics does not mean, as is often supposed, that he advocated a form of caesaro-papism. Although he continued the theocratic tradition of earlier writers, he also followed them in excluding the realm of the spirit from the jurisdiction of the prince. One of the most interesting parts of Joseph's teaching was his doctrine of the tyrant. Although he rejected in general the view (held, according to him, by "certain unseemly" people) that earthly authority had been established by the devil, he made an exception. "If there is a king who, while reigning over men, allows himself to be reigned over by detestable passions and sins, by avarice and rage, cunning and falsity, pride and fury, or, worst of all, by unbelief and malediction, then such a king is not God's servant but the devil's, and not a king but a tyrant." And Joseph's conclusion was: "Thou shalt not obey such a king or a prince, leading thee to impiety and cunning, even if he tortures or punishes by death."

The distinction between king and tyrant, commonly drawn in medieval Western Europe, was well known in Russia, mainly from the writings of St. John Chrysostom and St. Basil the Great. It was implied in the political teachings of St. Vladimir, Hilarion, St. Theodosius, and Vladimir Monomakh and is much in evidence in the chronicles. The chronicles sometimes explain tyrannical rule empirically (e.g., a prince, having reached old age, lost his grasp of affairs and surrounded himself with unworthy advisers), but generally Russian writers before Joseph of Volok regarded tyrannical rule as God's punishment for the people's sins and (like the majority of writers in the West) preached obedience and prayer for deliverance. Joseph's theory of rightful disobedience to a tyrant was the first such theory in the history of Russian thought. It is rather similar to the teaching on this subject of St. Thomas Aquinas, while Joseph's definition of a tyrant as a servant of the devil is identical with that of Bracton, but there is no direct evidence that Joseph of Volok was familiar with their writings.

In his later years, Joseph seems to have abandoned his doctrine of disobedience, but it was further developed by his pupil and follower Metropolitan Daniel. According to him, God had established earthly authority as a revenge upon malefactors and as praise for benefactors: If a man ignores the fear of God he should remember the fear of earthly rulers, so that, fearing them, people should not "swallow each other like fishes." But princes and rulers have power only over the body, not over the soul. Therefore, if they order a man to kill or to perform other actions harmful to the soul, it is not proper to obey them, even though they may torture one's body to death. "God created the soul free and autonomous," capable of distinguishing between good and evil. Thus it is not only the tyrant who is not to be obeyed, but also a king who, though generally righteous, orders in a particular case something that is harmful to the soul. The historian must note, however, that Daniel's activities as a Metropolitan did not conform with his theory of resistance to the unrighteous commands of a ruler.

Daniel's insistence on autonomy of the soul was soon contradicted in an anonymous tract known as *Conversation of the Miracle-Makers of Valaam*. The argument is interesting: "Had God created man autonomous, He would not have established emperors and grand princes and other authorities, and would not have divided one state from another." States and state authority were thus needed because man was not autonomous and had to be guided. This idea was later utilized by Ivan the Terrible. The author of the *Conversation* was against the participation of clergy in state government and against possession by the Church of villages, for such possession involved civilian jurisdiction over the inhabitants. For a monarch to countenance this meant to renounce his authority, to neglect his duties.

Joseph's and Daniel's doctrine of rightful disobedience greatly influenced the thinking of the Old Believers—the conservative part of the Church led by the Archpriest Avvakum, which rejected the correction of liturgical texts and of the ritual undertaken by Patriarch Nikon in the seventeenth century with the support of the Czar, who tried to enforce acceptance of the changes. Peter the Great's break with many Muscovite traditions finally convinced the Old Believers that not only the official Church, but also the reformed Russian state, was the work of the devil.

The Church party that opposed the Josephians is traditionally known as the Nonacquisitors, for it condemned monasterial land holding. Their spiritual leader was Nil of the Sorka, the promoter in Russia of contemplative monasticism and one of the most attractive figures in the history of Russian thought. Greatly influenced by the Hesychastic movement in the Greek and southern Slav churches, he put the highest value on "thoughtful prayer," and in the statute for the monks written by him he avoided any direct prohibitions or commands, making instead suggestions—based on a remarkable knowledge of human psychology—on how to master various passions. Each individual was himself to judge how far he could go along the path suggested in the statute. It is not known whether Nil favored administrative measures against heretics, but his followers, while not opposing imprisonment for the unrepentant, insisted that those who had repented should be received back into the Church. One of the preconditions for the contemplative life was renunciation of worldly riches, not only by individual monks (which Joseph of Volok also insisted upon), but by the Church as a whole—a doctrine very similar to that of William of Ockam and the Spiritual Franciscans in the West. Thus it came about that, in spite of their dislike of administrative measures, the Nonacquisitors did not oppose confiscation of monasterial lands. Lacking interest in formal arrangements, Nil and his followers did not apply their principles of freedom and toleration to problems of state form and governmental institutions. Thus we find crystallized in Josephians and Nonacquisitors respectively two sets of intellectual and political attitudes, which we shall meet repeatedly in later Russian thought: on the one hand, practicality based on formal discipline and in constant danger of degenerating into ritualism or brutality, and on the other, humane benevolence appealing to inner freedom and toleration and in constant danger of escaping into pure contemplation or abstract theorizing.

The official theory of Muscovite autocracy was finally elaborated by the Grand Prince Ivan III (sometimes called the Great), perhaps the most outstanding of the Muscovite rulers. When, in 1478, the Novgorodians came to the conclusion that they had to submit to the Grand Prince but nevertheless tried to remain "free men," Ivan III declared that the grand princes wished to have the same kind of sovereignty over Novgorod—which was their "patrimony"—as they had over Moscow. The Novgorodians pleaded ignorance of the Muscovite traditions and asked for the retention of the judicial authority of their mayor, for a fixed tax, for fixed conditions of military service, etc. Ivan's answer was remarkable: "Now you are instructing me, are setting limits to our sovereignty; where then is my sovereignty?" He proceeded to abolish the citizens' assembly and the office of mayor as being incompatible with his sovereignty; then, by a unilateral gesture, he granted some concessions, but refused to regard this whole arrangement with Novgorod as a contract. In his diplomatic correspondence, Ivan III expressed the view that there should be only one ruler in a realm and no vassal princes, and when it was suggested to him that the German Emperor might be persuaded to offer him the title of king, he replied: "We have been by God's grace sovereign in our land from the very beginning, from our first forefathers, and are ordained by God . . . and ask God to let us and our children be forever as we are now, sovereigns in our land, and as for ordination, neither have we wanted it from anyone in the past, nor do we want it now." Ivan III's concept of sovereignty, which can be traced back to the idea that a prince is an emperor in his own realm, rather than to the notion of Moscow as the Third Rome, explained the use, increasingly frequent during his reign, of the titles "Czar" and "Autocrat." The terms "autocrat" and "autocracy," which in Russian are exact translations from Greek and which (like the word "czar") had occasionally been used by ecclesiastics before, were identical in their meaning with "sovereign" and "sovereignty."

The theory of Muscovite autocracy reached its extreme point in the writings of Ivan the Terrible, chiefly in his correspondence with foreign royalties and with Prince Kurbsky. In his letters to Queen Elizabeth of England and to the kings of Poland and Sweden, Ivan the Terrible maintained that elective monarchy and the limitation of the power of the monarch by assemblies of his subjects were incompatible with the monarch's sovereignty, that the first reduced him to the position of a benefice-holder and the second, figuratively speaking, to that of a chairman of a rural district council. Ivan's political philosophy was set out in greater detail in his two letters to Prince Kurbsky, the first of which was made public. They reveal a strong caesaro-papist streak in his thought: "I try industriously to instruct people in the truth and the light so that they should know the true God . . . and the sovereign given to them by God." All subjects are equal before the Czar in that they are all obliged by God to be the Czar's slaves. It is proper for Czars to be attentive, sometimes very mild, at other times furious; for they must treat good people with mercy and mildness, but evil ones with fury and torture. He who lacks this ability is not a Czar. The main criterion for distinguishing good subjects from evil ones is whether they carry out the wishes of the sovereign. Those who do are his "well-wishers." "To our well-wishers . . . we grant all kinds of great beneficence, but those who find themselves among opponents . . . receive punishment according to their guilt." However, the Czar's power of life and death over his subjects, though it has no external limitations, is not purely arbitrary, since it must be both purposeful and unselfish: Its purpose is to maintain and increase the glory and well-being of the realm and to carry out God's will. In judging himself by these criteria, Ivan alternated between self-glorification and self-abasement, the important theoretical implication here being that a sovereign may fall far short of the ideal and that it is his personal responsibility to aspire to the ideal.

Autocracy as understood by its chief protagonists—Ivan III, Joseph of Volok, and Ivan IV—made great strides in the fifteenth and sixteenth centuries, but it would be wrong to assume that it was able to assert itself as the sole effective force in the political life of the country. Several traditional institutions proved strong and tenacious enough to withstand for a long time the encroachment or onslaught of the autocracy.

The judicial authority of the Church in matters of religious beliefs and practices, of marriage and inheritance, and in all matters affecting Church people (clergy, monks, people resident on Church lands, and those living on Church charity), established by the Church Statute of St. Vladimir, remained essentially intact despite occasional interference on the highest level by the grand princes. Judicial authority in this case was in fact also legislative, since the Greco-Roman canon law was constantly adapted to changing Russian conditions and views through partial revisions of the manuals in use, authoritative interpretations by metropolitans and archbishops, and the practice of jurisdiction in bishops' courts. A Church council (e.g., that of 1503) could make decisions contrary to the wishes of the grand prince with his acquiescence.

The feudal institution of immunity exempted from princely jurisdiction and administration (i.e., tax-collecting) another large category of the prince's subjects—all tenants (gentry and peasants), slaves, and other persons resident on the patrimonial estates of the magnates—although jurisdiction in the most important criminal cases was gradually transferred to crown courts. Relations of an even more feudal nature prevailed in those cases in which minor apanage princes, forced to surrender their principalities to the grand prince, received them back as fiefs or were compensated by fiefs elsewhere. Tatar princes entering Muscovite service also sometimes received fiefs. Notwithstanding Ivan III's theoretical arguments against having more than one ruler in a realm, he himself, his son, and even Ivan the Terrible carved out apanages for their younger sons. Finally, the grand prince's lieutenants in the provinces were regarded as benefice-holders, and in practice their judicial, fiscal, and military duties were not very different from those of the magnates in the latter's immunized patrimonial lands.

The magnates' service to the grand prince, traditionally based on a free contract, became obligatory by the sixteenth century, but at the same time the magnates evolved a complicated system of precedence, or seniority (*mestnichestvo*), based partly on descent and partly on merit, which had to be taken into account in all senior appointments and therefore limited considerably the sovereign's freedom of action until it was abolished in 1682. The magnates' council survived all the tribulations of Mongol domination and the rise of autocracy and remained indispensable at the central government level (except for a period in the reign of Ivan the Terrible). The composition of the council was changed through the addition of former apanage princes or their descendants, who now formed the upper layer of the magnates and, at the opposite end of the hierarchical scale, of the upper ranks of the grand prince's own gentry and of his senior clerks. But the functions of the magnates' council remained essentially the same —to advise and assist the sovereign in legislation, administration, and jurisdiction and to share with him the responsibility for all major decisions. Moreover, in the middle of the sixteenth century, under Ivan the Terrible, the Council of the Land—the representative assembly that had existed in an embryonic form in the last decades before the Mongol conquest—was revived. It was usually constituted as three estates sitting simultaneously but separately—the Church council, the magnates' council, and the elected representatives of the provincial gentry, townspeople, and sometimes even peasants—and it was convoked from time to time, especially in the seventeenth century, to deliberate and decide on matters of particular importance (such as the election of a new Czar after the Time of Troubles, or the passing of a new Code of Laws).

A new and pragmatic turn was given to the theory of autocracy in the middle of the sixteenth century by I. S. Peresvetov. A member of the Russian gentry from Lithuania with considerable experience in various campaigns in central Europe, he entered Muscovite service and in 1549, after a period of frustration, submitted two petitions to Ivan the Terrible in which, drawing attention to his grievances, he also put forward his views on good government and suggested far-reaching reforms. He further elaborated his ideas in a number of other writings, some of them allegoric in form. Little is known of Peresvetov's later life, but his views clearly expressed some of the feelings and aspirations of a social class whose significance was increasing—the gentry—and they may have influenced the Czar himself, who kept Peresvetov's writings in his library. The main foundations of good government are, according to Peresvetov, justice and freedom. Justice is more important than faith: "God loves justice, not faith." The Orthodox Greeks had "read the Gospel" but did not carry out God's will, and thus they had proved less acceptable to God than had the Turks, who, though they did not follow the true faith, had carried out justice. The injustice of the Greeks had consisted in the limitation of the power of the Byzantine emperors by the magnates, who in their handling of state affairs had been motivated by selfish interests and who had oppressed the people. Hence a necessary condition for the realization of justice is that the monarch should be active himself and his power unlimited: "If a king is mild and quiet in his rule, his realm will be impoverished and his glory will diminish. If a king inspires fear and is wise, his realm will expand and his name will be glorious in all lands." Fear of the king is a necessary condition for justice, since only this fear can ensure the integrity of administration and of the courts: "A realm without fear is like a horse without a bridle." Peresvetov therefore recommends the death penalty for a variety of crimes, especially for offenses (like the taking of bribes) committed by officials. As for corrupt magnates, they deserve burning. Freedom is no less important than justice: "God created man autonomous and ordered him to be his own master, not a slave." "If a country is enslaved, every kind of evil is done in that country: theft and robbery and abuse and great impoverishment to the whole realm, by which they incur the wrath of God and serve the devil." Slavery should therefore be abolished. The concept of freedom is introduced by Peresvetov in discussing the problem of the armed forces. "If the people in a realm are enslaved," he wrote, "they are not courageous: for an enslaved man is not afraid of shame, nor does he gain honor for himself." The army should consist not of magnates and their retainers, but of warriors freely entering the service of the Czar. Free warriors are the best supporters of the Czar's power. Conversely, it is the quality of the service rather than birth or wealth that should determine the social position of the Czar's subjects, and this applies not only to the military field but to state service in general. Courts of law should be reorganized in such a way that, instead of provincial lieutenants who themselves receive the court fees and the fines imposed upon offenders, there should be specially appointed salaried judges. In order to strengthen the authority of the Czar and provide the state treasury with the money necessary to maintain the class of salaried warriors and officials, Peresvetov suggested a centralization of the financial system—all taxes and other public revenues should go into the Czar's treasury.

Peresvetov's views are in several respects remarkably similar to those of his older contemporary Machiavelli. There is a stronger theological element in Peresvetov's argument, but expediency and the lessons of history loom as large as they do in *The Prince*. The use of allegory gives Peresvetov's political pamphlets a medieval air, in contrast to Machiavelli's scientific reasoning. But Peresvetov's views on the expansion of the state as the proper aim of the ruler's policies, on justice based on fear, his ideas on freedom, on the need for wide popular support for the prince's power, on centralized finances and judiciary, the elimination of all vestiges of feudalism, these are the same as Machiavelli's. The modernity of Peresvetov's thinking comes out clearly in his advocacy of reforms. Political writers in Russia before him, and even his contemporary Ivan the Terrible, usually argued from tradition and custom, even though on occasion a fictitious tradition had to be invented for the sake of argument. Peresvetov was the first writer to break with this medieval approach.

Theories of Shared Power (Sixteenth and Seventeenth Centuries)

As we have seen, advocates of autocracy had to contend with formidable institutional obstacles. But there was also no lack of theoretical opposition. The opposition came from different sources and took different forms. There was nostalgic longing for lost freedoms and republican institutions on the part of some Novgorodian and Pskovian writers. There were anarchist leanings among the heretics (who are briefly discussed on p. 114). But most of the opponents of autocracy advocated some form of sharing of power between the monarch and other persons or institutions.

The most persistent opposition to autocracy, naturally enough, came from the class that had most to lose, the magnates, whose views were most eloquently expressed by Prince A. M. Kurbsky. The descendant of a minor branch of the Rurikids, Kurbsky had been a Muscovite commander in the campaign that had led to the conquest of Kazan' in 1552 and during the first part of the Livonian war, but fearing disgrace, he had fled to the Polish Commonwealth, Muscovy's enemy in the war. While there, he wrote several letters to Ivan the Terrible in which he attacked the Czar and his policies. His letters, like those of the Czar to him, were intended to be public statements, and in them, as well as in a number of other writings, he developed a political theory sharply opposed to that of autocracy. Kurbsky shared his correspondent's views of the personal responsibility of the monarch, and in arraigning Ivan's terroristic policy Kurbsky pictured him as a tyrant. But, like Joseph of Volok before him, he did not preach tyrannicide. The only form of resistance to the tyrant that Kurbsky specifically justifies is emigration. Defending himself against the charge of treason, he said that an oath of loyalty under compulsion was a sin on the part of the person resorting to compulsion, and that he who does not flee from persecution is like a person committing suicide. The evil, however, was not confined to Ivan's personal characteristics but lay in the autocracy itself. To Kurbsky, responsible power was limited power, and the way to limit it was to share it with the magnates, as had previously been done by Muscovite grand princes. Tradition was an important element in Kurbsky's views on good government. A considerable Latin scholar, who had while in exile made many translations from Latin into Russian, he quoted Cicero on the nature of a properly constituted political community: "What is a city? Every collection of fierce and primitive people? Every multitude of robbers and runaways gathered into one place? Surely you will deny this. For it was not a city at that time when the laws had no force in it, when the courts of justice were abased, when the custom of the fathers had been extinguished. . . ." If pagan philosophers, Kurbsky commented, basing themselves on natural law, were able to come to such wise conclusions, surely Christians should accept and apply them.

Kurbsky's views are sometimes likened to those of his anti-absolutist contemporaries in Western Europe, such as George Buchanan. They did indeed have in common the antiabsolutist tendency, the alternative to be preferred—effective estates of the realm—and the turning to classical antiquity for inspiration, but the specific lines of argument of the West European humanist antiabsolutists were not very similar to Kurbsky's.

While Prince Kurbsky, objecting to autocracy, advocated the sharing of power by the Czar and the magnates, an anonymous tract dating probably from the same period (known as *Another Version of the Conversation of the Miracle-Makers of Valaam*) went further in its demands for popular participation in the government. The strength and well-being of the realm, according to the author of this tract, depended not on the bravery and military exploits of the monarch but on his wisdom. A wise Czar should have a permanent "universal council" consisting of representatives of all his towns and districts, of "people of all grades." In addition to this body, there should be another council, consisting of "men of reason, wise and reliable leaders" who are close to the Czar and whom he should consult daily.

Practical steps to curb autocracy and to give the idea of shared power a basis in written law were made during the Time of Troubles at the beginning of the seventeenth century. The most interesting document from this point of view is the text of the agreement concluded in 1610 by the magnates' council, apparently authorized by the Council of the Land, on the election of the Polish Crown Prince Wladyslaw as Czar. Wladyslaw was bound by this agreement not to harm the Orthodox faith in any way and not to interfere in the affairs of the Church, not to seize Church or monasterial lands or the patrimonial lands of the magnates, not to change the traditional customs and norms of the Muscovite State, not to take anybody's life without a proper trial before the magnates' council, not to introduce new taxes without consultation with the magnates' council, and not to change the law code except upon deliberation in both the magnates' council and the Council of the Land.

Several other important political ideas were generated by the turmoil of the Time of Troubles, though they were usually implied in major political actions rather than advanced in a theoretical form. These were the ideas of the magnates' council acting as a provisional government during an interregnum, and of the Council of the Land in times of crisis exercising the old right of the citizens' assembly to elect princes (now applied to the election of Czars); acceptance of elective monarchy as an expedient; the idea that in the presence of sharp internal dissensions a foreign prince should be elected Czar in preference to native candidates; and finally, the idea that, if everything else failed, public authority reverted to the population at large to be exercised through the citizens' assemblies of Moscow and other principal cities. None of these ideas was really novel; all had been intimated by past Russian history. Common to all of them were the underlying notions of exceptional circumstances and overwhelming necessity, of conciliar solutions being preferable in such conditions, and of the ultimate and residual powers of the totality of citizens—notions that had been given currency in Western Europe by the Conciliar Movement two centuries earlier.

The period immediately following the Time of Troubles brought to the fore a quite different type of sharing of powers— the sharing of temporal power between the Czar and the Patriarch of Moscow. Patriarch Philaret, the father of the young Czar Michael Romanov, immediately upon his election assumed the title Great Sovereign, which had hitherto been reserved for the Czar. There were thus two Great Sovereigns in Moscow, and until the death of Philaret, all state papers were issued in both their names. When a magnate, concerned about his rights of precedence, claimed in 1621 that to represent the Patriarch at a state function was less dignified than to represent the Czar, and instituted formal proceedings, Michael delivered a remarkable judgment, saying that his father was just as much a sovereign as himself and that their sovereign majesty was indivisible.

The title Great Sovereign was assumed again by Patriarch Nikon, who did not refer to the precedent of Philaret, but in the preface to a prayer book authorized by him in 1655 advanced a doctrine of equality of the Czar's and the Patriarch's powers.

As the basis of his argument Nikon used Emperor Justinian's Sixth Novel, which had previously been interpreted in Russia as providing for harmony between the two powers, not their equality. Later, however, Nikon changed his views and developed a comprehensive theory of the supremacy of spiritual over temporal power, the Church over the State, and the Patriarch over the Czar. He advanced several arguments for the postulate that priesthood was superior to kingship. The origin of both powers was different, for although both had originated from God, priesthood had come from Him directly, during Moses's forty-day conversation with Him and through Christ's laying of hands on the Apostles; whereas the power of the king, according to Nikon (who here had in mind the establishment of the kings of Israel), though also given by God, had been given in anger and fury. And in the contemporary world, Nikon declared, the grace of the Holy Ghost descends directly upon bishops, while the king has to be anointed by a bishop: "The smaller is blessed by the greater," he concludes. So much for the origin. Nikon derives his next series of arguments from the purposes of spiritual and temporal power. The king is responsible for the bodies of his people, the priest for their souls; the king may remit material debts (Nikon probably had in mind the remission of taxes), while the priest can remit sins. The king has the power of reward and punishment, but these rewards and punishments have no eternal significance and are subject to reconsideration on the Day of Judgment. Obligations imposed by the priest, on the contrary, even if wrongly imposed, remain valid in Heaven. Finally, according to Nikon, the primacy of spiritual power was evident from history—God since antiquity had preferred the priests, and so also had kings themselves. To prove the latter point, Nikon quoted in full the famous Charter of Constantine the Great to Pope Sylvester (which had already been proved a forgery), and referred to Justinian's Sixth Novel and to the example of St. Vladimir of Kiev. Not only was the Church, in Nikon's view, completely immune from any interference by the Czar, but even in secular matters the Czar had virtually no independent authority and was in reality an agent of the patriarch who had ordained him.

The idea itself of the supremacy of spiritual over temporal

power was not new in Russia; as we have seen, it had been held by Metropolitan Alexius three centuries earlier. But Nikon was the first person in Russia to uphold the papo-caesarist theory of the medieval Roman Church, using essentially the same arguments that had been used by the papist party in the West. Nikon's views were defended at the Russian Church Council in 1667 by a number of bishops, but the majority of the Council was against them and they were condemned. However, the Council refused to endorse the opposite doctrine, conveyed in a message from the Patriarch of Constantinople, of the unlimited power of the Czar in matters of Church organization and discipline, and reaffirmed instead the traditional Russian view of the interdependence of both powers.

3. Petrine Russia

THE REIGN of Peter the Great (1689–1725) brought about changes in the field of political thought similar to the changes taking place in the social and economic life of the country. Peter's aim was to modernize the economy and the administration in order to enable Russia to realize its potentialities and take a place among the European powers equal to that of the most advanced countries. Modernization meant a great acceleration in the introduction of West European techniques, procedures, and ways of thought that had been slowly going on since the late fifteenth century, and progressive Westernization was the most outstanding feature in the development of political thought throughout the eighteenth century and the first quarter of the nineteenth. For seven centuries, Russian thought had been basically oriented toward Byzantium and Russia's own past; now it was inspired by the ideas and doctrines current in contemporary Western Europe. Individual schools of political thought in Russia were also related to corresponding West European trends. The three main schools that emerged in the eighteenth century and exercised great influence on all subsequent thought in Russia were those of enlightened absolutism, constitutionalism, and radicalism.

Several of Peter the Great's practical policies were of particular significance for the future development of Russian political thought. His economic policy was strictly mercantilist; it was continued by his successors and created the same problems for the adherents of liberal policies in the nineteenth century as those confronting liberals in Western Europe. In place of the late seventeenth-century combination of a gentry militia and regular units of mercenaries, Peter created a national army based on conscription. In the process of streamlining the administration, he gave final shape to the three social groups that dominated the social scene in Russia until at least the middle of the nineteenth century: the nobility, the civil servants, and the serfs. The nobility was created through amalgamation of two estates: the patrimony-owning magnates and the fief-holding gentry. The term "magnate" was abolished, and so was the distinction between patrimonial estates and fiefs, both merging in the concept of landed property, which was treated as patrimony but could not be alienated. All nobles were under the obligation of lifelong state service, either military or civil (until they were relieved from this obligation by Peter III in 1762). A unified system of state bureaucracy was created, with fourteen ranks of civil servants from minor clerk to chancellor, the bureaucratic career being open to anyone. A state servant who reached officer's rank or its equivalent in the civil service, was ennobled. Peasants living on both patrimonial and infeudated estates, who had originally been free tenants, had been finally tied to their landlords by the Conciliar Code of 1649, and this interminable hereditary bondage had made their position very similar to that of the slaves. Peter the Great amalgamated both groups into one estate of serfs when he introduced the poll tax and subjected to it, together with other nonprivileged estates, the slaves who had hitherto been free from taxation or any other direct obligation to the state.

Enlightened Absolutism

Peter the Great himself adhered to the views that were later termed enlightened absolutism. Indeed, the very idea of a reforming absolute monarch emerged in Western Europe under the influence of his personality and activities. This was the first case of a direct impact of Russia on West European political thought (except for the notion of the "Muscovite threat," which had been propagated by Muscovy's western neighbors—the Teutonic Order, Poland, and Sweden—since the sixteenth century). Unlike his contemporary, Louis XIV, author of the famous phrase *"l'état c'est moi,"* Peter looked upon himself as the servant of the state, giving expression to his views, for example, in the proclamation that was read to the Russian troops before the battle of Poltava. The purpose of public authority was, for Peter, to further the welfare of the state and the people, and the means of achieving this end was the absolute monarchy. Accordingly, the Russian Czar was officially described (in the Military Criminal Code of 1715) as an "autocratic monarch who does not have to give account of his deeds to anyone in the world, but has the power and authority to govern his states and lands as a Christian Sovereign, according to his will and judgment." And in fact, Peter was the first Russian monarch to rule without the assistance of either the Council of the Land, which had become defunct before his accession, or the magnates' council, which he himself discarded. Upon the victorious conclusion of the Northern War in 1721 (as a result of which Russia replaced Sweden as a great power), Peter was acclaimed by the Senate,* in the name of "all ranks of the Russian people," as "Peter the Great, Father of the Fatherland, Emperor of All Russia." The official reasons for this appellation as stated at the ceremony were that the title of emperor had already been held by Russian monarchs for several centuries and had been recognized by many foreign potentates (implying that the Senate was merely substituting the Latin *imperator* for the Russian *tsar'*) and that the attribute "great" was already being widely applied to Peter, so that the only innovation was the title "Father of the Fatherland," which was being accorded to Peter following ancient Greek and Roman examples. Peter's merit was to have raised the Russians from obscurity to the stage of glory before the whole world, "so to speak, from nonexistence to existence," and to have introduced them into the society of political peoples. In his short and simple reply, Peter stated that he wanted the whole people to know what God had done for Russia through the war and the peace that had just been concluded; that, hoping for peace, one should not become slack in military matters if one wished to avoid the fate of Byzantium; and that everyone should work for the common welfare to alleviate the lot of the people. The mixture of Muscovite traditions, the Renaissance cult of classical antiquity, and modern West European concepts that made up Peter's political philosophy could not have been better illustrated.

* A new body, consisting of senior officials, which in a sense was a successor to the magnates' council.

The theory of enlightened absolutism was further developed and propagated in Peter the Great's time by a group of adherents and active participants of his policies colloquially known as "the learned team," especially by the leading figure of this team, Archbishop Theophan Prokopovich (1681–1736). Prokopovich was a Ukrainian and in a way his pre-eminence among the ideologists of the time was a continuation of the Ukrainian and Belorussian intellectual influence characteristic of the second half of the seventeenth century. Born in Kiev to the family of a minor merchant, he was educated at the Academy there, continuing his education in Poland—where he converted to Greek Catholicism—and then in the St. Athanasius College in Rome, a special institution for Catholics of the Eastern rite. However, on his return to Kiev he reverted to Orthodoxy and remained a strong anti-Catholic throughout his life. He became a monk and a lecturer at the Kiev Academy and quickly rose to its rectorship. An admirer of Peter's, he attracted the attention of the Czar by his vocal support of Peter's activities, was called to the new capital of St. Petersburg, created Archbishop of Pskov, and became Peter's chief adviser and spokesman on ideological and theological matters. Especially important was Prokopovich's role in the reform of Church administration, when the Patriarchate of Moscow was abolished and replaced by the Most Holy Synod consisting of bishops but headed by a lay official as the representative of the Czar, who thus became the head of the Church. This arrangement reflected Prokopovich's general Protestant inclinations for which he was often criticized.

Prokopovich developed his theory of enlightened absolutism in several sermons, letters, official documents, and in a special treatise on the subject written at Peter's request and entitled *The Truth of the Monarch's Will* (1722). Like most eighteenth-century theorists, he based his views on the notions of natural law and social contract. A theoretical consideration of the problems of state and government should, according to Prokopovich, start from common sense or natural reason. It was common sense that induced man to exchange conditions of natural freedom for a social union —the state. At first, the people were sovereign in the state, but then, following God's direction, they decided to entrust state

power to one person, the monarch, and having done so they cannot annul this contract or in any way limit the monarch's power.
Drafting the new Church Statute, Prokopovich coined the formula that remained in use throughout the imperial period: "The
Emperor of All Russia is an autocratic and unlimited monarch.
To obey his supreme authority, not only from fear, but also from
conscience, God himself commands." Two other forms of government besides monarchy were possible—aristocracy and democracy
—but because of the fragmentation of authority that both involved Prokopovich considered them harmful. Monarchy, he
held, can be either hereditary or elective, but the former is preferable because it is more stable: The office of the monarch is
filled immediately upon becoming vacant, without any interruption; the heir, knowing he will inherit, can prepare himself for
the task; and the reigning monarch would naturally wish to leave
the state to his heirs in good condition. There is, however, one
defect in a hereditary monarchy based upon primogeniture—the
throne may fall to an obviously incapable person. Prokopovich
therefore maintained that the monarch should have the right to
designate as his successor any member of his family, no matter
what the degree of relationship. Such designation occasionally
had been practiced in Russia from the late fifteenth century,
justified by Byzantine precedents, but Prokopovich was the first
to justify it on general grounds, and his doctrine of designation
was intended to be a theoretical justification of Peter's law of
succession, which remained in force during the whole eighteenth
century. Prokopovich's views on the positive tasks of government are easily predictable. Having received his absolute power
from the people, the monarch must use it for the common good,
and to this end he must not only institute firm administration
and just courts of law, but also do everything he can to spread
education, since, according to Prokopovich, all social ills—poverty, vice, and crime—are due to ignorance.

The theory of enlightened absolutism was the prevalent political doctrine in eighteenth-century Russia and had among its adherents such outstanding public figures as the scientist and poet
M. V. Lomonosov and the Empress Catherine II.

The last major writer who can be regarded (though with serious reservations) as a representative of the theory of enlightened absolutism was the poet and historian N. M. Karamzin (1766–1826). Born in a noble family (probably of Tatar descent) in the Middle Volga area, he was educated at a private boarding school in Moscow, belonged in his youth to the group of Moscow Freemasons around the publisher Novikov, and in 1789–90 undertook a journey to Western Europe, visiting Germany, Switzerland, France, and England. Soon after his return to Russia, Karamzin was acclaimed as the leader of a new, sentimental movement in Russian literature and as a reformer of the Russian literary language, which he successfully freed from the weight of the Church Slavonic tradition. He founded and edited the literary and political journal *Messenger of Europe,* the first influential monthly journal in the country, thus inaugurating what remained throughout the nineteenth century the chief forum of public discussion in Russia. The last twenty-three years of his life Karamzin devoted to writing his *History of the State of Russia,* holding the title of Imperial Historiographer—the only official position he ever held, having consistently declined all offers of high political office.

Karamzin's interest in political theory was awakened by the French Revolution and by the arbitrary regime of Emperor Paul in Russia (1796–1800), and he expressed his views in his *Letters of a Russian Traveler,* his *History,* and above all in the *Memoir on Ancient and Modern Russia,* which was presented to Emperor Alexander I in 1811, but not published until a quarter of a century later. Karamzin's political thought was influenced by the study of Russian history and by earlier eighteenth-century writers, notably Montesquieu. The most recent student of his political ideas, Professor Richard Pipes, finds no indication of influence by contemporary Conservative thinkers like Burke or de Maistre, although Karamzin knew the latter personally.

Karamzin valued above all the freedom of the individual to pursue his private interests—economic, intellectual, aesthetic, etc. This freedom cannot be enjoyed without a civil order, which in turn can only be maintained by a strong state power. Anarchy is therefore the worst state of affairs, to which even despotism is preferable. But the arbitrary rule of a despot is a bad basis for a stable civil order, which must have a firm foundation in laws. Beyond this, the form of government is of secondary importance, and Karamzin's views on the suitability for a particular country of republican, aristocratic, or monarchical government are rather similar to those of Tatishchev (whom we shall consider in the next section) and Montesquieu. Monarchy (Karamzin used the term autocracy) is the form suitable for Russia; moreover, it accords with the Russian tradition and is the only legitimate form in Russia. Legitimacy and an established order are always to be preferred to upheavals and experiments that endanger the established freedoms. Karamzin perceived such a danger in Speransky's reform plans, and his *Memoir* was aimed at influencing the Emperor against them.

Though at first he shared the national nihilism characteristic of the Enlightenment, Karamzin gradually moved, under the influence of his historical studies, to an appreciation of and respect for national traditions in general and the Russian past in particular. Although a people should learn what is good from other peoples, it should not renounce and reject its own cultural heritage as Peter the Great had done. This is a position very similar to that taken up in the seventeenth century by A. L. Ordin-Nashchokin, and in the eighteenth century to a greater or lesser extent by, among others, Shcherbatov, Kozel'sky, and Fonvizin, with whom we shall deal in the next two sections.

Combining some of the traits of enlightened absolutism, liberalism, and cultural nationalism (or "Russophilism," as it is sometimes called), Karamzin became a forerunner of the liberal conservatives of the nineteenth and early twentieth centuries.

Early Constitutionalism

The first author to revive the constitutionalist idea in the new era of enlightened absolutism was I. T. Pososhkov (1652–1726). The son of a silversmith from a village near Moscow, he had a career typical of many enterprising bourgeois of the time, combining various jobs for the government (designing equipment for the Mint, holding a state monopoly for the sale of vodka in Novgorod, etc.) with private business enterprises and speculations of his own. A lively and fertile mind, he found time despite all his practical preoccupations to reflect on general problems of morals, government, and the economy, expressing his views on these subjects in submissions to influential people, in correspondence with a Church dignitary, and in several treatises, of which the *Book on Scarcity and Wealth* is deservedly the best known. It was finished in 1724, when the author was over seventy, and was intended as a summing-up of all his main ideas. The book was supposed to be presented to the Emperor, but there is no evidence that Peter in fact saw it before his death in 1725. Soon afterward, Pososhkov was arrested, apparently in connection with a charge of fraud. He died in prison, and the book remained unpublished until 1842, although several copies were made during the eighteenth century and it attracted the attention of Lomonosov among others.

According to Pososhkov, state power is established by God for the general good of the people. In Russia, it is the power of an autocratic monarch and not an aristocracy or a democracy. This is as it should be, for only an autocratic monarch can be free from attachment to any particular group or class in society and therefore act justly toward all his subjects; Pososhkov deplored the situation "among foreigners," where "kings have not the same power as the people, therefore kings cannot act according to their own will, but their subjects have the power, and above all the merchants"—an observation the more remarkable in coming from one who was himself a merchant. However, in one sphere he suggested a modification of the autocratic principle and an adjunct to the monarch's power. The most important and urgent task of government in Russia was a thorough scrutiny and reappraisal of the existing laws and the compilation of a new code in place of the Conciliar Code of 1649. And for this task, Pososhkov thought that a representative assembly should be convened, consisting of deputies elected by all the estates of the land, from the higher clergy and nobility down to the state peasants and the serfs. Such an assembly should sit in one chamber, deliberate, and produce a new code; this code should then be implemented for a trial period, during which it should be open to every kind of criticism and suggestions for improvement. The final stage should be the confirmation of the new code by the Emperor in accordance with the outcome of such a referendum. Pososhkov justified this rather cumbersome procedure, which he called "perfect general consultation," on two grounds. If the new laws were to be in the interest of the whole people, it was essential that all groups and points of view in society should be represented. And a task of such magnitude could not be successfully carried out without the participation and the "free voice" of many people, since God had not given any one man the necessary ability but had divided it among many "like pellets." Pososhkov's idea of an elected representative constitutional commission, a kind of *ad hoc* Council of the Land, obviously suggested by the role of the latter in passing the Conciliar Code of 1649, was later taken up, and two such commissions met in the 1760's, one consisting of representatives of the nobility and merchants, the other of all estates except parish clergy and the serfs.

A new legal code was an essential but not a sufficient means of establishing justice, for Pososhkov thought that judicial reform was also necessary. The general requirements put forward by him for the ensuring of judicial impartiality are that there should be only one system of courts, and not special courts for the different social estates; that access to the courts should be easy for all; and that the courts should be independent except from "God and the Czar." The selection of judges is important. It is preferable that there should be three judges in each court, drawn from among the state officials, the military, and the merchants respectively; if no state officials are available, a member of the minor nobility might be appointed, but the higher nobility should be excluded, since they normally do not care for the interests of the common people. For the same reason as Peresvetov before him, Pososhkov thought that the higher nobility should not be drawn upon for the state administration.

But Pososhkov's ideas about a single representative chamber and equality before the courts did not mean that he had in mind the abolition of the different estates. On the contrary, he assigned specific functions to each of them, thus sharpening the distinctions between them. The function of the nobility was state service, both civilian and military (though, as we have seen, he regarded the higher nobility as unsuitable for civilian administration); the merchants, and they alone, should carry on the country's industry and commerce, to the exclusion of both the nobility and the peasants—a demand that was repeated by merchant deputies in the Commission for drafting a new Code of Laws which sat in 1767–68. Pososhkov drew up a detailed program of economic policy that a good government should pursue, a policy typically mercantilist in all its essentials, although there is no evidence that he had read the contemporary West European economic literature. So concerned was he with the progress of industry in Russia that, in addition to many other protective and stimulating measures, he suggested that merchants should be allowed to round up vagrants and beggars and register them officially as their serfs for work in their factories. Children also should be used as a labor force. Pososhkov's ideas about policy toward the peasants were more original. The function of the peasants was, in the case of serfs, through socage, to enable the landlords to devote themselves to state service; in the case of state peasants, to contribute to the revenue through the payment of taxes. The importance of these functions demanded that the peasants be able to perform them, and hence they should be kept from impoverishment. The landholdings of the serfs should be consolidated and clearly demarcated, and their obligations to the landlords should be strictly regulated by the state in direct proportion to the size of their holdings. As for state taxes, Pososhkov was strongly opposed to the newly introduced poll tax (which was in fact inequitable) and thought that it would be desirable to return to household taxes, which should be more rationally calculated on the basis of the size of landholdings. Another cause of peasant poverty was idleness, and to counter this, peasants must be forced to work by the landlords and the police. The harsh treatment of peasants, vagrants, and children recommended by Pososhkov reflected his general conviction that administration must be ruthless in pursuing its aims; the most extreme manifestation of this conviction was his view that the state had a duty to exterminate heretics.

At the time when Pososhkov was writing his *Book on Scarcity and Wealth,* another, much more far-reaching, constitutional plan was maturing in the mind of Prince D. M. Golitsyn (1665–1737).

A member of one of the foremost aristocratic families of Russia, Prince Golitsyn, after studying naval affairs in Italy, had made a distinguished career in state service—as Ambassador in Constantinople, Governor of Kiev, and President of the Chamber College (Board of Revenue). He was an assiduous student of legal and political theory and his large library included the works of Machiavelli, Grotius, Puffendorf, Locke, Tomasius, and other sixteenth–early seventeenth-century writers, including a score of books on aristocracy and the English Constitution. Dissatisfied with the practice of absolute monarchy, involving as it did arbitrariness on the part of the monarch and his favorites, Golitsyn decided to work for the establishment of a constitutional regime in Russia. The first practical step in this direction was made in 1726, almost immediately after the death of Peter the Great, with the setting up of the Supreme Privy Council of six members (later increased to eight), holders of the highest ranks in the civil service, to legislate together with the Empress (Catherine I) and under her chairmanship. Besides transferring the legislative power of the monarch to a collegiate institution, this act separated the legislative power from the administrative. But the new arrangement did not function satisfactorily. Golitsyn, who was one of the Supreme Councilors, continued to work on his plan, taking as a model the Swedish Constitution of 1720. An opportunity to act was provided by the succession crisis after the death of the adolescent Emperor Peter II, in 1730. Having decided to install a niece of Peter the Great as Empress, the Supreme Councilors proceeded to impose "conditions" severely limiting her power. Empress Anne (a childless widow) promised not to marry again and not to nominate a successor, and, in effect, to rule together with the Supreme Privy Council, since the armed forces were to be under the control of the Council, and the Empress was forbidden without the consent of the Council to start a war or conclude a peace treaty, to introduce new taxes or to spend the state revenue, to promote to the military or civilian ranks above colonel or to make important appointments, to deprive noblemen of life or property without trial, or to grant land or villages. A failure to comply with these conditions would deprive the Empress of her crown.

The "conditions" provoked the combined opposition of the adherents of absolutism inspired by Prokopovich and of the more radical constitutionalists among the gentry, an opposition that succeeded in wrecking the work of Golitsyn and his friends. The main accusation against them was that of aiming at an oligarchy, a rule by a few aristocratic families, and indeed the "conditions" lent themselves to such an interpretation. But they had been conceived merely as the first stage in a constitutional reform, and Golitsyn's full plan envisaged a somewhat wider sharing of powers. Apart from the Council (whose ten to twelve members were to belong to the highest nobility), it provided for a Senate of thirty to thirty-six members for preliminary consideration of problems to be presented to the Council, a Chamber of the Gentry with 200 members for the defense of the rights of this estate in case of their violation by the Council, and a Chamber of Town Representatives, two from each town, to deal with commercial affairs and the interests of the common people. These parts of Golitsyn's plan were not made public, and the ensuing misunderstanding contributed to the failure of the whole enterprise.

The more radical constitutional proposals already referred to were those of V. N. Tatishchev (1686–1750). A nobleman by birth, he apparently received no systematic education and began his career as an army officer. But he read extensively, especially during official trips to Sweden. Transferred to the civilian administration, he combined scholarly work with his official duties in the Mint, in the mining administration, and later as a provincial governor. He took an active part in the political events of 1730, and was the principal author of the document entitled "The Unrestrained and Concerted Discourse and Opinion of the Congregated Russian Gentry on State Government." Later Tatishchev laid down his general political views in two works: *A Conversation Concerning the Usefulness of the Sciences and the Schools* (1733) and *History of Russia* (completed in 1739), neither of which was published in his lifetime.

Tatishchev was a member of Prokopovich's "learned team," and his political theory, though rather more elaborate, was similar to that of Prokopovich and equally based on the doctrines of natural law and social contract. Of the originators of these doctrines he esteemed Grotius and Puffendorf highly but deplored

the influence of John Locke, thus revealing his preference for
theories that stressed the obligations of citizens rather than their
rights. States must be guided in their policies by natural and civil
law and must aim at the common good. Tatishchev saw the state
as the last—logically and chronologically—in a system of "subordi-
nations" that had gradually limited the original freedom of man,
it having been preceded by the family and the city. Family, city,
and state were natural forms of bondage, made inevitable by the
need for survival; parallel with them there had developed voluntary forms of bondage, resulting from free contracts between individuals and giving rise to class differences; peasant serfdom was
such a voluntary bondage. The historical process consisted of
progressive enlightenment, and the principal stages in this process
(at least for Christian peoples) were the invention or acquisition
of the art of writing, the coming of Christ, and the introduction
of printing; Tatishchev compared these three stages with youth,
manhood and maturity in the life of an individual. Although the
general course of history was the same for all peoples, national
peculiarities were not excluded. Thus Russia had developed somewhat differently from Western Europe: Princely feuds and the
Tatar yoke had delayed the progress of enlightenment, the people's minds had remained immature and full of superstitions,
which enabled the clergy to retain their hold over them, while
Peter's reforms opened up a new era of enlightenment and progress. Unlike Prokopovich, Tatishchev regards all three main forms
of government—monarchy, aristocracy, and democracy—as legitimate, but suitable for different states: Small states can afford a
democratic government, bigger states that are not threatened by
invasion from abroad can have an aristocracy, while large states
exposed to aggression must have a monarchy. Other forms of government, such as constitutional monarchy, are irregular and extraordinary. Thus England has a combination of all three forms:
monarchy (the King), aristocracy (House of Lords) and democracy
(House of Commons). The Russian constitutional crisis of 1730
created an extraordinary situation, which on the one hand demanded clear answers to a number of fundamental questions and
on the other justified extraordinary solutions. Tatishchev summarized the problems involved under four headings. First, to

whom does the power belong in the case of the death of a sovereign without heirs? His answer was that in such a case death releases the subjects from their oath and power falls to "the people in general"; existing institutions merely retain, for the purpose of keeping public order, such powers as they had had under the laws in force prior to the crisis. To the second question—who, in such a case, can change a law or an old custom or introduce a new one? —he gives the answer: nobody, except by the volition of the whole people. The election of a new monarch must, according to natural law, be by the consent of all subjects, some of them acting personally and others through delegates. By arrogating to themselves the right to decide on the succession, the Supreme Councilors violated the rights of the gentry and of "other ranks," who should defend this right as far as they can in order to uphold the principle. If the "ancient autocratic government" was to be changed, what form of government would be the best, considering the "condition of the people"? As a matter of principle, Tatishchev considered a change of the monarchical form of government unnecessary and harmful. But since a woman had been elected to the throne, temporary constitutional arrangments had to be made to help her, for "being a female person, she is unsuited to such many labors and, moreover, lacks the knowledge of laws." Finally, Tatishchev proposed a draft constitution to be considered by a commission of at least a hundred representatives of the gentry, which should be called immediately. The draft envisaged the abolition of the Supreme Privy Council and the substitution of two chambers "to assist Her Majesty." The first chamber, called Upper Government, or Senate, should consist of twenty-one members (with not more than one member of any one family) and have legislative and administrative functions. Draft laws should be prepared by colleges (government departments) or their individual members and presented to the Senate, which after due deliberation should give the law final shape and present it for confirmation to the Empress. A special concern of the Senate should be to ensure fair practices in the Secret Chancellery (political police), for which purpose two members should be delegated each month. The Lower Government should consist of 100 members and deal with the "internal economy"; it should be divided into three sections sitting in rotation for four months at a time. Three times a year a plenary session of the lower chamber should be called, for not longer than a month, to decide on important matters, and extraordinary plenary sessions should be called if a war breaks out, the monarch dies, etc. Both chambers should sit together as the electoral college for the election of members of each chamber; such combined sessions would also make the highest military and civilian appointments (with the participation, in the first case, of all generals, and in the second of heads of all government departments). Tatishchev's draft further proposed extensions of the privileges of the gentry and some improvements in the conditions of the clergy and the merchants.

Having allied themselves with the absolutist party against the seemingly oligarchical project of the Supreme Councilors, Tatishchev and his fellow constitutionalists in fact merely helped to reestablish autocracy.

The striving of the nobility to consolidate and safeguard their privileges was, in Russia as elsewhere, one of the strongest impulses of constitutionalist thought. The most outstanding advocate of the claims of the nobility in the second half of the eighteenth century was Prince M. M. Shcherbatov (1733–90). A member of an old aristocratic family, Shcherbatov received a good education at home, served in the Guards as a young man, was a deputy in Catherine II's Commission on the new code (1767–68), later held appointments as official historiographer, Master of the Heralds, and President of the Chamber College, and died as a Senator. In his submissions to the Commission and in speeches during its proceedings (where he emerged as the best orator and the leader of the nobility party), in his *History of Russia from the Earliest Times,* his social utopia "The Journey to Ofiria of Mr. S., a Swedish Gentleman," and in many articles and pamphlets (some of which, like the "Journey," were not published in his lifetime), Shcherbatov developed a comprehensive system of political views centered upon the idea of the nobility as the dominant class. Like most writers in the eighteenth century, Shcherbatov appealed to the notions of natural law and social contract. All men were equal by nature, but the conclusion drawn from this by the "modern philosophers" that all men should be socially equal was

chimerical. In accordance with natural law, some people were
destined to be rulers and chiefs, others to be "good executors,"
while a third group were to be "blind actors." The decisive feature
was upbringing, and only the hereditary nobility could provide
for their offspring the kind of upbringing necessary for the ruling
class. One of the experiences necessary to prepare them for participation in the business of government was the managing of
their own serfs—or slaves, as Shcherbatov preferred to call them—
to whom fell the fate of being "blind actors." Shcherbatov attacked Peter the Great's principle of ennobling for merit, though
he was prepared to accept it provided that the upper layer of the
nobility, the strictly hereditary aristocracy, was given even greater
privileges than the nobility in general. Nobles should have an exclusive right to own land and slaves, and all state and former
Church lands (secularized in 1764) should be sold to them. Somewhat inconsistent with the general idea of strict functional differentiation between the estates was Shcherbatov's insistence that
nobles and their serfs should have the right to engage in industry and commerce to the detriment of the interests of the merchants. The rights of each estate, according to Shcherbatov, are
rooted in the social contract: "Peoples, in choosing chiefs for
themselves, had no other purpose but to sacrifice a part of their
liberty in order to safeguard the other part of it." Criticizing Catherine II's Charter to the Nobility (1785), he pointed out that several of the privileges listed in it were not privileges at all, since
they were essentially basic human rights. Speaking of the necessity
to safeguard the civil order, he suggested the participation of solicitors or counsel for defense in all criminal trials, and the introduction of the English institution of habeas corpus. Many of
Shcherbatov's positive ideas on government are found in his
utopia. The ideal Empire of Ofiria is a constitutional monarchy,
the principles of which, inscribed on the walls of the imperial
palace, are: "Not the people for the kings, but the kings for the
people, for the people were there before the kings"; "The king
should be the first to obey the laws of his country, for he is king
according to the law, and in destroying the power of the laws he
destroys the obedience of his subjects to himself"; and "Kings are
neither artisans, nor merchants, nor solicitors, they do not feel

many of the needs felt by their subjects and are therefore unsuitable themselves to draw up laws." Shcherbatov constructed a complicated system of government for Ofiria, with many features borrowed from the plans of Golitsyn, Tatishchev, and Pososhkov, and with the addition of a vigorous local government, strictly separate from crown officials and based on the local corporate bodies of each of the free estates (the nobility, of course, having the major voice). All proceedings in the central and local assemblies and in the courts are open to the public, and this has an important educational function, helping to acquaint the population at large with the laws and their application. Education in general has a high priority among the tasks of government: It is free and compulsory, each estate has its own schools, but the laws of the country are taught in all. (Though earlier, Shcherbatov had argued that the "lower orders" in Russia should not be educated since education might awaken in them the spirit of disobedience.) Shcherbatov's concern for the rule of law did not mean that he favored liberal laws. On the contrary, the lives of the Ofirians are often regulated in the minutest detail, and there exists a special moral police—the priests, who, in accordance with Shcherbatov's deistic standpoint, are elected public officials. However, one field of social relations must, according to Shcherbatov, remain free from government interference—relations between the nobles and their serfs: Any interference here would tend to loosen the bond between them, whereas it is in the general interest that this bond should be strengthened. Many of Russia's ills (vividly described by Shcherbatov in his pamphlet *On the Deterioration of Morals in Russia*) he traced to the upheaval and the adulteration of Russian life caused by Peter the Great. This view was not uncommon, but Shcherbatov was probably unique in going further back and dating the beginning of the rot from 1682, when the magnates' system of precedence was abolished and high appointments became in consequence open to people of lowly origin.

If Shcherbatov deliberately acted as a spokesman of the nobility, his contemporary and fellow constitutionalist S. E. Desnitsky (ca. 1740–89) did not intend to further the interests of any particular class, but he is rightly considered by Soviet historians as essentially bourgeois in his views. A Ukrainian burgher by birth,

Desnitsky was educated at Moscow, St. Petersburg, and Glasgow universities (he was a pupil of Adam Smith at Glasgow), and upon his return to Russia in 1767 he was appointed Professor of Law at Moscow University. He was a prolific writer and translator, translating among other works the first three volumes of Blackstone's *Commentaries on the Laws of England.* Desnitsky was undoubtedly an original, though not very influential, thinker. He developed his ideas on government and politics in introductions and notes to the works he translated, in his university lectures and speeches, some of which were printed, and in the submission on the *Establishment of Legislative, Judicial, and Punitive Authority in the Russian Empire* (1768), which he hoped might be of help to the Commission on the new code then sitting. Desnitsky subscribed in a general way to the doctrine of natural law, but he criticized Grotius and Hobbes for overstressing, in different ways, the role of monarchs, and Puffendorf for his abstractness. He leaned on Hume's philosophical and political writings and on Adam Smith's *Theory of Moral Sentiments,* praising these authors as great philosophers who were most helpful in any study of law and government. Desnitsky limited the sphere of the natural rights of man to bare necessities of physical survival, and he laid stress on man's acquired rights. These had been acquired in the course of history, and Desnitsky traces their development, making use of ethnological as well as historical material. Humanity, propelled by the constant striving toward a higher state, which is inherent in man's nature, had in the course of its history run through four stages. The main feature of each stage was its predominant economic structure. The first stage had been one of hunting and gathering wild fruits, next came the pastoral stage, followed by the agricultural, and finally by the commercial stage. Legal institutions and forms of government were largely dependent on the stage of economic development; thus property developed with the transition to the third stage, that of agricultural settlement, there having been no conception of material things attaching to people in the first stage, and only the phenomenon of ownership inseparable from possession in the second. The right of property began with the house and was then extended to land; it was quite justifiable, having arisen in consequence of productive effort. The right of property reaches its final perfection in the commercial stage of development. The most perfect society is that which has the most perfect property rights, and therefore the commercial stage is the final stage in social development. Its social and legal principles are: open paths to happiness for everyone (he who carries the greater burdens having greater privileges, honor, and dignity); establishing the rights that belong to everyone, from the first to the last man; appropriate and just punishments for sins; permitting both parties before the court to have a free and public voice, so that justice is not done secretly but openly and publicly, limiting both the judge and the person before the court, so that neither can transgress his respective limits. However, Desnitsky allows that the commercial stage is not without its vices—monopolistic concentrations of capital, and the possible deterioration of morals (due to luxury) and of government.

Desnitsky's views on the origin of the state were rather unusual for his time and are of some interest. The notion of social contract is absent from his writings. According to him, statehood developed gradually as a result of the inequality of men. There were three kinds of inequality: physical, intellectual, and material. Physical inequality mattered most at the early stages when the strongest and bravest became "chiefs of peoples." Moral and intellectual superiority acquired greater importance later and produced diplomats and military leaders. Finally, material inequality arose after the appearance of property, and wealth became the main source of social prestige and political power. Feudalism in Western Euope and medieval political institutions in Russia had been based on land ownership. The modern commercial economy was the most solid foundation for a state, because commerce developed strong centripetal forces. On the other hand, the government may become corrupt and insecure at the commercial stage and even turn into a democracy or an aristocracy. The republican (Desnitsky uses the term as a synonym for democratic) form of government is an unstable one, since the egalitarian sentiment may become excessive and universal participation in government is likely to lead to disobedience. Desnitsky favored a limited monarchy and suggested the establishment in Russia of a senate of 600–800 members elected on a property franchise. Among his other practical suggestions were: local government in major towns, with municipal councils elected by merchants and resident noblemen in a fixed proportion; trial by jury; magistrates' courts for petty cases; the reintroduction of the death penalty for murder (capital punishment had been abolished in Russia in 1754); a prohibition on selling serfs without land and on splitting serf families by sale; a more equitable system of taxation, including the progressive taxation of property and a heavier sales tax on luxury goods.

If Desnitsky's approach was theoretical, that of Speransky, the great statesman of the reigns of Alexander I and Nicholas I, and the last constitutionalist thinker to be considered in this section, was primarily practical, though he always justified his practical measures or suggestions by general guiding principles and considerations. M. M. Speransky (1772–1839), son of a village priest from the Vladimir Province in central Russia, was educated at the theological seminaries in Vladimir and St. Petersburg, taught mathematics, physics, rhetoric, and philosophy at the St. Petersburg Seminary for a short time, then almost by accident joined the civil service and within a few years had reached the highest rungs of the bureaucratic ladder. He took an increasingly prominent part in the administrative reforms of the early years of Alexander I's reign until he became the most influential adviser of the Emperor. Falling suddenly from favor in 1812, he spent several years first in banishment and then as a provincial administrator, but eventually returned to the capital and in the 1830's accomplished the enormous task of the codification of Russian laws (all attempts at which, for more than a century, had been unsuccessful), earning the name of the Russian Tribonian. Speransky's views on political matters found their expression, apart from his practical activities, in many official memoranda, in private notes, and in his correspondence with friends. The views themselves stemmed from his acquaintance with the classics of political thought (we find references to Plato, Aristotle, Cicero, Bacon, Grotius, Puffendorf, Hume, Ferguson, Montesquieu, Blackstone, Bentham, etc.), his knowledge of Russian legal history, his observation of political development in contemporary Europe, his own rich political and administrative experience, and (increasingly as time went on) his religious beliefs (Speransky was a Christian mystic and, like the Old Believers, considered the official Church to be the work of Antichrist).

Speransky was the first post-Enlightenment thinker in Russia (perhaps in Europe) who saw the ultimate task of government in Christianizing social life. "People who maintain that the spirit of the Kingdom of God is incompatible with the principles of political societies are wrong," he wrote. "I do not know a single state problem that could not be reduced to the Gospel." Natural law is the moral order established by God, which finds its expression in people's consciences, their convictions, and customs. But this theocratic bent is absent in Speransky's official memoranda before banishment; these are brilliant short essays on the main problems of political theory and their argument is purely utilitarian, based on the notions of nature, social contract, and general will. The argument runs roughly as follows. Each state possesses three kinds of forces given to it by nature: the physical or personal powers of each member of the state, the powers of industry or of people's labor, and the powers of popular esteem or honor. If there was only one state in the world and if it consisted of equally strong and equally just individuals, there would be no need to have a government. But this is probably a utopia. Government is the means by which the person, the property, and the honor of everyone are safeguarded, it is chosen by the people and given for this purpose a part of the people's powers. Entrusting one individual, or a number of them, with the task of government, the people may leave to them the choice of ways in which this task should be performed. This is the despotic form of government, irrespective of whether it is autocratic or republican. The despotic was probably the only form of government in the world for a long time, since it is most similar to the patriarchal order in a family. But gradually the peoples began to realize that the powers given to their governments could be used against themselves, and they found it necessary to specify the aims and the basic rules of government. These specific aims and rules make up the constitution of a state. A government based on a constitution is either a limited (or genuine) monarchy or a moderate aristocracy. Sometimes Speransky uses the term "republic" as synony-

mous with constitutional government. Even with the best intentions a despot cannot be just, for he would have to be almost a
god to achieve this. It is inconceivable that an enlightened and
commercial people should choose to live in normal times under a
despotic government, and therefore no despotic government is
legitimate among such peoples. But there are always two constitutions in a state: the external and the internal (what we should
now call the formal constitution and the constitutional reality).
The former does not determine the latter and may indeed be fictitious, the government remaining in fact despotic. Speransky
gives a vivid description of such a fictitious constitution: an apparently free legislative body that is in fact completely dependent
on the autocratic power; executive power that according to the
letter of the law is responsible, but according to its spirit is completely independent; and a judiciary ostensibly free but in fact
tied in such a way that in its essence it is always in the hands of
the autocratic power. The internal (or genuine) constitution is
the actual distribution of powers in the state and in particular a
precise limitation of the general will and of the powers of the
government, so that it should only have what is necessary and
sufficient for its efficient functioning. Entrusting more powers to
the government means taking them away from the people, since
the total amount of powers in the state at any given time is a definite quantity. (Politics consists in establishing the exact quantities
of each kind of powers and in making use of them on the basis of
this knowledge.) If in a concentrated form these powers produce
the state authority, in a dispersed form they produce the rights of
the subjects. Each citizen's rights consist of his share in the enjoyment of the powers that have been left to society after the alienation to the government of a part of the original total enjoyment
of his powers by each man in the precontract anarchic state.
There are two kinds of rights: political rights, which determine
the subjects' share in the exercise of state authority, and civil
rights, which determine the degree of their freedom in respect of
their persons and property. There are therefore two kinds of liberty in society—political and civil. Political liberty exists when the
classes that make up society participate to a greater or lesser extent in the exercise of state authority, while civil liberty is the in-

dependence of each class from the arbitrariness of another class in matters of personal and property obligations. Conversely, there can be political and civil slavery. There have been states with the highest degree of political liberty, but never one with perfect civil liberty. A certain amount of civil liberty can exist without political liberty, but it cannot be secure; the only real guarantee of civil liberty is political liberty. But the latter cannot be established quickly by the will of a benevolent despot or of a revolutionary minority. The state must be ripe for political liberty, that is, the common opinion, or popular spirit, must long for it. The most that a benevolent despot can do in the absence of such a longing is gradually to introduce constitutional forms and thus familiarize the people with the notions of rights and liberties.

Turning from theory to historical reality, Speransky found that constitutional governments had existed in the Greek republics and in republican Rome; the despotic system had established itself in the Orient; while in Europe, the feudal system had established itself after the fall of Rome. The feudal system was based upon autocratic power, but this power, though not limited by law, was limited by the fact of its physical fragmentation. Crusades in Western Europe and campaigns against the Tatars in Russia had facilitated the elimination of feudal fragmentation and the concentration of autocratic power; the introduction of regular armies and regular taxation completed the unification, and the feudal system was replaced by a new one, for which Speransky suggests the name "feudal autocracy." But the passage of time and the progress of civic education had strengthened the republican—or constitutional—sentiment, which in the end prevailed, first in England, then in Switzerland, Holland, Sweden, Hungary, the United States of America, and finally in France. In most of these countries the constitutions were genuine, but in France, at the time of writing (1809) it was fictitious. Russia was at the autocratic, or despotic, stage, and at first Speransky said that Russian society consisted only of two kinds of slaves: slaves of the autocratic power and slaves of some of these slaves (serfs). The second type of slavery was especially intolerable because the peasants were the most useful part of the population, while the landlords were parasites. There was no political or civil liberty in Russia, the rights of the nobility and the townspeople being fictitious. But later Speransky changed his mind and considered the civil rights of the nobility, merchants, burghers, and state peasants to be genuine. Russia was ripe for transition to the constitutional stage, and this transition should not be delayed, for otherwise there would be a violent revolution.

Speransky drew up several plans for constitutional reform, that of 1809 being the most comprehensive. He envisaged a hierarchy of "legislative" assemblies on four levels—from rural district to the empire as a whole—all of which, except the rural district assemblies, would be elected on indirect franchise, with the lower assemblies acting as electoral colleges for the higher. There were also to be courts (with different jurisdictions) on each of the four levels, judges being elected by the respective assemblies from among the most prominent residents. But otherwise there was to be a strict and genuine division of powers. All Russian subjects were to have general civil rights, though all were to be subject to state service of some sort. Nevertheless, there were to be three legal classes or estates. The nobles were to have the privileges of choosing their state service and of owning inhabited land; they were also to have political rights, subject to property qualifications. Members of the middle classes also were to have political rights, subject to the same property qualifications, but no privileges in the field of civil rights except that they could be ennobled. Finally, the "working people" (peasants living on land belonging to the nobles, hired laborers, and domestic servants) were to have no political rights, even if they possessed property in the form of capital; the acquisition of land was to qualify them for transition to the middle classes. The problem of the distribution of rights turned out to be the most difficult for Speransky, and he changed his mind more than once. At first he had recommended a division of Russian society into two classes, an aristocracy (after the English pattern) as guardians of the constitution, and commoners; toward the end of his life he expressly repudiated the property franchise. But by that time he had come to the conclusion that Russia was not yet ripe for constitutional government, and that only preliminary steps, such as codification, were appropriate. His great reform plan remained on paper.

Early Radicalism

Modern radicalism in Russia dates from the second half of the eighteenth century, and the first writer we have to consider here is Ya. P. Kozel'sky (ca. 1727–after 1793). A Ukrainian nobleman educated in Kiev and St. Petersburg, he spent most of his life in government service but devoted much time to writing; he published school textbooks, translations from the French (including two volumes of selections from the *Encyclopédie* on philosophy and related subjects), German and Latin with introductions and critical notes, and original essays, of which *Philosophical Propositions* (1768) is the most important. It is a brief philosophic encyclopedia, the second part of which, devoted to "practical" (or "moral") philosophy, contains under the headings "Jurisprudence" and "Politics" a system of ethics and political theory; Kozel'sky hoped that the book might influence the work of the Commission on the new code then sitting.

Kozel'sky found that the only "substantial" writers on matters of moral philosophy were Rousseau, Montesquieu, Helvetius, and the third Earl of Shaftesbury (whose *Inquiry Concerning Virtue* Kozel'sky knew in an anonymous French edition). Rousseau in particular seemed to him worthy of immortality, "a highflying eagle" who had surpassed all previous philosophers. But Kozel'sky does not follow his authorities blindly—he tests their propositions and rejects them if they contradict his own guiding lights. He argues from divine, natural, international, and civil law (most often natural and civil), and the argument is basically utilitarian. Kozel'sky took well-being, defined as constant happiness, to be the aim of each individual and each people, and, since the original natural state of mankind had been lost forever, the most appropriate means toward this aim were virtue and reason. Virtue, defined as strict adherence to justice toward humanity as a whole and to each member of it, was the highest moral value; Kozel'sky is at pains to repudiate the rival claims of reason, deploring the fact that they are more widely accepted by his contemporaries. Politics is the science concerned with realizing righteous intentions by the most appropriate and at the same time righteous means; politics teaches men to be and to appear virtuous. Politi-

cal authority and obedience are treated as resulting from a particular kind of contract. Rulers should rule their subordinates with
love and justice and promote their well-being, while the subordinates must in return love, honor, and obey the rulers as the
people in whose hands their well-being lies. Politics as applied
to rulers is the art of ruling subordinates in such a way as to
earn their love and respect; here Kozel'sky argues against the
view that the common people should not concern themselves with
politics. Having lost, through social contract, his natural freedom
and natural equality, man has acquired instead moral freedom
and moral and legal equality—people in civil society are equal by
contract and by right. Turning to forms of government, Kozel'sky
names democracy (direct), aristocracy, monarchy, and despoty,
quotes Rousseau on reasons for preferring elected aristocracy (a
representative republic) to direct democracy and for rejecting
hereditary oligarchy, and Bielefeld as preferring monarchy to
despoty. Kozel'sky's own preference for a republican form of government becomes obvious when he quotes Montesquieu on the
bases of each form—virtue as the base in a republic, honor in a
monarchy, and fear in a despoty. Having given Montesquieu's
description of the "fundamental laws" of a republic, he adds
that in his own view there were two fundamental laws in a monarchy, namely that people's social status was determined by their
worthiness and merit, and that the monarch introduced new laws
and abolished old ones for the right reasons. Kozel'sky was opposed to a hereditary nobility, though he thought that differences
of status were inevitable in a monarchy. Although he does not
say so, it is clear that he considered the Russian government to
be despotic. He reproves Montesquieu for saying that it was
difficult or even impossible to be virtuous under an autocratic
government: This kind of thing should not be said openly; it
was better to suggest in public that people could be virtuous
under any government if they tried and to express the hope that
in time this would result in moral improvement. Kozel'sky considered property to be inviolable, but he was against great social
and economic inequality and preferred a society of moderately
well-off, industrious, and peaceful people; of the existing states,
Holland seemed to him to be the nearest to this ideal. It would

be desirable to arrange society in such a way that no member of it should be a burden to the whole nor should society as a whole be a burden upon any of its members. People greatly wronged by their superiors become vindictive if they have an opportunity for vengeance, rather like a river held back by a dam becomes destructive; if this happens, they can in justice be considered almost guiltless. But in general Kozel'sky was against abrupt changes of any kind, and relied primarily upon education as a vehicle of moral and social improvement. However, it was impossible, according to him, to "polish" a people without lightening their burdens.

Kozel'sky's views on some other economic and social matters deserve attention. They were clearly anti-Mercantilist. The wealth of nations, he wrote, consisted of the industry of their peoples and was not to be measured in gold or silver. Price was an arbitrary measure to facilitate equivalent exchange, and money was merely metal tokens invented for the purpose of indicating price. Everyone should work, with eight hours as a desirable working day, dividing the remaining time between sleep and leisure—leisure should be used only for rest and innocent enjoyment. Self-employed people should be required to supply yearly reports on their work, as do public employees. Everyone should be sufficiently well off to eliminate the necessity for indebtedness. Gifts should be forbidden by law because of their demoralizing effect; however, if a man was in dire need through misfortune, such as fire or theft, the government—society as a whole—should compensate him. Finally, Kozel'sky was strongly opposed to militarism and the conquest of foreign territories, branding them as requiring human sacrifices to greed and aggrandizement (Shcherbatov and Desnitsky were also opposed to aggressive wars, but neither denounced them so persistently and emphatically); it is particularly noteworthy that Kozel'sky, twelve years before the publication of Abbé Raynal's *Histoires des deux Indes,* attacked the colonial policy of the European powers in America, while Desnitsky seemed to approve the Russian conquest of Alaska. For defensive purposes, Kozel'sky favored, instead of conscription, a combination of a regular army consisting of people who had chosen the military career with military training for all citizens.

There is no doubt that Kozel'sky's *Propositions* had a considerable influence on the further development of political thought in Russia, although the views he advocated were (and often still are) connected in the public mind with the name of N. I. Novikov (1744–1818), a journalist and publisher, the head of the Moscow Freemason group, who did much to propagate them and restated them fairly comprehensively in his treatise "On Trade in General" (published in 1783 in the "Supplements" to his newspaper *Moscow Record,* which had a circulation of 4,000). Novikov was imprisoned during the last years of Catherine II's reign, and this made him especially popular with Russian radicals.

But the man to whom the honor is usually given of having been "the first Russian radical," the founder of the revolutionary tradition in Russia, is A. N. Radishchev (1749–1802). The eldest son of a rich, noble family, Radishchev was educated privately until the age of thirteen, then served as a page at Catherine II's court, was sent to the University of Leipzig in 1766, and upon his return to Russia five years later entered government service, ending up as Director of Customs in St. Petersburg. His famous book *A Journey from St. Petersburg to Moscow,* published anonymously in 1790, was confiscated; the author was soon identified, charged with incitement to rebellion, sentenced to death (Catherine II had reintroduced capital punishment for high treason), but reprieved and banished for ten years to eastern Siberia. Emperor Paul brought him back from banishment, and under Alexander I he was appointed to the commission on codification of laws, but his efforts on behalf of the peasants proved futile, and he committed suicide.

Apart from the *Journey,* Radishchev wrote notes to Abbé de Mably's *Observations sur les Grecs* (which he translated in 1773), the poem "Liberty" (written in 1783 and published as a part of the *Journey*), a treatise *On Man, His Mortality and Immortality* (written in banishment, it reveals the author's great erudition and philosophic ability), and several articles, official memoranda, and drafts. In his political thinking Radishchev in all essentials followed Kozel'sky, both in substance and in procedure, selecting, as Kozel'sky had done, the more radical elements in the teachings of Helvetius and Rousseau, with the addition of Locke, Mably, and Herder, and adapting them to his own basic attitudes. These were his abhorrence of serfdom and of autocracy, both of which he castigated vividly and vigorously. The strong emotional appeal of Radishchev's writings (he was the originator of the radical wing in Russian Sentimentalism) and his own tragic fate are principally responsible for his fame. He believed in a circular, or pendular, movement of history, in which freedom born out of tyranny in its turn gives birth to slavery. But despite this immutable law of nature, people should guard freedom if they have had the good fortune to gain it. In the history of Russia, autocracy was not a permanent feature. It had been preceded by the democracy of the citizens' assemblies, which had survived longest in Novgorod. This city had flourished as long as it remained a free republic and had sunk to insignificance and dreariness with the establishment of autocracy. Already in his translation of Mably's *Observations,* Radishchev had substituted "autocracy" for "despotism," adding a note in which he wrote: "Autocracy is a condition that is most contrary to human nature. . . . We cannot grant unlimited power over ourselves. . . . If we live under the authority of laws, this is not because we inevitably have to do so, but because we find it to our advantage. If we give to the law a part of our rights and of our natural power, it is in order that they should be used in our interest; we make a *silent* contract with society about this. If it is broken, then we also are released from our *obligation.* The injustice of a sovereign gives to the people—his judge—the same (or an even greater) right over him as the right over offenders that the law gives to him. *The sovereign is the first citizen of the society of the people.*" This rejection of autocracy in principle grew in the *Journey* into a call for its overthrow and a glorification of regicide as the culminating point of a victorious popular revolution. This was the first appearance of the idea of tyrannicide in the history of Russian political thought. Radishchev praises Cromwell for having, through the execution of Charles I, taught succeeding generations how peoples can avenge themselves, and at the same time condemns him as an evildoer who, having seized power, suppressed the people's freedom. Extending Kozel'sky's notion of legitimate revenge in the direction of political revolution, Radishchev extended it also in the direction of social revolution, a revolution of serfs against their masters, whose massacre would not deprive the country of much valuable human material. All cultivated land should belong to those who toil on it, and if they are organized in village communes that periodically redistribute the land according to the number of able-bodied adults in each family, this, though bad for agriculture, is "good for equality." Such were Radishchev's chief legacies to subsequent generations of Russian radicals and revolutionaries, almost all of whom have regarded him as their intellectual forefather.

Similar, though more moderate, views were held by D. I. Fonvizin (ca. 1745–1792), who is principally known as one of the great Russian playwrights. A nobleman of German descent, he was educated at Moscow University and was an influential official in the College (Ministry) of Foreign Affairs, as well as one of the leading figures of the literary world. His most important political work is the *Discourse on Unchangeable State Laws,* written in 1782–83 on the instructions of his superior, Count N. I. Panin, the head of the diplomatic service and leader of the liberal opposition to Catherine II. In the *Discourse,* Fonvizin spoke of a state (obviously Russia) that was neither despotic (because the nation had never given itself over to the sovereign to be ruled by him arbitrarily) nor monarchic (because it had no fundamental laws) nor aristocratic (because its government was a soulless machine moved by arbitrary decisions of the sovereign) nor democratic (for a land where the people, creeping in the darkness of the deepest ignorance, were silently carrying the burden of cruel slavery could not even resemble a democracy). The government form to be preferred was constitutional monarchy, and on this point Fonvizin was less radical than Kozel'sky, Novikov, or Radishchev. His views on monarchy are an interesting mixture of the doctrine of social contract with the old teaching of Joseph of Volok. A just and humble monarch was "God's likeness," the successor on earth of God's authority; a monarch lacking these qualities was not a monarch but a tyrant and his subjects were morally free from any obligation toward him. In stating the consequences of this release from the obligations of obedience, Fonvizin is more direct and outspoken than Kozel'sky, though less so than Radishchev in his "Liberty." It was well known that all human societies were based on mutual voluntary obligations, which were destroyed as soon as they ceased to be observed. Obligations between a sovereign and his subjects were equally voluntary. Every authority "not graced by the Divine qualities of justice and mercy, but causing offence, violence, tyranny" came not from God but from people who had been compelled by the misfortunes of the times to yield to force and to debase their human dignity. If a nation found the means to break its chains by the same right by which these chains had been laid upon it, then it should break them. The case was clear: Either the nation had the right to regain its freedom or else no one had had the right to deprive it of its freedom in the first place. Although Fonvizin's *Discourse* was not published at the time, it became known through handwritten copies and later had some influence upon the Decembrists, two of whom were Fonvizin's nephews.

The Decembrists (so called because they attempted a *coup d'état* in December, 1825) were the first modern revolutionary movement in Russia. Almost all of them were young army officers, and most were nobles. They had fought in the Patriotic War of 1812 against Napoleon, taken part in the subsequent West European campaign, and served in the Russian army of occupation in France. One of their leaders, Colonel P. I. Pestel' (1793–1826), ascribed the spread of revolutionary ideas in Russia at the beginning of the nineteenth century to two factors: the study of political theory ("Political books are in everybody's hands; political sciences are taught everywhere.") and foreign (European and American) examples ("Political news is spread everywhere . . . these events familiarized the mind with revolutions, with the possibilities and opportunities of carrying them out."). Both fitted the same pattern: "Every age has its own distinguishing feature. The present is distinguished by revolutionary thoughts." Describing his own conversion to revolutionary ideas, Pestel' spoke of the impact on him of the outcome of the French revolution: "The majority of basic institutions introduced by the revolution were retained and recognized as good things when the monarchy was restored. . . . This made me think that revolution was apparently not as bad as it had been made out, and might perhaps even be very useful, this thought being further strengthened by the consideration that those states that had not had a revolution continued to be deprived of such advantages and institutions."

However, unlike Radishchev, the Decembrists did not cherish the prospect of a bloody revolution. "Terrible happenings in France during the revolution made me seek a means of avoiding such a course," wrote Pestel'. And, as one of the Decembrists put it, since the indignation of the people, caused by exhaustion and by the abuses of the authorities, was threatening a bloody revolution, "the societies decided to avert a greater evil by a smaller one." They decided upon revolution by an enlightened minority, and it was natural to think of a military coup—many, if not most, of the enlightened young men of the time were army officers, while the many coups in eighteenth-century Russia had made such actions familiar. The question of regicide was discussed among the Decembrists, but it was rejected. But the problem of means did not end there. By deciding to form a secret society (after the examples of the Freemasons and of the German patriotic anti-Napoleon society Der Tugendbund), the Decembrists at the outset accepted deception as a legitimate means of political struggle, thus inadvertently following Joseph of Volok's views on cunning. And their pretense to be acting in favor of Grand Duke Konstantin was a mild form of the device applied by the imposters of the Time of Troubles and by Pugachёv. Having rejected terror, the Decembrists nevertheless accepted the idea of a revolutionary dictatorship. They intended to establish, after a successful coup, a provisional government that would decree a number of far-reaching reforms before the convocation of a constituent assembly; the task of the latter would be to consolidate measures worked out in advance and carried out by the revolutionaries. Two aspects of the idea of revolutionary dictatorship are of interest here. First, it is a variation of the idea of benevolent despotism, which in Russia can be traced from Hilarion's approval of forcible conversion to Christianity, through Joseph of Volok's and Pososhkov's views on the treatment of heretics, and Peresvetov's and Ivan the Terrible's conceptions of the rights and duties of the monarch, to the enlightened absolutism of the eighteenth and early nineteenth centuries. On the other hand, the idea of revolutionary dictatorship reflects the belief, widely held in the Age of Enlightenment, in social reform through legislation. These were the ideas on revolution held by all, or most, Decembrists. But a movement involving several hundred participants and sympathizers (500 people were under investigation after the failure of the attempted coup, and more than 100 were found guilty) could hardly be expected to be homogeneous, and in fact we find several trends among the Decembrists, ranging from the comparatively moderate position that had earlier been taken up by Fonvizin to one approaching that of Radishchev.

The more moderate trend found its best expression in the constitutional draft of N. M. Murav'ëv (1796–1843). It envisaged a constitutional monarchy with a strict division of powers, a two-chamber legislature based on property franchise, full civil rights and equality before the law for all citizens (peasants were to be freed without land), habeas corpus, trial by jury, and elected police officials. An interesting feature of the draft was that it proposed a federal structure of government: Russia was to be divided into a dozen states, with their own legislative and executive authorities enjoying some measure of autonomy. If the imperial family did not accept the constitution after the coup, they were to be expelled from Russia and the country was to become a republic. The more radical wing of the Decembrists upheld the republican idea as a matter of principle. Their most outstanding leader was Pestel', who wrote a document entitled *Russian Truth* (recalling the medieval Code of Laws), in which, as in the case of Speransky's drafts, specific constitutional proposals are preceded by a theoretical treatise on government. This part of the document contains a section on the "aristocracy of wealth," which gives an extremely interesting assessment of the position and role of the nineteenth-century bourgeoisie: "The distinguishing feature of the present century is an open struggle between the people and the feudal aristocracy, during which there begins to arise an aristocracy of wealth, much more harmful than the feudal aristocracy, since the latter can always be shaken by public opinion and is therefore to some extent dependent on it; whereas the aristocracy of wealth, owning this wealth, finds in it a tool for its intentions against which public opinion is completely powerless, and by means of which it makes the whole people . . . completely dependent upon itself." Pestel' rejected the idea of property franchise and foresaw universal male suffrage. The Russian republic, according to him, was to be a unitary state with a single-chamber legislature, a directly elected executive, and a kind of constitutional court that was also to have the power of appointing army commanders in chief. All the peoples of Russia were to lose their national identities and be assimilated, with the exception of the Poles, who were to become independent. A part of the land belonging to the landlords was to be nationalized (with compensation) and divided into "communal" and "private" land, the former to be given to rural communities which were to put it freely at the disposal of the peasants, and the latter to be sold to private buyers and subsequently to be treated as a commodity. Private societies of every kind were to be forbidden on the grounds that if their aims were legitimate, these aims would in any case be furthered by the government; and if they were not legitimate, people should not be permitted to pursue them.

The Decembrist movement, despite its total failure, played a very important role in the history of Russian political thought. Its main contribution was that it gave an example of practical revolutionary activities that inspired future generations of radicals. The five hanged leaders of the society were the first martyrs of Russian radicalism. Many of the Decembrists' ideas were picked up by later revolutionaries. But the movement and its attempted coup also influenced the thinking of the opposite camp, the adherents of the autocracy, and especially Emperor Nicholas I, whose accession to the throne the Decembrists had tried to prevent.

4. The Theory of Official Nationality and Its Antidote

THE YEAR 1825 may be regarded as marking the end of the Petrine period in Russian political thought. The impetus given to it by Peter's reforms was spent. Trends of political thought that had emerged under the influence of seventeenth-eighteenth century West European writings, on the assumption that the ideas of their authors, being of a universal nature, were directly applicable to Russia, came to a rather inglorious end. Enlightened absolutism proved unable to overcome the national sentiment and, in Karamzin's thought, succumbed to it. Constitutionalism, faced with the apparent "unripeness" of Russia, was even less successful in holding its ground. And radicalism collapsed at the first attempt to turn the theory into practice. The fact that all three trends crumbled just when they seemed to be on the point of winning made their failure all the more painful. Russia suddenly seemed to have reached a dead end. Rationalism itself, in some measure common to all three trends, no longer inspired any trust, since it had clearly failed to grasp the human and historical reality. It yielded to the mysticism of the Freemasons, Alexander I, and Speransky, and to the atheism and materialism of some of the Decembrists, but the new metaphysical props were unable to sustain the old political doctrines.

Yet the state existed and had to be governed—but on what principles? And the failure of the eighteenth-century doctrines had to be explained, the condition of Russia had to be understood—intellectual curiosity and emotional involvement demanded it. Two ways out were suggested in the late 1820's–early 1830's, and both proved fruitful for future political thought.

The Theory of Official Nationality

The political doctrine that was later christened by historians the Theory of Official Nationality was formulated in 1832 by S. S. Uvarov (1786–1855), a man of noble birth and many gifts who had the reputation of being "the best-educated man in Russia." He had a varied experience in government service, was for many years President of the Academy of Sciences, and from 1833 to 1849 Minister of Education. Uvarov restated his doctrine several times, in almost identical terms, in official circulars and reports during the period when he was in charge of education. It was based on three concepts—orthodoxy, autocracy, and nationality—and these three words became the battle cry of its adherents. Orthodoxy meant devotion to the teaching and ritual of the Russian Orthodox Church, a reaction to the skepticism of the eighteenth century and the mysticism of the early nineteenth, a return to the spiritual roots of pre-Petrine Russia, an attempt to rebuild a bridge to the spiritual world of the mass of the people. The affirmation of the principle of autocracy meant an end to the liberal policies and the juggling with constitutional projects characteristic of the early years of Catherine II's and Alexander I's reigns, a return to the old Muscovite notion (recently reaffirmed by Karamzin) of autocracy as the basic and permanent feature of Russian statehood, to a view of the Czar's authority that was certainly shared by the vast majority of his subjects. Finally, nationality, the least clear of the three principles, was interpreted by Uvarov as devotion to the Russian national heritage and the spiritual make-up of the people, a refusal to trust Western Europe as a model for Russia, or West European theories (most of them regarded in any case as intrinsically harmful) as at all relevant for Russia; it also implied a concern for the interests and well-being of the people. The author of this doctrine of denominationalism, authoritarianism, and intellectual and cultural conservatism was widely known to be a skeptic in religious matters, a liberal in his political views, and a cosmopolitan in his tastes and style of life (he always wrote in French or German). Uvarov was not, of course, the first public figure in Russia to display such incongruity between his public utterances and his private beliefs (the sincerity of both Catherine II and Alexander I, for instance, has been questioned), but he was probably the first Russian politician to make Joseph of Volok's precept of perfidy the key to his whole political doctrine.

Not all adherents of the doctrine had the same manipulative attitude toward it, and one of these "dissenters" was the Emperor Nicholas I himself. His approval of the doctrine gave it the official position it enjoyed, but he himself sincerely believed in the principles it enunciated, and throughout his reign faithfully endeavored to implement them. Indeed, the most recent student of the Theory of Official Nationality, Professor N. V. Riasanovsky, rightly regards Nicholas as its real inspirer, a man who had always held the views that were woven into a doctrine by the versatile Uvarov. The doctrine, as formulated by Uvarov, did not imply a rejection of Peter the Great's reforms—these were regarded as irrevocable, and the contemporary Russian Empire was seen as a happy blend of pre-Petrine and Petrine features. Indeed, Nicholas I continued the Petrine policy of borrowing useful techniques from Western Europe and established in Russia a political police on the French model. Nor did Uvarov propagate obscurantism or demand the cultural isolation of Russia; he specifically intended the autocracy to be enlightened. But his doctrine did lend itself to obscurantist, isolationist, and retrograde interpretations, and censorship of the press, restrictive educational policies (especially after Uvarov's resignation as Minister), and attempts to isolate Russia from the West European germs of Liberalism and Socialism were characteristic features of Nicholas I's reign, particularly after the 1848 revolutions in Western Europe.

Accepted by Nicholas I, the theory of orthodoxy, autocracy, and nationality survived as the official political doctrine at least until the revolution of 1905, if not until February, 1917. In practice it fared rather badly under Nicholas I's successor, Alexander II, whose reign was marked by the great liberal reforms of the 1860's and 1870's, but it was faithfully adhered to by the two last emperors, Alexander III (1881–94) and Nicholas II (1894–1917). Indeed, during these two reigns the court and government circles laid increasing stress upon the pre-Petrine roots of the

existing political order. The practical policies of the period between the assassination of Alexander II in 1881 and the revolution of 1905 were oppressive and obscurantist: curtailment of
local government and of the autonomy of the universities that
had been introduced in the 1860's; increasing discrimination
against Jews and increasing Russification of national minorities;
frequent bypassing of the reformed, modern judiciary by the
imposition of states of emergency. The political police resorted,
albeit on a modest scale, to the employment of *agents provoca-
teurs*—a practice that had been recommended by Joseph of Volok.
Although Nicholas II was compelled by the revolutionary events
of 1905, especially by the general strike in October, to grant a
constitution, the Russian Emperor was described in the Constitution itself as an autocrat. The legal significance of this definition
was not clear, but there could be no doubt that it was intended
to convey the impression that the Russian monarchy still adhered
to the principle of autocracy. The Constitution left executive
power entirely in the hands of the Emperor, so that the government was not responsible to the State Duma (the legislative
assembly) until the end of the monarchy.

The active adherents of the theory of Official Nationality
formed a number of militant right-wing organizations, of which
the most important was the Union of the Russian People. The
best-known leader of the Union (though he later left it) was
V. M. Purishkevich (1870–1920), a landowner from Bessarabia
and one of the most brilliant orators in the Duma. Nicholas II
himself was an honorary member of the Union. The Union made
much propaganda use of the so-called "Protocols of the Elders of
Zion," a forged document purporting to show the existence of an
international Jewish conspiracy aimed at establishing Jewish
domination throughout the world. Gangs of Union adherents
(colloquially known as the Black Hundred) organized pogroms
of Jews and students. Purishkevich was so appalled by the dis-
repute into which the royal family's favorite Rasputin brought
the monarchy in the years after 1905, that in 1916 he took part in
his assassination. But nothing could now save the monarchy, and
its fall in 1917 signified the collapse of the theory of Official
Nationality.

Several monarchist organizations were formed after the Civil War by the *émigrés* abroad, and some of them still exist. They have invariably idealized conditions in pre-1917, and especially pre-1905, Russia, and have usually maintained that both revolutions and the Communist regime were the work of some alien, sinister forces, most frequently identified as Jews and Freemasons. This view has little factual basis as far as Jews are concerned; but in regard to the Freemasons, the theory—though for long held to be disreputable because it was advanced only by these extremist right-wing groups—has been recently proved (by G. Aronson) to be partially correct. A Masonic organization, which is briefly described on pp. 110 and 207, did in fact play an important part in preparing the 1905 and February 1917 revolutions. The "Jew and Freemason" theory of Bolshevism was adopted by the German Nazis and used in their propaganda in Russia during World War II, however without any appreciable success.

Chaadaev

The most extreme reaction to the trend of thought that resulted in the formulation of Uvarov's doctrine in the 1830's came from P. Ya. Chaadaev (1793–1856). A nobleman with excellent education, first at private schools and then at Moscow University, he became a cavalry officer and took part in the campaigns against Napoleon that brought him to Paris. Returning to Russia, he joined one of the Decembrist organizations but he happened to be abroad in 1825 and therefore took no part in the uprising. His thinking took a pessimistic turn after the suppression of the movement, and in 1829, in a mood of near despair, he wrote (characteristically in French) his main work, *Philosophical Letters*. They were circulated in handwritten copies until 1836, when the first *Letter* was published in Russian in a liberal monthly journal. The effect was later likened by Herzen to that of a bomb explosion. The journal was immediately forbidden, and Chaadaev himself was officially declared to be insane and put under medical care. In these conditions he wrote the *Apology of a Madman,* in which he further developed his ideas, giving them, however, a rather unexpected optimistic twist.

Chaadaev's historiosophic and political doctrine has been described (by Herzen) as "revolutionary Catholicism." The ultimate source of human destiny is for him divine providence, working through religious ideas given to humanity and embodied in the general human reason from which individuals derive their own spirituality and reason. Human history consists essentially in the development of ideas that move people to action. The divine idea has found its most perfect expression in Christianity, which preserved its true nature in Roman Catholicism, and thanks to Catholicism, Western Europe has had a rich intellectual life. Eastern Christianity, on the contrary, had become a ritualistic ornamental adjunct of the sterile Byzantine state, and it was Russia's greatest misfortune that she had accepted and lived under this form of Christianity. As a result, Russia had no feudalism, no renaissance, and played no part in the modern intellectual movement toward individual freedom—in short, no history. The ignorance, barbarism, and slavery of the Russian past and present do not constitute history. However, this lack of history, Chaadaev argued later in the *Apology,* could turn out to be Russia's hope: If she recognizes the futility of attempts to continue following a different road from that of the West, and wholeheartedly and unreservedly joins Western Europe, then the very absence of established forms and traditions may enable her to move faster than other countries in the realm of ideas and, perhaps, to make her own unique contribution to future European history.

Although Chaadaev did not develop a specific doctrine of state and government, his brilliantly and forcefully expressed views inaugurated a new phase in Russian political thinking. Like the Romantic doctrines in contemporary Western Europe, they undermined the basic assumption of the Enlightenment that obscurantism had been reigning until the emergence of modern rationalist thought, which was equally applicable to all problems and situations and was bound to lead all humanity into the kingdom of reason. Although both historical nihilism and rationalist optimism were present in Chaadaev's thought, both had lost their absolute character and become circumscribed and conditional. No further step in political thinking in Russia could be made without testing the validity of Chaadaev's contentions, and the different conclusions at which people arrived in this process laid the basis for the main divisions in Russian political thought throughout the nineteenth century.

The doctrine of Official Nationality, accepting in full and justifying the existing state of affairs, and Chaadaev's total rejection of both, supplied the two extreme positions from which and between which Russian political thought moved during the nineteenth century. Russia's identity or similarity with Western Europe, or, conversely, its distinctiveness, was the problem most hotly debated, and the different views taken upon this point formed the essential background of most of the rest of political thinking. The result of this basic orientation was, not surprisingly, that for several decades after the 1830's, the main division in public opinion was between the Westernists and their opponents, who came to be known as the Slavophiles. Neither camp was homogeneous, the Westernists in particular including a variety of trends derivative from different West European models. The Slavophiles were at first a more coherent school, and they developed their specific doctrine earlier than the Westernists, because they obviously could not merely take over any of the party programs current in the West.

5. Slavophilism

THE INTELLECTUAL movement that came to be known as Slavophilism was not restricted to the sphere of politics and political thought but embraced theology, philosophy, historiography, literary criticism, and later even the natural sciences. But because of the nature of the Slavophile doctrine itself, these various fields of intellectual activity were regarded as closely connected and political implications were never far from the surface. Three trends can be distinguished within the Slavophile movement in the wider sense during the six decades of its existence: the original Slavophilism, the so-called "soil-bound" school, and Pan-Slavism.

Classical Slavophilism

The recognized head of the Slavophile school, and in many respects its most outstanding representative, was A. S. Khomyakov (1804–60). Of a noble family, he received an excellent education at home and at Moscow University, where he read mathematics. He spent his life, apart from a short period in the army, as a country squire managing his estate in the summer, and debating in the Moscow salons in the winter. Khomyakov impressed his contemporaries, supporters and opponents alike, as a man of great erudition, original and sharp mind, clear and firm convictions, and one whose actions were in complete harmony with his beliefs. Although he was brilliant in oral debate, writing did not come easily to Khomyakov, and apart from his unwieldy *Notes on World History* (which were published in three volumes after his death), his writings mainly took the form of private letters or comments upon other people's articles; it is remarkable, for example, that his theological views (and Khomyakov is now widely regarded as the most important modern Orthodox theologian) were developed mainly in his correspondence (particularly with William Palmer, a Fellow of Magdalen College, Oxford).

Khomyakov was not directly interested in politics and his views on the subject were for the most part an incidental outcome of his ecclesiological, anthropological, and historiosophic doctrines. For Khomyakov, the basic reality in this world was the Church, conceived as a free community of naturally diverse individuals the purpose of which is the attainment of truth. Truth can only be attained through the application of all one's spiritual forces— will, reason, and faith—not by an individual seeking truth in isolation, but in a free community with others of similar disposition. This is the essence of Khomyakov's ecclesiological principle of "conciliarism" (*sobornost'*)—free unanimity in the pursuit of truth. There are two different spiritual types, which can find their expressions both in individuals and in groups. One of them seeks and treasures freedom and strives to attain as complete freedom as possible in this world—that is, free community of faith, reason, and will ultimately realized in the Orthodox Church. The other spiritual type is one that tries to escape from the responsibility of freedom into the realm of necessity. The way of this escape is fragmentation, the divorce of man's spiritual powers— will, reason, and faith—from each other, reliance on one or other of them alone, subordination to external authority based on one of them. Historically, the spiritual principle of freedom (which Khomyakov called Iranian) had found its expression primarily in Ancient Greece and later in Orthodox Christianity and in the communal spirit of the Slav peoples. The principle of necessity (called Kushite by Khomyakov) found one of its main expressions in Ancient Rome, with its excessive reliance on reason and on the external authority of law. These Roman qualities were taken over by the Roman Catholic Church, which was both reasoning and legalistic, and largely conditioned the spiritual and therefore the social and political development and make-up of the West European peoples. The Reformation, Protestantism, modern science and philosophy, liberal economic doctrines, revolutions and parliamentary institutions—all these were signs of progressive fragmentation and of the tendency to shield oneself behind an external authority of one kind or another. Khomyakov was not

80 · RUSSIAN POLITICAL THOUGHT

anti-European and did not find everything in Western Europe reprehensible. Many aspects of English life, in particular, appealed to him, and he treated the English jury system, like the Russian peasant commune (*mir*), as an example of the realization in public life of the principle of conciliarism.

Russian historical development, thanks to the communal spirit of the people and to the Orthodox Church, was different from that of Western Europe and, Khomyakov thought, much closer to his own ideals. The Russian state was founded not by conquest but by an invitation to the Scandinavian princes and peaceful acceptance of their authority. When the Rurikid dynasty came to an end, a new dynasty, the Romanovs, were installed by the whole people acting through the Council of the Land. The Orthodox Church did not aspire to temporal power and there was no rivalry between the Church and the State, as there was in the West, the relations between them being usually harmonious. Peter the Great had destroyed the former harmony by subordinating the Church to the State, by forcibly introducing administrative practices alien to the communal spirit of the people, and by alienating through cultural Westernization the upper strata of Russian society from the majority of the people, who retained their old ways. The cultural benefits of Westernization should be retained, but in order to heal the spiritual damage caused by it, the government and the educated society should return to the spirit of the Orthodox Church and free communal life. In the field of government, in particular, bureaucracy and intolerance should be abandoned and free public opinion should sustain the monarch in carrying the burden of rule, which has been entrusted to him by the people.

The classical Slavophiles were a remarkably homogeneous group. They were members of a small number of noble families, often related to each other, from central or eastern Russia. They were educated at Moscow, which remained their intellectual home, St. Petersburg being regarded as a symbol of the alienation and corruption of Russian public life by the hostile West. Although most of them spent some time in government service, these periods were usually short, and since they were all comfortably off they could afford the life of independent gentlemen of learning and letters. They published several journals, but more often than not each new publishing venture soon ran into trouble with the censorship and was forced to close down. Their degree of interest in political matters varied, but generally speaking the younger generation of Slavophiles was more politically minded and more active in the political field. The brothers Aksakov— Konstantin (1817–60) and Ivan (1823–86)—were the chief public spokesmen of the movement, Ivan in particular playing a role of popularizer similar to that of Novikov in eighteenth-century radicalism. Their constant themes were rejection of the ways and fashions of the West and often strong hostility to it (perceived as a reaction to the hostility of Western Europe toward Russia); rejection of both the regimentation of the life of the country (dear to the hearts of the government and the proponents of the official political creed) and also of any constitutionalist tendencies, which appeared to them as attempts by the nobility to establish, contrary to the Russian tradition and spirit, a privileged position for themselves in public life; freedom of public opinion and of the press. The political formula of the Slavophiles, developed mainly as a result of K. S. Aksakov's studies in Russian history, was "Plenitude of power for the Czar, freedom of opinion and counsel for the land," that is, for the people. This formula had, they maintained, been operative in Russia from the Kievan period until the introduction of West European absolutism by Peter the Great, and Russia should return to it. The Slavophiles were keenly interested in the reforms of Alexander II, several of them were deeply involved in preparing and implementing the emancipation of the serfs, and from the 1860's on, they took an active part in the new local government.

One of the most politically active of the Slavophiles, and certainly the most effective of them in practical politics, was Yu. F. Samarin (1819–76). A Hegelian in his early youth, Samarin turned Slavophile under the influence of Khomyakov and remained his great admirer; he was the first to call Khomyakov a Doctor of the Church. Apart from Khomyakov's teaching, Samarin's political views were influenced by his study of the history of church and state relations in Russia, of the reforms in Prussia under Baron vom Stein at the beginning of the century, and, among West

European writings, especially by L. von Stein's *Socialism and Communism in Present-day France* (1843). Practical experience also played an important role: as a landlord and in the course of his duties as a government official, Samarin familiarized himself thoroughly with all aspects of the peasant problem, and an official mission to the Baltic provinces of the Russian Empire gave him a welcome opportunity to study at first hand the problem of national minorities. Finally, his frequent travels in Western Europe gave him much material for thought. Samarin was convinced that the power of the Russian Czar should be unlimited, but he was equally convinced that it should rest upon the recognition of a wide sphere of freedom for the Czar's subjects. As for all Slavophiles, the problem of the Church was of great importance for him. The West had failed to establish the right relationship between Church and State, had failed to escape the choice between the alternatives of domination by the Church and negation of the State, as with the Roman Catholics, or domination by the State and negation of the Church, as with the Protestants. Russian history had proved that there was another solution. The Church always recognized the State, but the reverse was not always the case, and recognition by the State was not necessary for the Church. In this lay its freedom, which could not be taken away by any earthly power. For the sake of preserving this freedom, the Orthodox Church must not try to enlist the support of the State in the struggle against other religions or denominations. The normal relationship between Church and State in the Orthodox world was mutual recognition. Such a harmony had existed in Russia before it was disturbed by Roman Catholic influence, which gave to the Moscow Patriarchy a papist aspect and created among the clergy a political party hostile to the state. The ecclesiastical reform of Peter the Great and Theophan Prokopovich had been a natural reaction, but they went too far toward the Protestant extreme. This one-sidedness should be recognized as a necessary but ephemeral historical stage on the way to re-establishing the original harmony. In L. von Stein's book, Samarin found what for him was a translation of Khomyakov's spiritual principles of social life into the language of politics: a sharp distinction between state and society, between political and social problems, and an advocacy of social justice. Samarin's impressions of the Baltic provinces seemed to him to confirm the basic Slavophile views. The German minority there, basing its claims on the right of conquest, maintained the old feudal system, which hindered the economic development of the region and perpetuated oppression and exploitation by the nobility of the peasants, mainly indigenous Latvians and Estonians who, though personally free (serfdom had been abolished in the Baltic provinces under Alexander I), had no land and were forced to rent it from the German landlords; the medieval guild system in the towns was similarly hindering free economic development.

Such was the theoretical and practical equipment that Samarin brought to what became his main contribution to Russian political thought—the part he took in the emancipation of the serfs. Having established his reputation as an authority on the problem (through a number of privately circulated papers and memoranda, since discussion of this subject was forbidden in the press), Samarin was invited as an outside expert to join the committee officially entrusted with preparation of the reform. The distinctive contributions of Samarin and one or two fellow Slavophiles who were associated with the work were two: One was the decision not merely to free the serfs personally, but, in order to avoid their proletarianization, to transfer to them the title of a part of the land belonging to their masters. A minimum allotment was granted free of charge, while ownership of larger allotments was to be acquired through a system of redemption payments, described by a recent student (D. J. Footman) as a kind of hire-purchase; landlords were at once compensated by the government for the alienated parts of their land. The other, even more specifically Slavophile, contribution was the decision to transfer the land allocated to the ex-serfs in those parts of Russia where village communes existed not to individual peasants but to the communes, which would hold the title and periodically redistribute the land among peasant households. The bases of distribution could be different, according to the will of the commune, and they did vary in fact (according to the number of "mouths," of able-bodied members of the household, etc.), but it was the principle of communal ownership which was dear to the

Slavophiles and which they succeeded in implementing, at least in central Russia.

In their determination to meet Chaadaev's challenge and to test the validity of his contentions, the Slavophiles attempted a deeper understanding of the Orthodox Church consciousness, a comparative study of manifestations in the history of the world of the two opposite spiritual principles—freedom and necessity— an understanding of the Russian past in terms of these principles, a reconstruction from historical and contemporary evidence of an ideal, peculiarly Russian, way of life, and an elaboration of a positive program of fuller realization of this ideal through the gradual elimination of what appeared to them to be alien features in the social and public life of Russia (serfdom, Western-type absolutism based on regimentation, subjection of the church, press censorship, etc.). It is usually pointed out that the Slavophiles were influenced in their approach by, and directly borrowed many of their ideas from, the German Romantics and Idealists (Herder, Friedrich Schlegel, Schelling, Hegel), through whose intellectual school they all passed. But it should also be emphasized that the Slavophiles leaned, in their speculations, on the Eastern Fathers of the Church; that, all their exaggerations notwithstanding, they resuscitated the authentic tradition of Metropolitan Hilarion (his views on slavery and freedom, on Russia as a pre-eminently Christian country, on relations between Church and State) and the dualistic tradition in the pre-Petrine Russian political practice and thought (princes' and citizens' assemblies in Kiev and Novgorod, Czar and Council of the Land in Muscovy). Three specific Slavophile ideas were destined to survive their originators and to make a considerable impact on later thought: the principle of conciliarism, the notion of the communal spirit of the Russian people, and the idea that Russians shared their peculiar characteristics with other Slavs.

Pan-Slavism

Although a certain Pan-Slavic tendency can be discerned in the original Russian chronicle, Pan-Slavic sentiment contributed little or nothing to Russian thought during the late Middle Ages and the Muscovite period. The Pan-Slavic theory of J. Križanić, the seventeenth-century Croat Jesuit, fell upon deaf ears in Russia at the time, though one can hear its echo in a manifesto to the Balkan Slavs that Peter the Great issued during his war against Turkey, and in a similar manifesto of Catherine II's. Modern Pan-Slavism was also not of Russian provenance, having originated among the southern and western Slavs in the first half of the nineteenth century. But it gradually found adherents in Russia. The first significant group were the members of one of the Decembrist organizations, the Society of United Slavs. They envisaged, in case of a victory of the revolution in Russia, the liberation of the western and southern Slavs and the creation of a democratic Slavic federation in which Russia would be an equal member. After the failure of the Decembrists, the Pan-Slavic idea was picked up by the conservative M. P. Pogodin (1800–75), Professor of History at Moscow University (born a serf), who is usually counted among the chief (and sincere) upholders of the theory of Official Nationality. Pogodin became the chairman of the main Pan-Slavic organization, the Moscow Slavic Benevolent Society (founded in 1857), and he was succeeded in this position by Ivan Aksakov. Most other Slavophiles were members of this society, although, despite their name (which was given to them by their opponents), they generally took little interest in the actual life of non-Russian Slavs. Unlike the informal but compact circle of the Slavophiles, the Pan-Slavic society was rather loose and heterogeneous. It aimed at asserting and demonstrating the cultural and political solidarity of the Slavs by such means as holding the Second Pan-Slavic Congress in Moscow in 1867 (the First had been held in Prague in 1848) and championing the cause of the southern Slavs during the Balkan wars of 1875–78. These last years saw the climax of the Pan-Slavists' influence, which had aroused considerable public interest in Russia and succeeded in making the government accept as its official aim the liberation of southern Slavs from the Turkish yoke. Aksakov's speeches were reported in newspapers throughout Europe and he was widely regarded abroad as the spokesman of the Russian government. This illusion was shattered in 1878, when the government, having liberated Bulgaria (an act for which Alexander II once again earned the appellation Czar-Liberator—having first been so called for liberating the serfs in Russia), agreed at the Berlin Congress to return half the territory to the Ottoman Empire. Aksakov denounced the government in a famous speech, as a result of which the Moscow Slavic Society was suppressed and Aksakov himself ordered to leave Moscow.

This moderate Pan-Slavism, which for a brief period became popular (and was revived during both world wars), must be distinguished from the extreme Pan-Slavist theory that is chiefly associated with the name of N. Ya. Danilevsky (1822–85), though it had a few other prominent adherents, including the great poet F. Tyutchev. Danilevsky was the son of a general, a zoologist by training and profession, and a leading anti-Darwinist. In his book *Russia and Europe* (1869), he advanced one of the first theories of cultural types or civilizations as the principal divisions of mankind by analogy with the different species of a genus. Cultural types were conceived by him as self-contained and self-sufficient entities that could exist side by side or replace each other, but the cultural substance of a type could not be transmitted to a successor. Europe is one of such cultural types (Romano-Germanic), and its claim to universality is unfounded and preposterous. Russia is not a part of Europe, but, together with other Slavs, forms a cultural type of its own, and in describing it Danilevsky follows the Slavophiles. Each cultural type may excel in one or more of the main fields of human endeavor: religious, cultural in the narrow sense, political, or social and economic. Only one type, however, the Slavic, has the potentialities that enable it to develop in all four directions, and thus, for the first time in history, to produce a fully balanced civilization. But in order to develop these potentialities to the full, the Slavs must liberate themselves from their German and Turkish masters and must join Russia to form one great Slavic empire headed by the Russian Czar. Russia, as the largest and the only independent Slavic country, is under an obligation to act for the achievement of this aim, and Russian foreign policy must be entirely subordinated to this task. The only valid criterion for a correct foreign policy is whether a given step furthers or hinders the attainment of Slavic unity, or whether it is indifferent in this respect. Other countries and their policies must also be judged from this point of view alone, for one's cultural type is the highest unity, to which one can and should subordinate other interests and considerations. In its political aspect, Danilevsky's theory was a revival, with a new theoretical justification, of Križanić's views of two hundred years earlier.

The "Soil-bound" School

If the Pan-Slavic trend was an extension of the Slavophile movement in one direction, the "soil-bound" school, similarly basing itself on some of the main tenets of Slavophilism, extended it in other directions. The Pan-Slavists clung to one of the weakest aspects of the Slavophile theory—the peculiar features supposedly common to Russia and the other Slavs. The writers of the "soil-bound" school, on the contrary, were inspired by two points that were among the Slavophiles' strongest tenets. One of them was that Russians should know their own country, study it, and base their judgments on the realities of Russian life. Following this approach, the writers of the "soil-bound" school took upon themselves the task of "fusing" the educated stratum with the "popular principle." They wanted to "return to the soil" from which Peter's reforms had alienated the upper classes. This appeal, formulated in the early 1860's by F. M. Dostoevsky (1821–81), gave the trend its name. The other starting point of the thought of this school was the Slavophiles' concept of freedom.

Not Dostoevsky, but his contemporary A. A. Grigor'ev (1822–64), was the first leader of the school. They had much in common. Both belonged to the nobility, but, unlike the Slavophiles, not to old and wealthy families. Both had to earn their living, both became professional writers and journalists, and both led very unsettled lives. In their youth both belonged to the radical circles of the 1840's and were arrested in connection with the Petrashevsky case. But Grigor'ev was soon released, while Dostoevsky spent several years in prison and banishment. In the 1850's, Grigor'ev was the leading figure on the journal *The Muscovite,* and in the 1860's, they cooperated on the journals that were edited by Dostoevsky. Probably the most important of Grigor'ev's political writings was an article he published in 1863 under the title "Sad Reflections on Despotism and on Voluntary Slavery of Thought." It begins with the declaration: "There are people who, not only in accordance with the spirit of the time, but according to their personal taste hate . . . the word *slave,* but who also equally hate the famous formula of all theorists, from the great theorist Caligula to the other great theorist Robespierre," i.e., the formula which Grigor′ev quoted as a motto of the article, *"Liberté, égalité, fraternité—ou le mort!"* "What are such people to do," he asks, "at a time when a merciless logical dilemma is erected everywhere?" Grigor′ev loves and respects the Slavophiles, whom he calls representatives of a serious and honest trend, but for him Slavophilism is still a theory, like radicalism. True, the Slavophiles' notion of freedom (and here Grigor′ev specifically referred to Samarin, who had expressed the belief that a human thought should be allowed to destroy itself if it was wrong and not be put down by others) was infinitely superior to that of the radicals, who were intolerant of any view that differed from their own. But the Slavophiles were aristocrats, out of touch with the real life of the common people, especially the townspeople.

Dostoevsky was, of course, a far greater thinker than Grigor′ev. But he thought primarily in images and developed his political philosophy above all in his great novels (particularly *The Possessed* and *The Brothers Karamazov*) and in such works as *Notes from the Underground.* In comparison, his more overtly political writings, such as the *Diary of a Writer,* are of lesser importance. There have been many attempts to interpret Dostoevsky's thought, but it seems that nobody succeeded in understanding it better than V. S. Solov′ëv, who was very close to Dostoevsky during the last years of the latter's life. Summarizing Dostoevsky's social philosophy in the first two of his three memorial speeches, Solov′ëv shows that the initial impulse in Dostoevsky's thought was his compassion for the sufferings of those who were wronged and humiliated in contemporary society. And his first reaction was to join those who sought to put things right through a change, by violent means, in the external conditions of people's lives. While being punished for this attempt, Dostoevsky came into closer contact than before with other sufferers, and as a result of learn-

ing the state of their minds he came to the conclusion that it was
wrong for an individual to make up his own social ideal and
criminal to try to impose it upon others. To construct an ideal of
one's own appeared to him as an act of self-deification. Dostoevsky contrasted the homemade truth of an individual or group of
people with the Christian religion, which was accepted and preserved by simple people. He demanded from an individual the
moral feat of renouncing his self-made ideal and returning to the
Christian ideal of the people, not, however, because it was popular or national, but because it was a universal truth. Thus the
Church was the ideal society for Dostoevsky (as it had been for
St. Augustine), and all social and public life should be essentially
identical with the life of the Church. Belief in the Church among
the Russian people corresponds to the belief in socialism in Western Europe. But whereas European Socialists demand a leveling
down to a general state of material satisfaction, this "Russian
Socialism" raises everyone to the level of the Church as a spiritual
brotherhood, albeit while preserving external inequality of social
status. The possession of the truth cannot be the privilege of one
people, any more than it can be the privilege of an individual.
In order to approach the ideal, not only must individuals renounce
their private ideals, but the people as a whole must renounce and
shake off whatever may be incompatible in its make-up with the
religious truth. Dostoevsky did not idealize the Russian people,
although he believed that Russia had a special mission in the
world and was capable of fulfilling it. Unlike the Pan-Slavists,
who deplored the weakness of national egotism among the Russians, Dostoevsky saw in this weakness a sign of Russia's greatness.
Dostoevsky saw in the Russians two especially valuable features: an
unusual ability to absorb the spirit and ideas of other peoples—
a capacity for spiritual transsubstantiation (especially manifest in
the poetry of Pushkin)—and, even more important, the realization
of one's own sinfulness, an inability to accept one's imperfection
as the norm, a thirst for purification. Dostoevsky maintained,
therefore, that, despite their apparent bestiality, the Russian people carried in the depths of their souls a different image, the image of Christ. When the time came, they would reveal this other
image to all peoples, would attract them all to this image, and

thus fulfill their mission. The world could not be saved by force, the coming together should be effected freely, for if unity is imposed by blind instinct or external compulsion it is the unity of an ant heap, which was, for Dostoevsky, the opposite of his ideal. There must be a free agreement to unite.

It is hardly necessary to say that Dostoevsky himself practiced his belief in freedom. He was a free thinker, and it is debatable whether his views are compatible with the Christian dogma, which demands the rendering unto Caesar of what is Caesar's. But there is no doubt that in his striving toward a sanctification of social life, he reverted to the tradition of the medieval Church, which worked for a replacement of an externally imposed law by an innerly accepted truth. Dostoevsky was preceded on this path by Speransky and also Gogol', though the latter, like the medieval thinkers, held the existing state to be sanctified and, unlike Dostoevsky, did not aim at a transfiguration of it. Dostoevsky's indebtedness to the Slavophiles is obvious. But whereas Khomyakov had conceived the Orthodox Church and the communal spirit of the Slavs as parallel phenomena, though stemming from one source, their relationship was for Dostoevsky a causal one. In his famous speech, shortly before his death, at the ceremony of unveiling the Pushkin monument in Moscow, Dostoevsky, in asserting that the peculiarity of the Russian people lay in their universality, overcame the basis of the division between the Slavophiles and the Westernists. The immediate emotional impact of the speech was great, but, having recovered from its spell, most of the adherents of both trends returned to their separate paths. V. S. Solov'ëv was one of the very few thinkers who understood Dostoevsky's message in the spirit of its author, and two decades passed before it dawned upon a somewhat wider circle—the so-called "Landmarks" movement. During the twentieth century, Dostoevsky's ideas have had a greater influence abroad than in Russia—partly through his own writings and partly through those of his followers, especially Berdyaev.

6. *Westernism*

WESTERNISM in the broad sense (either asserting that Russia was essentially identical with Western Europe or that Russia should follow and imitate it) was the dominant trend in Russian political thought during the nineteenth and the beginning of the twentieth centuries, dominant in the sense of having more literary voices than any of the other trends. The basic Westernist orientation almost inevitably led to endeavors to identify with greater precision exactly what it was that one admired in Western Europe or thought Russia to have in common with it. And so it was natural that the Westernists, after an initial brief period of comparative unity in the 1830's and early 1840's (in the face of the Slavophiles and the adherents of the theory of Official Nationality), then split into several trends, which roughly corresponded to the political trends and parties of Western Europe, and frequently identified themselves with these. More often than not there were personal and political contacts with like-minded people in West European countries, which were highly valued by the Russians concerned though not always by their foreign counterparts.

Conservatism

Westernist Conservatism stood very close to the Official Nationality theory and had many points of contact with the later Slavophiles, but it was distinguished from both by the Westernist Conservatives' belief that what they valued and advocated neither was nor should be specifically Russian, that they had common ground with the Conservatives of Western Europe.

The first leader of the Conservative trend among the Westernists was M. N. Katkov (1818–87). The son of a minor government official of recent and even doubtful nobility, he was educated at Moscow and Berlin universities, and in 1845–50, was Associate Professor of Philosophy at the former. Having lost this position when the government ordered that the teaching of philosophy be entrusted to theologians, he exchanged the academic career for that of a publicist, and from the 1850's until his death he was editor and publisher of the daily newspaper *Moscow Record* and the monthly journal *Russian Herald*. Having in his youth belonged to the Stankevich circle, which we shall deal with at greater length later in this chapter and which was mainly devoted to the study of contemporary German philosophy, Katkov remained an adherent of Schelling's organicist views. They were later reinforced by his admiration for England, mainly the pre-reform England of the early nineteenth century. It is customary to divide Katkov's publicistic activities into two periods: a liberal period until the Polish uprising of 1863, and a reactionary one afterward. Although there is some basis for such a division, it is too rigid and, as Professor M. Raeff has pointed out recently, does not do justice to Katkov's continued liberal views on many matters after 1863. It was only after the assassination of Alexander II by the revolutionaries that his writings acquired a definitely reactionary character. Katkov's regular editorials in the *Moscow Record* over a quarter of a century were a running commentary on every conceivable aspect of Russian politics. He was an outstanding journalist, forceful, frank, and outspoken, and gradually acquired a standing and influence unique in the history of the Russian periodical press. He was widely regarded abroad as a mouthpiece of the Russian government, but he was in fact an independent public figure, and his relations with the government were not always happy. More than once he ran into trouble with the authorities, although on the other hand even ministers (of an autocratic government!) were sometimes afraid of his criticisms.

Pointing to the example of England, Katkov held that national solidarity and cohesion of the national body were compatible with a thoroughgoing individualism and with laissez-faire economic policies. He was a firm adherent of the principles of civil liberty and equality before the law, and he persistently attacked the remnants of serfdom found in the legal disabilities of the ex-serfs. He saw in the village commune in particular a major obstacle to economic and social progress, and during the 1860's and 1870's, he campaigned for its abolition, crossing swords with its Slavophile defenders, though in the 1880's he withdrew this demand as being of lesser importance than the need for political stability. The absence of the legal privileges and disabilities of different social estates would lead to the estates being distinguished simply by their material positions, and Katkov advocated easy social mobility, solely on the basis of merit (here again the English aristocracy served him as an example). He was perhaps the first influential journalist in Russia to realize that the country had entered upon the path of capitalist development, to welcome it, and to understand its consequences—such as the development of a labor movement. Following Desnitsky and the early Speransky, Katkov thought that property was the natural qualification for an active participation in public life. However, he drew very narrow limits for such participation. Like the Slavophiles, he upheld freedom of the press, and through his own activities greatly widened the field of public affairs that could be treated by the press. But he was in favor of limiting the functions of the local government bodies to purely economic matters and argued that there was no need for these bodies to be elected. It would be better if their members were appointed by the crown, as justices of the peace were appointed in England, from among better-off citizens, and served voluntarily without remuneration. In the 1880's, he sharply attacked the existing local government for "parliamentaristic tendencies" and various government departments for tolerating this. Even the new courts, which he had welcomed earlier, were denounced by Katkov in the 1880's as being subject, through the jury system, to the opinions of "the street." Katkov had always upheld absolute monarchy (despite his intensive study of Blackstone and admiration for England), but he fought fiercely against bureaucracy and thought that the country could and should be governed by the Czar with a minimum of officials; in this he stood closer to the Slavophiles than to the proponents of the official doctrine. A problem that was constantly in the forefront of his interests was that of national minorities. It had already been raised by Samarin, but Katkov (himself of half-Georgian extraction) was the first consistent advocate—after the Polish uprising of 1863—of administrative, legal, and cultural assimilation of the minorities (except the Poles, to whom he was prepared to concede cultural autonomy). He went so far as to maintain that since Russian administration was riddled with Poles and Baltic Germans, the country was living under a foreign yoke and that most of its ills were due to Polish or German intrigues. It is remarkable, however, that despite this extreme nationalism he was completely free from anti-Semitism and advocated the abolition of anti-Jewish laws. Two more of his interests deserve attention. In the field of education he was one of the chief advocates of a classical curriculum in state secondary schools, and he contributed to the reversal of the government's policy, which had earlier suspected classical education of fostering republicanism and had considered the natural sciences to be safer. In foreign affairs, Katkov at first defended the alliance with Germany and praised Bismarck, but he later changed his sympathies and advocated an alliance with France, which was in fact effected soon after his death.

Probably the most influential Conservative thinker of the late nineteenth and early twentieth centuries was K. P. Pobedonostsev (1827–1907), who, unlike Katkov, never changed his standpoint. He was educated at the School of Jurisprudence in St. Petersburg, which had been founded by a relative of Nicholas I in order to train future servants of the state in an antibureaucratic spirit and thus to counteract the growing bureaucratization of public life. Pobedonostsev proved to be a worthy alumnus. He held the chair of civil law at Moscow University in 1860–65, but left the academic career for a high judicial appointment and soon afterward became a Senator (i.e., member of the Supreme Court), a member of the Council of State (a consultative body that assisted the Emperor in legislation), and in 1880 was appointed Procurator of the Holy Synod (that is, minister for the affairs of the Orthodox Church), remaining in this post until 1905. He was tutor in law to Alexander III and Nicholas II when they were heirs to the throne, and both remained under his influence, especially Alexander III, during whose reign Pobedonostsev was the most influential member of the government and the chief inspirer of its reactionary policies. Apart from books on civil law and legal history, Pobedonostsev published a new translation of Thomas à Kempis' *Imitation of Christ* and a volume of political essays under the title *Moscow Collection* (1896), which ran through several editions, was soon translated into foreign languages, and is the best-known comprehensive statement of the Westernist Conservative position. Pobedonostsev's favorite among modern political writers was Carlyle, from whom he borrowed many of his ideas; conversely, the circle of Carlyle's admirers in England procured the English edition of *Moscow Collection* (*Reflections of a Russian Statesman*, 1898).

The starting point of Pobedonostsev's reasoning is man and his spiritual make-up. The greatest need of man is communion, and a man's religion is his greatest treasure, which he will never subject to external control. Therefore, the state power has to tread carefully in approaching this sphere. But this does not mean that the Church as a "gathering of Christians who are organically bound together by unity of belief into a God-established union," and the state as "society organized into a civic union," should stand side by side in mutual indifference. Such alienation is contrary to the striving of the human spirit for unity. Not only must the state be overtly religious, but it must be denominational, because even people of other denominations and faiths will be more inclined to trust a government of believers than an irreligious and indifferent one. The Church has an important role in public life, for on it falls the double duty of implanting in the people a respect for law and the authorities, and of implanting in authority a respect for human freedom. Although the modern state (like the medieval Church) is a compulsory and inescapable union, the state power, however strong, is based upon nothing else but a community of spiritual self-consciousness between the people and the government. The main task of the supreme power in the state is to select people for public appointments. If it fails in this task, laws and institutions, however good they may be, lose their importance, for the government will be judged by its agents. With the passing from the historical scene of the hereditary aristocracy with its automatically assumed right to govern, there has appeared a new aristocracy of wealth, and the state power must be on guard against this, since to succumb to it means to serve egotistic sectional interests. Independence from such sectional interests is one reason why a monarchy is preferable to other forms of government; and a monarchy is also best suited to uphold the law and to avoid arbitrariness.

The concept of law, according to Pobedonostsev, has two aspects. On the one hand, a law is a rule, an external regulation of human activity. On the other hand, it is a commandment, and it is on the concept of commandment that the moral consciousness of law is based. The Ten Commandments remain the basic type of law. Irrespective of sanctions, of punishment for violating the regulation, the commandment has the power to evoke man's conscience by establishing from above the authoritative distinction between equity and iniquity. In relation to the state power, law is, or should be, the norm directing the will and the acts of the authorities, which are there for the purpose of satisfying essential needs of the population and for keeping the order that is necessary for the defense of the rights of each and all. The law must guard the freedom of the people to live in accordance with their traditions and customs. To be effective, a law must respond to the people's real need in the sphere to which it relates, it must fully correspond to the conception of truth and justice that exists in the soul of the people. But the law must not narrowly circumscribe the functioning of the authorities; it must leave room for decision and action prompted by a sense of duty; it must not weaken the energy of the administrator. If only for this reason, it would be desirable that the number of laws be small, but there is another and more important reason—the legal position must be easily understandable to simple people if the administration of justice is to serve its purpose. Custom is preferable to written law, but if there is to be written law it must be carefully prepared and must fit easily into the existing system of law and government. In his demand that there be few written laws and that the law be comprehensible to simple people, Pobedonostsev stood close to the Slavophiles and very far from Speransky, who had held that the demand for simplicity and comprehensibility of the law must yield before the necessity of narrowing the limits of arbitrariness and that multiplication of laws was an inevitable consequence of the increasing complexity of modern life.

Pobedonostsev also spoke of the progressive complexity of life, but he had no sympathy for it. In general, he found the state of humanity in his time depressing. He attributed its sad state to a great extent to modern political trends and government systems. Political rights in antiquity meant that every citizen was entitled to contribute to the conduct of public affairs according to his ability and circumstances. Political authority in medieval Europe grew spontaneously out of custom, without any premeditated plan or principle. The French Revolution swept away the old institutions and put in their place abstract concepts. Each of the three concepts in the slogan *"Liberté, égalité, fraternité"* had healthy aspects, he thought, but their interpretation by liberals, democrats, and socialists was false and the effect pernicious. Freedom as understood by the liberals meant unrestrained self-seeking, the reign of greed, corruption of the people by an irresponsible press, and the proliferation of lifeless, abstract, and mutually incompatible "principles" and "ideals." Pobedonostsev especially disliked the doctrine and practice of democracy. Democrats are wrong in equating freedom with equality, for there is abundant historical evidence that freedom does not depend on equality, while equality does not at all necessarily result in freedom. Freedom here means civil freedom, for Pobedonostsev scorned political freedom. Investing the supreme authority in the totality of voters led to infinite fragmentation of it. Each voter, possessing a minute fraction of power, can do nothing with it but put it at the disposal of a reckless manipulator, be it an individual or a party. Standard practices of such manipulators were bribery and terror, and to these propaganda had been recently added. Having thus secured the necessary majority of votes, the winning party would exploit its power for selfish ends. Parliamentary governments always acted in the interests of a party or company. Finally, the socialist ideal involved intolerable regimentation of citizens' private lives. Pobedonostsev believed that Russia was following the same dangerous path that had been and was being trodden by West European countries (except England, which had managed to preserve some of her healthy organic traditions) and the United

States, but that in this respect it was fortunate that Russia was lagging behind.

Pobedonostsev's remedies for stopping the rot were stubborn resistance to all liberalistic, democratic, and socialist tendencies; recognition that service was the only legitimate moral foundation of state authority; and gradual training, beginning at the parish level, of dedicated and responsible public workers. Having proved their worth, these people might in the future be delegated to take part in conducting the affairs of the nation as a whole. The path to genuine progress was not by an extension of voting rights, but by the sustained efforts of able, informed, and virtuous individuals on all levels of national life. The practical effect of Pobedono-stsev's activities and influence was almost totally negative, and his name remains a symbol of the oppressive and retrograde policies of Alexander III's reign.

The third outstanding representative of Westernist Conserva-tive thought, L. A. Tikhomirov (1852–1923), started his political life as an active revolutionary. Joining the Populist movement in the 1870's, he put his faith in a popular rebellion, was arrested, and spent five years imprisoned in a fortress. Upon his release, Tikhomirov, disillusioned by the passivity of "the people," was one of the first in the Land and Freedom organization to turn to the idea of a *coup d'état* by the revolutionary intelligentsia. As a member of the famous Executive Committee of the People's Will Party, he condoned its terroristic activities, though he opposed terrorism in principle. He was the leading theorist of the party, drafted its program and edited its publications, and at the same time, living underground, contributed to legally published radi-cal journals. The futility of the assassination of Alexander II finally disillusioned him; he emigrated to France in 1883 and soon ceased participating in underground work. His *Russia, Po-litical and Social* was written from a revolutionary point of view (there is an English translation by Marx's son-in-law E. Aveling, 1888), but in 1888 he published a brochure under the title *Why I Ceased to be a Revolutionary*. He was pardoned and allowed to return to Russia, and the government kept its commitment not to subject him to an interrogation that might involve the betrayal of his former associates in the revolutionary movement. Tikhomirov became a regular contributor to the *Moscow Record* (which continued the Katkov tradition) and then its editor and publisher, and he later combined his position as a leading publicist of the Right with a high-ranking appointment in government service. The books written by him during this period—*Monocracy as a Principle of State Constitution* (1897) and *Monarchical Statehood* (1905)—are among the best expositions of the monarchist principles. Despite his political apostasy, he retained the personal respect of the revolutionaries, was not molested, even after 1917, and was allowed to die in peaceful obscurity.

The reversal of his political allegiance did not result from, or bring about, a complete change in Tikhomirov's political views. On the contrary, there was much in his views that remained constant, and, as he himself maintained (and this contention has been confirmed by a recent student, Dr. K. Tidmarsh), these constant elements were more fundamental to Tikhomirov's thought than what was discarded or acquired through his conversion. Even as a revolutionary, he laid stress on the positive, constructive aspects of the desired change, not upon the destructive element of revolution. This made it the easier for him to turn to the idea of a coup and a subsequent revolutionary dictatorship. It is not difficult to discern here Peresvetov's idea of benevolent despotism, which can appear with equal ease in the shape of an autocratic monarchy. What was important for Tikhomirov was not the appearance, but the nature, scope, and uses of power. If the aim is to eliminate the alienation of the government from the people, to stamp out injustices and corruption, and if it turns out that the revolutionary party, besides being weaker than the government, is afflicted by the same ills of lifelessness and corruption, then what can be more logical than to join the stronger side and try to achieve one's aims with the state authority as an ally, especially if the latter also has the additional advantages of legitimacy and enjoying the unreflecting confidence of the majority of the people? What was needed was neither revolution nor reaction nor progress towards an abstract ideal, but a steady evolutionary growth based on the firm foundation of the interests of the people and their genuine sentiments. Russia in particular, because of its cultural backwardness (which struck Tikhomirov by comparison with France), needed the positive creative work of every capable and patriotic citizen. As often happens, the concrete policies advocated by Tikhomirov fell far short of his clear and not unreasonable general propositions. In practical politics he became a mouthpiece of the extreme right—retrograde, obscurantist, nationalist, and even to some extent anti-Semitic. This, combined with the stigma of being a renegade, prevented Tikhomirov's more enlightened theoretical views from having a perceptible impact on public opinion.

While both Pobedonostsev and Tikhomirov were reactionaries in their practical politics, there were two outstanding progressives among the Conservative politicians of the late nineteenth and early twentieth centuries—Witte and Stolypin.

S. Yu. Witte (1849–1915), a nobleman of Dutch descent, grew up in a Slavophile milieu, and his German-sounding name was an embarrassment for him in his youth. He read mathematics at the New Russia University in Odessa and began his active life as a railway employee, quickly rising to become Director of the South-Western Railways. His efficiency and business acumen attracted the attention of Emperor Alexander III, who appointed him Minister of Transport in 1892 and Minister of Finance later in the same year. Witte occupied this key ministry for over a decade, vigorously continuing the policies, inaugurated by his predecessors Bunge and Vyshnegradsky, of rapid industrial development (with the help of protectionist tariffs, large foreign loans and extensive railway construction), strengthening the country's finances, and modern labor legislation. At first Witte neglected the peasants, among whom the poorer suffered from rural overpopulation in European Russia and the richer and more enterprising from low grain prices (caused mainly by American competition in the world market) and from the communal land ownership. But by the turn of the century he realized the importance of agriculture for Russia's economy and initiated the reforms in this field which are usually associated with the name of Stolypin. Constantly attacked by the extreme right and mistrusted by Nicholas II, Witte was relieved of his departmental duties in 1903 and received an honorific appointment as chairman of the Committee of Ministers—a body without a genuine corporate existence that was mainly used by the last emperors for discussing illiberal legislative proposals likely to be rejected by the Council of State. While holding this uncongenial appointment, Witte performed two great services to his country in 1905—negotiating an extremely favorable peace treaty with Japan and advising the Emperor to grant a constitution that would provide for a representative assembly with full legislative powers.

"By family traditions and temperament," as he put it, Witte was an adherent of absolute monarchy, and, as late as 1898, in a famous memorandum (first published by liberals abroad in 1902 under the title *Autocracy and Zemstvo**) he had argued that genuine local government was incompatible with absolutism. But he became convinced that the spread of representative government among civilized nations was an irresistible process, and at the critical moment during the 1905 revolution, when a general strike had brought almost the whole of industry, as well as transport and communications, to a standstill he submitted proposals for establishing a legislative State Duma.† After some hesitation, Nicholas II approved these proposals, and they formed the basis of the *Manifesto of the 17th of October* which granted the constitution. Witte was thus the father, albeit not a very enthusiastic one, of Russia's constitutional (or semiconstitutional) regime of 1906–17, which was briefly discussed in the section on the Theory of Official Nationality. For a short period in 1906, he was chairman of the Council of Ministers, i.e., the first constitutional prime minister; he tried to include prominent liberal politicians into his cabinet, but so strong was the enmity between even the moderate liberals and the bureaucracy of which they considered Witte to be a representative that they refused his offer. Nicholas continued to mistrust Witte, and he was soon dismissed and spent the rest of his life as a member by appointment of the reformed Council of State —the upper chamber of the legislature—opposing, presumably out of a sense of personal slight, the policies of Stolypin he himself had initiated. In the field of foreign affairs, Witte consistently

---

* *Zemstvo* (from the Russian word for "land") was the colloquial collective name of the local government bodies established by the reform of 1864.

† *Duma* ("deliberation") was an old term, used until the seventeenth century for the Magnates' Council; it had been revived by Speransky and was used for the municipal councils after the 1870 reform.

upheld the cause of peace, advocated the limitation of armaments, and was one of the first champions of European unification.

Witte's almost immediate successor as prime minister, P. A. Stolypin (1862–1911), a landowner with aristocratic connections, had been educated at St. Petersburg University, where he read science. He was Marshal of the Nobility in Kovno province (Lithuania) and was appointed governor of the neighboring province of Grodno in 1902, transferred to the same position in Saratov in the following year, and in 1906, after a short spell as Minister of the Interior, was appointed chairman of the Council of Ministers. Like Witte, he attempted to form a coalition government reaching as far left as the non-radical wing of the Constitutional Democratic Party, but the bulk of both conservative and liberal opinion was against such a coalition, and Stolypin's secret negotiations came to nothing. He nevertheless continued to seek parliamentary support for his policies and gradually won a measure of cooperation from the moderate liberals in the Third Duma.

Stolypin's speeches in the Duma show that he was a loyal supporter of the constitutional regime which he was determined to make successful, though when faced with what he considered to be a malicious obstruction, contrary to the spirit of the constitution (the left-wing majority of the Second Duma refused to strip of immunity its Social Democratic deputies, whom Stolypin wanted to put on trial for alleged connection with the party's illegal Military Organization), he did not hesitate to resort to a measure that was held by many to be unconstitutional—the introduction by decree, after dissolving the Second Duma, of new electoral regulations in 1907 that sharply restricted the franchise and ensured a right-wing majority in the Third Duma, which then made the corresponding changes in the law. In one of his speeches in the Duma, Stolypin coined the phrase that has remained as a motto of his political life; speaking of the radical majority of the intelligentsia, he said, "You want great disturbances. We want a great Russia." Stolypin's recipe for Russia's greatness consisted of the twin policies of firm suppression of armed uprisings and underground revolutionary activities on the one hand, and of removing the causes of popular discontent on the other. Legalizing trade unions, making labor relations in industry more orderly through the institution of elected shop stewards, preparing a scheme of sickness benefits with the funds to be administered by elected representatives of the workers—these and similar measures were to ensure that industrial workers should turn a deaf ear to revolutionary propaganda. But Stolypin's attention was mainly devoted to the peasants. He gave them freedom to leave the commune and to become full owners of their consolidated landholdings; removed other legal disabilities of the peasants; facilitated purchase by the peasants of land belonging to the nobility or the state; and initiated a big program of voluntary resettlement in Siberia of peasants from overpopulated areas of European Russia. All these measures were aimed at creating a strong class of well-to-do farmers who would run their farms on capitalist lines, thus simultaneously putting an end to traditional peasant discontent and raising the efficiency of Russian agriculture.

Hated by the revolutionaries and the extreme right-wing elements, Stolypin was assassinated by a Socialist Revolutionary terrorist who was also a police agent. But his policies were continued by the successive governments, though half-heartedly and often incompetently, so that by the time the monarchy fell in February, 1917, four-fifths of all agricultural land in European Russia was owned by the peasants (either communally or individually) and half of the remainder was rented by them from other owners; 2.5 million households (one-fourth of the total) had left the communes and twice as many cases were under consideration.

Liberalism

Almost every discussion of Westernism begins with a reference to the circle of students and young intellectuals that formed in Moscow in the 1830's around N. V. Stankevich (1813–40), a promising philosopher and historian who, despite his early death, earned for himself a firm place in the history of Russian thought as the inspirer and early guide of a whole galaxy of brilliant men. His main passion was the German idealistic philosophy, and, more than anyone else, he was responsible for the appearance in Russia of that strong Hegelian tendency which still dominates much of Russian thought. Some of the younger Slavophiles, including K. S. Aksakov and Samarin, originally belonged to the Stankevich circle, and indeed the split between the Slavophiles and the Westernists was partly an internal affair of the circle. The majority of its members took up the Westernist position, but gradually a division into a liberal and a radical wing became perceptible among the Westernists themselves. The leading liberals were Katkov (who, as we have seen, later developed into a conservative) and Granovsky, while the radicals, who will be considered in the next section, were headed by Bakunin and Belinsky.

T. N. Granovsky (1813–55) was educated at St. Petersburg and Berlin universities (Savigny and Ranke were among his teachers at Berlin), and from 1839, he held the chair of world history at Moscow University. Apart from lecturing to his students, he gave many public lectures which had a great impact upon public opinion. Lecturing chiefly on the Middle Ages, Granovsky impressed on his listeners the ideas of historical progress and of the transitory character of oppressive institutions such as slavery, serfdom, and absolutism. On the other hand, Granovsky rejected radicalism because of its subordination of human lives to abstract ideas. Ideas, he said in his lectures, are not Indian idols carried in a festive procession and crushing the superstitious worshipers who throw themselves under the wheels.

The theoretical leaders of what may be called classical Westernist liberalism in Russia were Kavelin, Chicherin, and Gradovsky. Like Granovsky, they were noblemen by birth and university teachers by profession. Kavelin and Chicherin belonged to the second, and Gradovsky to the third generation of Westernists. K. D. Kavelin (1818–85) received the Westernist creed from Belinsky, who was his private tutor, and although as a student at Moscow University he was in close touch with the Slavophiles, Belinsky's influence prevailed. But Kavelin did not follow his teacher into the radical camp. As a professor in Moscow and St. Petersburg and as a publicist, he consistently upheld liberal principles. His personal influence on Alexander II, which made Kavelin one of the chief inspirers of the great liberal reforms of Alexander's reign, was perhaps of particular importance. In philosophy, Kavelin turned from pure Hegelianism, which seemed to him too abstract, to what V. V. Zenkovsky has called "semi-Positivism"; Kavelin himself called his position one of Ideal-Realism and vigorously defended it in a controversy on problems of psychology against Samarin's metaphysics on the one hand and against materialism on the other. Primarily concerned with the freedom and autonomy of the individual, Kavelin conceived of historical development as a process of emancipation of the human personality. In a memorandum on the emancipation of the serfs submitted in 1855, he argued that serfdom was the main obstacle to progress in Russia and its continued existence was of great danger to the state. Like the Slavophiles, Kavelin insisted that the ex-serfs should be given land; but he also thought that the landlords should be fairly compensated, not only for the land but for the loss of the serfs' labor too. After the emancipation, Kavelin with equal energy advocated full legal equality for women and a wide competence for local government.

The most outstanding of the classical liberal Westernists was B. N. Chicherin (1828–1904). Coming from an old noble family (of Italian descent, but resident in Russia since the fifteenth century), he was educated at Moscow University, where Granovsky was one of his teachers, and for many years taught there himself. He was also active in local government, both in Moscow (of which he was Mayor in 1882–83) and in the Tambov Province of central Russia, where he lived on the family estate after retirement. Like Kavelin, Chicherin was jurist, historian, philosopher, and publicist in one person, and he distinguished himself in all these fields. In philosophy he was a strict Hegelian and argued against Positivism and Utilitarianism. As a historian, he joined Kavelin in developing the *étatiste* approach, i.e., regarding the state as the chief agent in history, and he soon became the acknowledged head of the *étatiste* school. Of considerable political significance was his so-called "decretal" theory on the origin of serfdom in Russia, according to which there had been a progressive "enserfing" of all the social classes by a series of government decrees in sixteenth- and seventeenth-century Muscovy; this had been necessitated by the historical conditions of the time, but modern conditions demanded a reverse process of emancipation, which, indeed, had started with the emancipation of the nobility

and the townspeople in the eighteenth century and must be concluded by emancipating the peasants. In his *Philosophy of Law*
(1900), Chicherin derived the concept of law from that of freedom, freedom itself being understood as the spiritual essence of
man. In his numerous writings on political science and on practical politics (*History of Political Doctrines*, 5 vols., 1869–1902;
Property and State, 2 vols., 1882–83; *A Course in State Science*, 3
vols., 1894–98; *On Popular Representation*, 1899; *A Number of
Current Problems*, 1862; *Problems of Politics*, 1903; etc.), Chicherin, like the Slavophiles, drew a clear distinction between society and state. But here the similarity ended. While the Slavophiles attached particular importance to the distinction between
organic communities and contractual associations, Chicherin
avoided this dichotomy and treated all the manifold groupings
composing society as associations of persons bound by diverse interests. The village commune in particular was in his view not
an organic growth permeated by a peculiar Slavic conciliar or
communal spirit, but an association created by the Muscovite
authorities for fiscal purposes—to ensure through collective responsibility the payment of taxes by all the villagers. The state
was defined by Chicherin as a union of free people bound by
law and governed by the supreme power in the interests of the
common good. There were thus four elements constituting a
state: authority, law, freedom, and the common good. The political ideal is a harmony of all four, and it is most likely to be
realized in a constitutional monarchy. Of the various forms of
popular representation, Chicherin favored a two-chamber system.
But Russia, according to him, was not yet ripe for representative
government and would for the time being have to make do with
a liberal absolutism; only at the turn of the century did he state
(in a pamphlet abroad) that the time had come for the introduction of representative government. Chicherin distinguished three
different types of liberalism—"street liberalism," bent on rebellion
and oblivious of the right of others to disagree; "opposition liberalism," which exhausts itself in negative criticism; and "conservative liberalism," which aims at establishing and securing genuine
freedom and therefore recognizes the need for a strong state authority, holds that rights are inseparable from duties (but also, of

course, vice versa), and moderates its demands according to the historical situation. Chicherin's antiradicalism found many expressions. He valued highly the positive qualities of the Russian nobility, pointing out that it was the only social group in Russia that combined wealth, education, corporate spirit, and experience in public affairs. He was an ardent individualist and anti-socialist, defended private property and the freedom of contracts, and opposed modern social legislation, which, in his view, was an unwarranted confusion of juridical law with moral law and of common good with charity. Chicherin rejected both the "night-watchman" view of the state and the subordination to it of all private activities. He formulated the ideal relationship between state and society as that of "a free society in a free state," while the actual variations in the relationship should be subject to the formula "the less unity there is in society, the more there must be in the state," or, in other words, the more independent and centralized must be the public authority. There was much room for positive action by the state, as was evident from the reforms of Peter the Great and Alexander II. But the most important and irreplaceable guarantee of freedom and law was absolute independence of the courts, and after the emancipation of the serfs this was the most urgent practical demand. Chicherin argued strongly against state interference in religious matters and against the established Church; for freedom of thought and speech; for autonomy of the universities; against the policy of assimilation of the national minorities propagated by Katkov and embarked upon by the government after the Polish uprising of 1863, especially in Alexander III's reign. He expected progress in international relations as a result of the further development of interdependent interests as well as from the application of moral principles to the sphere of foreign affairs.

The third classic of Westernist liberalism, A. D. Gradovsky (1841–89), Professor of Law at St. Petersburg University and one of the most influential legal theorists in Russia of his time, is frequently called "the Russian Benjamin Constant." Active at a time when Slavophilism had degenerated into Pan-Slavism or become almost indistinguishable from the doctrine of Official Nationality, he looked back on the classical Slavophiles with sympathy and understanding: the Westernism they had criticized was, Gradovsky wrote, a kind of internal emigration from the conditions of pre-reform Russia into abstract humanity, and although this was understandable, such internal *émigrés* were indeed cut off from the life of the country. Gradovsky was even more strongly opposed to abstract notions and ideals than Chicherin, whom he described as wanting to "transfer the Acropolis to Tambov." In considering problems of government, Gradovsky rejected both the constitutional schematism characteristic of the juridical approach and the notion of the spontaneity of social processes current among the sociologists; he adhered to the political approach, that is, he saw in government a field of free activity of individuals. Of Chicherin's four elements of the state, Gradovsky especially stressed freedom and law, and in describing the Russian government (in his *Principles of Russian Public Law,* 3 vols., 1875–81) he put the principle of legality before that of autocracy. In *The Public Law of the Foremost European Powers* (2 vols., 1886–95), Gradovsky gave a detailed survey of the historical development, and an analysis of the contemporary practice, of constitutional government, mainly in Britain. Apart from his major works, he published many articles, some of which were reprinted in two volumes (*Politics, History and Administration,* 1871, and *Difficult Years,* 1880). They were chiefly devoted to the main political trends of the time both in Western Europe and in Russia, and to the political aspects of the problems of nationality and national minorities. He was the first Russian scholar to give these problems (which had been dealt with in Western Europe by Buchez, Bluntschli, J. S. Mill, and others) an extensive and sympathetic treatment, free from any special pleading.

The chief carriers of the liberal tradition in the late nineteenth and early twentieth centuries were the so-called Zemstvo movement and the legal profession, the former striving to strengthen, extend, and defend against reaction the system of local government established by the reforms of 1864 and 1870, and the latter similarly working to safeguard, strengthen, and expand the modern judiciary created in 1864. A section of the periodical press also played an important part in disseminating liberal ideas, especially the monthly journals *Messenger of Europe* in St. Petersburg and

Russian Thought in Moscow. The pressure of liberal opinion for "crowning the edifice" of representative institutions by establishing a representative legislature increased steadily, until in 1904, an underground organization was set up under the leadership of I. I. Petrunkevich (1844–1928), the leader of the Zemstvo movement, and P. B. Struve, a former Marxist and Social-Democrat who had become a liberal. Called the Union of Liberation, this organization was to coordinate all the efforts aimed at a speedy establishment of a constitutional regime. The Union, together with the revolutionary Socialist parties, was instrumental in bringing about the 1905 revolution.

After the *October Manifesto,* which granted a constitution, moderate liberals (mainly landowners and businessmen), satisfied with what had been achieved, organized themselves into the Union of the 17th October (colloquially called the Octobrists). Its leaders refused to join Witte's government, but from 1907, being the strongest single party in the State Duma, the Octobrists to some extent supported Stolypin and his successors. The leader of the party, A. I. Guchkov (1862–1936), a wealthy industrialist, was chairman of the Duma Committee on Military and Naval Affairs and chairman of the Third Duma; during World War I, as chairman of the nongovernmental Central War Industries Committee (the War Industries Committees will be briefly described in the section on Technocratism), he did much to organize the country's resources for the war effort, while at the same time forming a conspiracy with other liberal and radical leaders, and with some of the generals, to force Nicholas II to abdicate and to make his successor agree to the formation of a government responsible to the Duma. After the February revolution of 1917, in which he played one of the principal roles, Guchkov became Minister for War and Navy in the first provisional government, but had to resign in May; the Octobrist party disintegrated during 1917.

But it was the Constitutional Democratic Party, not the Octobrists, that was the main party of the liberal intelligentsia. It was formed in 1905, and united the majority of the Union of Liberation with some of the members of a body called the Union of Unions, which for a short time during the revolutionary year 1905 had served as the central organization for a multiplicity of professional and other associations of the liberal and radical intelligentsia. The party maintained that a fully democratic system should be established in Russia without delay, with a Duma based on universal, equal, direct, and secret vote and a cabinet responsible to such a Duma. They also advocated agrarian reform, progressive social legislation, and cultural autonomy for non-Russian nationalities. The Constitutional Democratic Party was not homogeneous politically. Its right wing consisted partly of orthodox liberals, such as V. A. Maklakov, who continued the tradition of classical Westernist liberalism, and partly of the adherents of the Landmarks movement (which will be described in Chapter 10), headed by Struve. Among the left-wing majority of the party one could also discern at least two different trends. Comparatively weaker was that of the Populist Liberals, who were very close to the Liberal Populists (see Chapter 7) except that they did not in any sense subscribe to the socialist ideal. Many of them regarded A. I. Chuprov (1842–1908), a retired professor of political economy at Moscow University, as their intellectual leader.

The stronger of the two trends among the left wing of the Constitutional Democratic Party, the one that mainly determined the policy of the party as a whole and to which belonged the leader of the party, the historian P. N. Milyukov (1859–1943), was distinguished by its attachment to the doctrine of political democracy. Adherents of the democratic doctrine had not been very numerous in Russia until the turn of the century. Of the main political writers of the previous decades, only Dragomanov (see Chapter 8) and V. A. Gol'tsev (1850–1906), the editor of *Russian Thought,* had held it to be of primary importance. An attempt in 1894 to unite all the democratically minded elements in an illegal Party of the People's Right, came to nothing. The political Masonic organization formed in 1900–1901 and the Union of Liberation, of which the Masonic organization was the core, were the first strong organizations that were predominantly democratically minded, and after 1905 this role passed to the Constitutional Democratic Party. Constitutional Democrats were in a majority in the First Duma in 1906 and dominated its proceedings. A prominent deputy close to them was the political scientist M. Ya.

Ostrogorsky (1854–1920), whose pioneering work *Democracy and the Organisation of Political Parties* (first published in French, 1898, and in an English translation in 1902) had won him international recognition. After the dissolution of the First Duma, which had consistently refused to cooperate with the government, its Constitutional Democratic majority took the unconstitutional step of holding an unofficial session of Duma deputies, which adopted an appeal to the people not to pay taxes and not to report for military service until the government yielded and recalled the Duma. This appeal, drafted by Milyukov, fell on deaf ears. In the subsequent Dumas, the Constitutional Democratic Party was the chief party of the opposition. It actively participated in destroying the monarchy in February, 1917 (many Constitutional Democrats were in fact republicans), some of its leading members belonging to the political Masonic organization, referred to earlier, that took the lead in preparing the take-over of power. All the provisional governments in 1917 contained Constitutional Democratic ministers, though the leader of the party, Milyukov, like Guchkov, had to resign from the Ministry of Foreign Affairs in May under pressure from the Socialist parties. Constitutional Democrats took part in the election to the Constituent Assembly after the Bolshevik coup, but the party was suppressed by the Bolsheviks before the Assembly met.

The third influential liberal party of the constitutional period was the Progressive Party, which consisted principally of progressive businessmen and liberal intellectuals and was formed in 1912 through the fusion of two small groups with the characteristic names of the Party of Peaceful Renovation and the Party of Democratic Reforms (they had already formed one parliamentary party in the Third Duma). The theorist of the Progressive Party and its most outstanding political leader was M. M. Kovalevsky (1851–1916), historian, political scientist, and sociologist of international repute. A wealthy Ukrainian landowner, he had been educated at Khar′kov University and was Professor of Public Law in Moscow until summarily dismissed in 1887 by the Minister of Education as politically undesirable. He spent the following seventeen years abroad, lecturing at various European universities and founding the Russian Free High School of Social Sciences in Paris.

Returning to Russia in 1904, Kovalevsky combined a professor-
ship at St. Petersburg University with an active political life. The
landowners of his native Khar'kov province elected him to the
First Duma, but did not subsequently re-elect him, and he had to
be content with what was in his view a very inadequate substitute—
membership by election of the Council of State, where he was one
of the members representing the Academy of Sciences and the universities. Kovalevsky's great erudition in the field of political science enabled him to become a kind of theoretical mentor for the
majority of liberal politicians (his chief works in the field were
*History of Police Administration and Police Courts in English
Counties from the Earliest Times to the Death of Edward III.
Concerning the Problem of the Origin of Local Government in
England*, 1877; *Modern Custom and Ancient Law in Russia*, 1891;
The Origin of Modern Democracy, 4 vols., 1895–97; *Russian Political Institutions*, 1902; *English Public Law*, 1906; *From Direct
to Representative Democracy and from Patriarchal Monarchy to
Parliamentarianism. The Growth of the State and Its Reflection
in the History of Political Doctrines*, 3 vols., 1906). The Progressive Party occupied a position between the Octobrists and the
Constitutional Democrats, aiming at a fusion of all three into one
liberal party capable of forming a strong government backed by a
solid majority in the Duma; this aim was to some extent achieved
when the Progressive Bloc was formed in 1915. Progressive Party
members were active in the February revolution in 1917 and took
part in the provisional governments. Like all other non-Socialist
parties, the Progressive Party was suppressed by the Bolsheviks in
1918.

Non-Socialist Radicalism

Most post-Decembrist radicals in Russia were socialists or anarchists and will be considered in the following section and in the
chapters devoted to socialist and anarchist trends. But there was
also a brand of radicalism that did not quite merge into socialism
or anarchism. The father of this brand was D. I. Pisarev (1841–68).
An impecunious nobleman from central Russia, he was educated
at St. Petersburg University, where he read philosophy, and be-

came a professional journalist. Half of his active life (four and a half years) he spent in solitary confinement in a fortress for having written a revolutionary pamphlet calling for the overthrow of the Romanov dynasty. Fortunately, he was allowed to write while in prison, and the height of his influence coincided with the years of his confinement (1863–67), when, after the arrest and banishment of Chernyshevsky, he was the foremost radical publicist.

Pisarev's philosophical views were formed early and remained unchanged throughout his short life. He was a passionate materialist, individualist, and utilitarian. Because of his rejection on principle of all established authorities, liberals labeled his position as Nihilism, though he himself preferred to call it Realism. A belief in human reason, science, enlightenment, and the ensuing progress was never absent in his writings. But Pisarev's political views were not very definite or stable; a very young man, he was obviously still feeling his way. He admired the West European radicals, especially Heine, and was a declared revolutionary for a short period in 1862—a year when revolutionary feeling in Russia was stronger than at any other time in the decade. And roughly at the same time he was a socialist, pointing to Proudhon, Louis Blanc, and Lassalle as the people who were leading in the right direction. But both before and after 1862–63, while consistently protesting against any kind of oppression and exploitation, including capitalist exploitation, he was much more skeptical about both revolution and socialism. There is an almost Lockean identification of property with personal freedom in one of his articles. The socialist solution for the ills of society may be true, he wrote on several occasions, and if it is, good luck to the socialists; but it may be wrong, and Pisarev once expressed his horror at the thought of a thoroughly regimented socialist future —a horror that is usually associated with Dostoevsky's view on the matter. The "realists" do not have to be revolutionary socialist leaders. Growing in numbers and gradually forming a new enlightened "middle estate," they—the efficient gentlemen-farmers, progressive industrialists, and public-minded professional people —can and should by their example and by concerted public action transform the existing society into a better and a juster one. Their own interest, properly understood, will ensure that they do so. Certainly in an advanced country, such as England, Buckle and J. S. Mill are sufficient as intellectual guides.

Pisarev's writings continued to be read throughout the rest of the nineteenth century, and they influenced several generations of radicals, both revolutionary and reformist, as well as the less radical social reformers and the technocratists. The radical tradition was continued by a number of periodicals, but the non-socialist radicals never formed a political party of their own, though the radical strain was quite strong, as we have seen, in the Constitutional Democratic Party.

Early Socialism

The preoccupation of the members of Stankevich's circle with German idealistic philosophy, culminating in an infatuation with Hegelianism, makes it easy to understand the split among them in the 1840's into a moderate and a radical wing. The same was happening among Hegel's pupils in Germany, and the Russian left-wing Hegelians were closely following the speculations of their German fellows. Bakunin, indeed, participated in the activities of the German Left-Hegelians themselves. Like the latter, the Russians fell under the strong influence of Feuerbach's materialism and of the preaching of the French Socialists, especially Saint-Simon and Fourier. The development of Russian radicalism during the 1840's, 1850's, and 1860's was thus an almost exact parallel with the development of its German counterpart that led to the appearance of Marxism.

Socialism was not, of course, an entirely new idea in Russia. It had made its first appearance in the middle of the sixteenth century, when two rationalist heretics, M. S. Bashkin and Theodosius "the Squint," taught that slavery was unlawful since it contradicted the basic commandment to love one's neighbor. All people were equal, since they all possessed "spiritual reason." Everyone must renounce his personal property and give it to the community. There should be no earthly power among Christians, and therefore there was no need to recognize the state authority or to pay taxes; nor should the authority of parents be recognized. Finally, there must be no wars among Christians. The eighteenth-century founder of a sect called "the Runners," a soldier who is known only by his first name—Evfimy—taught that God had created everything as the common property of men, and he blamed moral misconduct, oppression, and wars on the establishment of private property. Some of the Decembrists had socialist leanings, which found their expression in Pestel's *Russian Truth*. Belinsky, Bakunin, and their fellow socialists among the Westernists could thus find some native predecessors, although their main inspiration undoubtedly came from abroad. Bakunin's socialism soon took an anarchist turn, and we shall consider his views in the chapter on Anarchism.

V. G. Belinsky (1811–48) was, together with Bakunin, the leading figure among the Russian Hegelians who embraced materialism and socialism. He was one of the first professional journalists in Russia and the first prominent representative of the type of people who thereafter predominated among Russian radicals of all shades—the so-called "intelligentsia of diverse ranks," that is, professional people of non-noble origin preoccupied with public rather than professional interests. Belinsky was a nervous, sensitive, and unstable person, liable to rush from one extreme to another, but he had a clear and powerful literary style and a genius for spotting literary talent and soon became the leading literary critic of his generation. In the conditions of the severe press censorship of Nicholas I's reign, literary criticism was almost the only form of expressing political views in public, and it was Belinsky who developed this art to perfection. He established as the chief criterion of literary merit the usefulness of a piece of literature as an instrument of enlightenment, edification, and instruction in social and political virtues. The application of this criterion by Belinsky himself was tempered by his fine artistic taste, but the principle proved disastrous when applied by his less gifted and more intolerant followers. Turning to the substance of Belinsky's political views, we find little that is new in comparison with the radicals of the eighteenth century and the Decembrists, and this is hardly surprising: social and political conditions in Russia had not changed much, and the tasks facing the radicals remained essentially the same. Hegelian influence reinforced the conviction that what was "not reasonable" was "not real" and was bound to be swept away by the progressive march of history. The socialist vision added to the attractiveness of the future and made the injustices and oppression of the present even more unbearable. But Belinsky, vacillating between revolution and peaceful progress, was not clear about the ways that history would take toward the future. In his published writings he confined himself to exposing the existing wrongs and preaching humanity and justice. The most comprehensive statement of his political views was his famous letter to Gogol'. The great writer, whose fame Belinsky himself had done his best to establish, was tending politically more and more toward the right, and in 1847 he published *Selected Passages from Correspondence with Friends.* The public at the time took this as a declaration of adherence to the Official Nationality doctrine, though it is now widely considered as a precursor of Dostoevsky's political thought. Belinsky's reply, which obviously could not be published at the time but was circulated in handwritten copies, is a spirited but completely negative attack on Gogol's position.

The third leading socialist Westernist of the 1830's and 1840's, A. I. Herzen (1812–70), was more definite than Belinsky in a preference for the revolutionary way. Herzen was a contemporary of Stankevich and Belinsky at Moscow University but did not belong to their circle, having a group of his own which was another important center of Westernists. Herzen also studied the German idealist philosophers, and later Feuerbach, but even before entering university he had read the main French philosophical and political writings of the eighteenth and early nineteenth centuries (which he had found in the library of his father, a wealthy nobleman), and the French influence remained decisive. Although relations between Herzen and the members of the Stankevich circle were very close and cordial, there was a basic difference in orientation. Herzen was far less interested in abstract philosophy than in social and political problems. The execution of the five leading Decembrists in 1826 made a great impression upon the young Herzen, and he swore to dedicate his life to their cause. Although there were periods in his later life when he seemed to think that peaceful progess was possible, he remained basically a revolutionary. Being, unlike Belinsky, a man of considerable private means, he did not have to earn his living, and he could have played a more active role in the intellectual and political life of Moscow and St. Petersburg; however, he was twice banished (on trifling grounds) for several years to small provincial towns, and in 1847, utterly disgusted with Russia, he went abroad never to return.

Herzen was not the first Russian political *émigré;* there are several well-known earlier ones, such as Prince Kurbsky (who produced a theoretical justification for political emigration) in the sixteenth century, the clerk G. Kotoshikhin, who emigrated to Sweden in the seventeenth century and left a description of Russia in the reign of Peter the Great's father, or the Decembrist N. I. Turgenev, who, being abroad in 1825, did not return and also wrote a book about contemporary Russia. But Herzen was the first to look on emigration as a base from which one could try to influence intellectual and political developments at home, and in this sense he was the father of the modern Russian political emigration.

Herzen's romantic Westernism received a great shock when, traveling through Western Europe after his emigration, and particularly during the 1848 revolution, which he experienced in Paris, he saw the egotism, vulgarity, and corruption not only of the bourgeoisie but also of the proletariat. After this, he no longer expected the light to come to Russia from the West, though he appreciated the far greater freedom enjoyed by the people in Western Europe. He still believed that the establishment of socialism was a necessary condition for a free and full development of the human personality, but he now thought that the prospects for socialism were far better in Russia than in Western Europe. His reason for this belief was the existence in Russia of an embryonic "socialist" institution—the village commune (*Letters from France and Italy* and *From the Other Shore,* both written in 1848–49; *The Russian People and Socialism,* 1851). By thus blending Westernist socialism with the Slavophile admiration for the peasant commune, Herzen originated the notion of a specifically Russian socialism, a notion that was later picked up by the Populists and became one of the chief planks in their creed. Herzen's concern for the individual human being tempered his socialism, however, and historians still cannot agree whether to

classify him as a socialist or perhaps as a liberal. Like his friend
Granovsky, he repudiated the idea that human beings could or
should be sacrificed for the sake of an abstract principle, even if it
is *salus populi.* "The liberty of the individual is the greatest thing
of all, it is on *this and on this alone* that the true will of the
people can develop. Man must respect liberty in himself, and he
must esteem it in himself no less than in his neighbor, than in
the entire nation."* Nor did he think that socialism would be a
lasting stage in the development of mankind, and in a famous
phrase he foresaw its end: "Socialism will develop in all its phases
until it reaches its own extremes and absurdities. Then there will
again burst forth from the titanic breast of the revolting minority
a cry of denial. Once more a mortal battle will be joined in which
socialism will occupy the place of today's conservatism, and will
be defeated by the coming revolution as yet invisible to us."†
Herzen's political views were based on his moral philosophy
which was of a kind uncommon in his time. He denied that it
was possible to devise a moral code that would either have universal validity or even be binding for any group of people. "The
truly free man creates his own morality"—anything else is either
idolatry or oppression.

Deprived of Russian citizenship for his refusal to return to
Russia, Herzen became a Swiss citizen, but he lived chiefly in
England. He maintained lively contacts with most of the contemporary revolutionary and socialist leaders (especially Proudhon
and Mazzini) except Marx. The antipathy was mutual: Herzen's
patriotism and quasi-Slavophilism seemed to Marx to be a betrayal of socialism in favor of official Russia, which was the chief
object of Marx's political attacks, while Herzen, on the other
hand, was repelled by Marx's dogmatism and intolerance. His
considerable private means enabled Herzen to establish the Free
Russian Press in London and to publish *The Bell* (1857–67)—
the first Russian *émigré* newspaper—which had much influence in
Russia, even in government circles, especially in the years preced-

* Alexander Herzen, *From the Other Shore,* transl. by M. Budberg (New
York: George Braziller, 1960), p. 12.
† Quoted by Isaiah Berlin in "Herzen and Bakunin on Liberty," in E. J.
Simmons (ed.), *Continuity and Change in Russian and Soviet Thought* (Cam-
bridge, Mass.: Harvard University Press, 1955), p. 487.

ing the emancipation of the serfs in 1861. Herzen's standing with the revolutionaries at home was uncertain during these years because of his ambivalent public attitude to the revolutionary path, and *The Bell's* pro-Polish stand in 1863 caused a rapid decline of its influence in Russia.

But Herzen's ambivalent attitude toward the revolutionary course around the year 1860 was more apparent than real, for at this very time he was taking part in working out a comprehensive revolutionary theory—not for publication but for the guidance of the practical revolutionaries who were then joining their efforts in an attempt to create a united underground revolutionary organization. Small revolutionary circles, consisting mostly of students, had existed in Russia throughout the 1830's, 1840's and 1850's, the most important being the Petrashevsky Circle in St. Petersburg whose members and sympathizers (including Dostoevsky and Grigor'ev) were arrested in 1849. But it seems that the man who gave more thought than anyone else to the practical problems of the revolutionary movement, the problems of organization, strategy, and tactics, was Herzen's old friend N. P. Ogarëv (1813–70). Ogarëv (a landlord who freed his serfs and gave them the land long before 1861) had been a member of Herzen's circle in Moscow in the 1830's, remained in Russia when Herzen emigrated, but joined him in London in 1856. While still in Russia he had taken every opportunity to familiarize himself with the Decembrist movement and met several of the Decembrists personally. He was also influenced by the book *Conspiration pour l'Egalité, dite de Babeuf* (1828) by Buonarroti, Babeuf's closest collaborator and later leader of the Italian *Carbonari*—a book that influenced many revolutionaries in Western Europe, including Blanqui and Marx. In the years between his emigration and the Polish uprising of 1863, Ogarëv drafted a series of papers on the revolutionary movement which were discussed with Herzen and with emissaries of the St. Petersburg revolutionary circle who, in 1861–62, formed an underground organization called Land and Freedom along the lines laid down in Ogarëv's drafts.

According to Ogarëv, an organization aiming at a social revolution must be a secret society. He traced the tradition of secret societies from the early Christians through the Reformation, the

Jesuit order, Freemasonry, and the French Revolution to the Decembrists. The society must have a self-appointed center consisting of a few people (Ogarëv called them "apostles"), among whom there must be specialists in all the main branches of science and learning but who must act unanimously, "as if they were one person." The center lays down the general direction of the society's activities and gives all the orders. It must have its own printed organ, which should be published abroad, out of the reach of the Russian censorship. (It was, in fact, Ogarëv who suggested to Herzen the publication of *The Bell,* and he wrote most of its theoretical articles.) In a large country like Russia the secret society must have local provincial centers situated in the focal points of the activities of the three potentially revolutionary groups in the country, i.e., the educated minority (universities and theological academies), the military (the headquarters of the more promising army corps) and "the people," mainly peasants (the towns and villages where large fairs are held). Ogarëv mentioned, as one of the organizational forms, innocent-looking subsidiary organizations (i.e., what would now be called "front organizations"); this technique had already been resorted to by the Decembrists, who had set up literary societies. Members of the society are essentially agents of the center of various degrees of initiation, from active members bound by promises of unconditional obedience to "unconscious agents" on the periphery, people who "act in the sense of the society without the need to know of its existence." Turning to problems of strategy, we find that Ogarëv discussed two forms of social revolution—gradual transformation and armed uprising. After some vacillation, he found them complementary rather than alternative: Gradual reforms are bound to be unsuccessful and therefore inevitably lead to violent revolution. Earlier he refers to the spread of Christianity as an example of successful gradual transformation effected by a secret society: "Finally . . . a Christian bishop crowns a Frankish king—and secret society turns into apparent Church, i.e., apparent authority." But as a rule, and especially in the Russian conditions of the time, an uprising is inevitable. At first Ogarëv, following the Decembrists, argued that it should be well organized in order to avoid bloodshed and plunder—this is the reason for bringing in the military, since only the troops can rise in an orderly fashion. The insurgent troops, commanded by officers belonging to the society, should march on Moscow and St. Petersburg, arousing the people on the way and being joined by volunteers. Such a movement can meet only insignificant opposition, argued Ogarëv. Later, however, he came to the conclusion that terror might be inevitable in the process of a revolution, terror resorted to by the insurgent masses (peasants and workers) in order to save the revolution.

Apart from the organizational work, the main field of the society's activities during the period of preparation is propaganda. The purpose of propaganda is twofold: to influence public opinion in the desired direction and to incite the popular masses to revolt. Both had already been realized and both kinds of propaganda used by the Decembrists. But while they had conceived propaganda primarily as personal example and personal persuasion, Ogarëv devised a comprehensive plan of printed propaganda with an encyclopedic list of problems to be dealt with.

Several of Ogarëv's tactical precepts also deserve attention. One is what was later called "utilization of legal facilities": when the society can, without endangering itself, institute something publicly, it must take the opportunity. A valuable "legal facility" to be utilized is the possibility of getting into important positions in the government apparatus in order to influence policy. To gain popularity, members of the society must also seek to get into positions where they can appear as champions of the people's interests. Making use of particularly dissatisfied minorities is another tactical measure recommended by Ogarëv: he mentioned sectarians, Cossacks, the workers of the Urals, Finns, Poles, Lithuanians, and Ukrainians. Ogarëv recommended opportunist tactics in propaganda and agitation. He warned against antireligious propaganda and against the use of abstract anti-Czarist slogans; for the time being, at any rate, propaganda among "the people" was to be concentrated upon such demands as communal ownership of all land, local and regional self-government, freedom of belief, and a convocation of a Council of the Land. Christian symbols and phraseology were freely used by Ogarëv in leaflets written by him. Finally, the revolutionaries must establish cooperation with liberal constitutionalists, since both have one aim in common—the abolition of autocracy.

Most of the members of the Land and Freedom organization were young people who had been directly influenced by N. G. Chernyshevsky (1828–89), the leader of the revolutionary movement in Russia in the 1850's and 1860's. Son of a priest from Saratov on the Volga, he had been educated at the local theological seminary and at St. Petersburg University, and he devoted his life to propagating revolution and socialism. His principal theoretical fathers were Feuerbach, the French and English socialist writers, and, in problems of economics, J. S. Mill, whose *Principles of Political Economy* Chernyshevsky translated, adding to it his own notes in which he gave Mill's views a socialist turn. According to Chernyshevsky, a social system based on exploitation was bound to perish because it was contrary to both reason and modern science and to the conscience of the people; it was bound to be succeeded by a socialist system, which was reasonable and corresponded to human nature. Although Chernyshevsky does not seem to have taken much note of Marx, his own speculations are often very similar to Marx's. Thus, although progress was based on intellectual development, the main aspect of progress, consisting in the acquisition and spread of knowledge, the intellectual development itself, "like the political and every other," depended on conditions of economic life; material conditions of existence played "perhaps the primary role in life" and were "the root cause of almost all phenomena in the other, the higher, spheres of life as well." The whole European society was divided in two parts, of which one was interested in preserving the existing state of affairs, when the fruits of the people's labor mostly fell into the hands of the few members of this part of society; the interest of the other part, which everywhere made up over 90 per cent of the population, consisted in bringing about a change, so that the laboring man should enjoy all the fruits of his labor and should not see them falling into the hands of others. While the mass of the people feels the need for a change in the system of the distribution of the fruits of labor and of such means of production as land and capital, there are also people whose intellectual and moral development reaches such intensity that the sight of injustices and lawlessness tortures them; these also desire changes, but conceive of them in a wider measure and think that just relations in the sphere of property must be supported by "various guarantees in the field of civil rights." (The meaning of this last phrase is not clear, but presumably Chernyshevsky had in mind some legal guarantees of communal or cooperative ownership.) People whose interests would suffer from such changes are trying to prevent them, resorting to police measures on the one hand and to spreading reactionary theories on the other. In these circumstances, the adherents of reforms split up into two parties, one hoping to persuade the powers that be to mend their ways, while the other thinks that this is childish. The moderates blame the adherents of radical measures for the policies of the reactionaries, instead of seeing the material interests behind these policies; indeed, the moderates tend to forget the striving of the mass toward a radical change of its material conditions, or, if they remember, they are hostile to such a change. Marx praised Chernyshevsky highly, and his views are now hailed by the Communists in Russia as the culmination of "pre-Marxist" social thought.

Of his Russian predecessors and contemporaries, Belinsky and Herzen made the strongest impact on Chernyshevsky. Following Herzen, he regarded the village commune as an embryonic socialist institution ("Critique of Philosophic Prejudices against Communal Land-Ownerships," 1858) and therefore laid special stress on the peasants as a revolutionary force, predicting a new peasant rebellion similar to those led by S. T. Razin in the seventeenth century and by E. I. Pugachëv in the eighteenth. In his dissertation *The Aesthetic Relations of Art to Reality* (1855) he gave a materialistic theoretical justification of Belinsky's utilitarian view of art, and he proceeded to apply this view in his articles on literature in the radical journal *The Contemporary*. Playing the leading role on the editorial board of this journal from 1854 until his arrest eight years later, Chernyshevsky displayed extreme skill in duping the censorship and succeeded in making *The Contemporary* into the foremost organ of revolutionary and socialist opinion in Russia. Chernyshevsky was irritated by the apparent instability of Herzen's revolutionism, but when it was decided to set up a revolutionary organization, he and his followers in fact cooperated closely with Herzen and Ogarëv, and it is quite possible (though there is no direct evidence) that some of the ideas that went into Ogarëv's theory had originated with Chernyshevsky. Arrested in connection with the discovery of the Land and Freedom organization, he wrote while in prison a novel (*What Is To Be Done?*) which depicted the life of dedicated socialists and played a great role in the intellectual and emotional development of future revolutionaries, including Lenin. Chernyshevsky spent nineteen years in banishment in eastern Siberia. Several endeavors by revolutionaries to prepare his escape failed, so that from the mid-1860's on he ceased to take an active part in politics; after his return to European Russia in the 1880's, he made no attempt to resume political activity, although he did not renounce any of his earlier convictions.

The revolutionary theory worked out by Ogarëv, Herzen, Chernyshevsky, and other leading participants of the Land and Freedom venture inspired, by way of oral tradition, the activities of the various revolutionary circles during the 1860's, and one of its most faithful and determined adherents was P. N. Tkachëv (1844–86). Of a noble but impecunious family, Tkachëv was expelled from St. Petersburg University for taking part in student disorders, was a member of a peripheral circle of the Land and Freedom organization and of several other circles in St. Petersburg during the 1860's, and was several times arrested and twice imprisoned before he escaped abroad in 1873. Living in Geneva and Paris, he remained a regular contributor to radical periodicals in Russia, at the same time publishing in emigration his own journal, *The Alarm Bell,* and later writing for a newspaper of the French Blanquists. The last years of his life he spent in a psychiatric hospital. Tkachëv was the first Russian politician to be seriously influenced by Marx. As early as 1865 he declared himself to be an adherent of Marx's teaching, saying that it had become the common property of all thinking and decent people and doubting whether an intelligent person could bring any serious arguments against it. "I think," he wrote again in an article published in 1869, "that all phenomena of the political, moral, and intellectual world are in the last analysis reduced to the

phenomena of the economic world and to the 'economic structure' of society, to use Marx's expression." Economic forces determined the life of society not through reason, which most of
Tkachëv's contemporaries among the Russian radicals regarded
as the chief regulator of human behavior, but through sentiments
and emotions. Tkachëv's views on the stage of economic development reached by Russia in the 1870's and on the significance of it
for the Russian revolutionaries were similar to those Marx
adopted a few years later. Russia was about to embark upon the
path of capitalist development, which would result in a stronger
and more stable government solidly supported by the bourgeoisie.
Russian revolutionaries must therefore strike while the government hangs in the air during the transitional period. On the
practical tasks of the revolutionaries, Tkachëv fully shared the
views formulated by Ogarëv. "The relation of the revolutionary
minority and the people," he wrote, "and participation of the
latter in the revolution, can be defined as follows: the revolutionary minority, having freed the people from the yoke of . . . fear
. . . of the powers that be, opens up for it an opportunity to reveal its destructive revolutionary force, and leaning upon this
force, skillfully directing it toward annihilation of the immediate
enemies of the revolution, the minority destroys the latter's protective fortress and deprives them of every means of resistance and
counteraction. Then, making use of its strength and authority, it
introduces new, progressively communist elements into the conditions of the people's life." Tkachëv propagated these views tire-
lessly in the 1870's, when the majority of revolutionaries in Russia had abandoned them. He wrote that *The Alarm Bell* "was not a
revolutionary agitation sheet; its task consisted merely in returning revolutionaries to those, solely correct, ideas and principles
of revolutionary activity from which they, under the influence of
the reaction, under the influence of anarchist and Lavrovist nonsense, had begun to turn away. These ideas and principles did
not contain anything new, but it was well to *be reminded* of
them. . . . It was enough to remind a small circle of revolutionaries of the forgotten ideas, and then the revolutionary practice
itself was not slow to prove that these ideas are reasonable and

practicable and to spread them among the majority of revolutionaries."

And in fact the People's Will Party, formed in 1879, adopted these ideas. They added to them, however, both in their theory and even more in their practical activity, the idea of individual terror against leading representatives of the existing regime in order to shake and disorganize it. Tkachëv opposed individual terror; he thought that disparate terroristic acts led only to the dissipation of the revolutionary party's forces and thus weakened it—the one form of individual terror he agreed to was that against police spies. The idea of terror against leading officials was partly an extension of the old idea of regicide, which had been revived by the student Karakozov who in 1866 made (on his own initiative) an attempt on Alexander II's life. But the leaders of the People's Will Party were also undoubtedly influenced by the doctrine that any means were permissible in the revolutionary struggle. This doctrine had been first advanced in Russia by Chernyshevsky's follower P. G. Zaichnevsky (1842–96) in the leaflet entitled *Young Russia* (1862), where he argued that only extreme measures could lead to success and that the government itself was not inhibited in its choice of means. In case of active opposition to the revolution, Zaichnevsky called for a total extermination of the "Imperial party." (Tkachëv in his early youth—according to his sister—had gone even further and had thought that in order to renovate the country it would be necessary to exterminate all inhabitants above the age of twenty-five!)

The doctrine of the admissibility of any means, of total moral indifference, was the cornerstone of the revolutionary views and activities of S. G. Nechaev (1847–82). He was associated with Tkachëv in fomenting student disorders in St. Petersburg University in 1869, and in the early 1870's he secured the support of Ogarëv and Bakunin. The device he most frequently applied was deception: In Switzerland he made Ogarëv and Bakunin believe that he had come as a representative of a Russian revolutionary organization, and upon his return to Russia he similarly mystified several young people by posing as an agent of the headquarters of an organization called Popular Revenge. Having formed a number of underground circles, he induced members of one of them to murder a fellow member whom he falsely accused of treason. Nechaev fled abroad, but was extradited as a common criminal and spent the rest of his life in prison. But the effect of the revelations in court about his activities was such that the majority of revolutionary-minded young people abandoned the very idea of a centralized conspiratorial organization, an idea which remained in disrespect during the 1870's until Tkachëv succeeded in winning new adherents.

7. *Populism*

THE TERM Populism is used by historians of Russia and Russian thought in three different senses. In the widest sense it includes all those thinkers and politicians who adhered to the idea of Russian socialism first advanced by Herzen, i.e., of socialism based on, or growing out of, the village commune. All the revolutionary socialists of the 1850's, 1860's, and 1870's belong to this category, as well as a bunch of revolutionary and reformist trends in the late nineteenth and early twentieth centuries. In a somewhat narrower sense, Populism includes all those who called themselves Populists, i.e., all the above-mentioned groups except the revolutionaries of the 1850's and 1860's, who in this case appear only as precursors of Populism. Finally, Populism in the narrowest sense includes only those writers and practical politicians who aimed simply at a truthful reflection of the genuine views and sentiments of "the people" themselves, that is, in fact, of the peasantry; it was this last group that (in the mid-1870's) first used the term Populism to describe its philosophy. This chapter will be devoted to Populism in the second sense. The most important feature common to all Populists in this category is not the name that they gave themselves (although it had a certain psychological importance), but the fact that they all adhered, to a greater or lesser extent, to the social philosophy of Lavrov, who can thus be considered as the real father of Populism.

Classical Populism

P. L. Lavrov (1823–1900), a nobleman by birth, received a military education and from the age of twenty-three was Professor of Mathematics at the Artillery Academy in St. Petersburg. Apart from mathematics, he wrote on military subjects and the history of science, on philosophy and sociology, but at first he did not concern himself with political problems. However, chiefly under the influence of Herzen and Chernyshevsky, he gradually became more interested in politics and finally joined the Land and Freedom organization. Arrested and banished after Karakozov's attempt on Alexander II's life, he fled to Paris in 1870, joined the International, and took an active part in the Paris Commune. Beginning in 1873, he published the journal *Forward!* in Geneva, which for several years was the chief organ of the Populist movement in Russia. In the 1880's and 1890's, he supported the People's Will Party, at first disapproving of terror but later justifying it. Although he wrote much and published several weighty volumes on the philosophy of history and on the history of thought, Lavrov's fame rests primarily on his *Historical Letters,* which, written in banishment, were first published in one of the radical journals and then, in 1870, as a separate pamphlet. Throughout the following decade this pamphlet served as the most important single source of inspiration for the Populist youth in Russia, and it was later reprinted several times as the main classical work of Populist thought.

The starting point of Lavrov's theorizing is the human personality with its varied needs and inclinations. Human activity has two aspects: perceiving means of achieving pleasure and escaping pain, and acting in order to achieve these ends. In the process of perception and acting, an individual forms for himself an ideal of human worthiness; this ideal becomes the main motive of the individual's behavior, while the individual's activity aimed at the realization of the ideal is the moving force of history. History appears to every man as a process of struggle between his ideal, held to be true, and other ideals, which are considered as wrong. The individual's ideal stands at the end of history, while everything in the past is evaluated, taken into account, or rejected in the light of the ideal. Thus history, according to Lavrov, is doubly subjective: because it is moved by human ideals and because it is studied in the light of such ideals. But not all ideals are of equal intrinsic value. The reason for this is that people's thinking is not uniform. The majority of people think passively, but there is a minority of critically thinking persons who are capable of forsaking personal advantage and of seeing the common good—"the development of personality in the physical, intellectual, and moral senses, the embodiment in social forms of truth and justice"—as their own ideal. The critically thinking persons do not necessarily do this—they may concern themselves with other fields of cultural endeavor, such as technology or science. This is also progress, but the price of this progress is great and constantly increasing. The soil upon which the educated minority grows is the passive majority, which lives in misery and suffers while it relieves the minority from cares and enables it to do creative work. Thus an enormous debt has been accumulated, which the critically thinking persons ought to repay, and the present task of every educated person is to pay back his debt. But although there is a moral obligation, there is no external necessity for an educated person to devote himself to the service of the common good, and everyone has to make a choice. If a person decides on service to the common good, his practical task is to help others to become critically thinking people. When a sufficient number of critically thinking people have been produced, they can effect a revolution that will eliminate material inequality and class differences—ills that have grown as a result of the temporary ascendancy of harmful ideals. Revolution will also destroy the existing state, which, having been created by social contract for the protection of everybody's safety, later degenerated into "a conspiracy of a few exploiters against the mass of the exploited." In his views on the class struggle and on the function of the modern state Lavrov came nearest to Marx, whom he respected highly and called his teacher. He took a great interest in the activities of the International and in the labor movement in Western Europe and glorified the Paris Commune as the first proletarian revolution. The aim of the hoped-for revolution was the same in Western Europe and in Russia—the abolition of "monopoly in all forms" and of "compulsory statehood" and their replacement by free associations of the working people. But whereas in Western Europe "the working people" means primarily industrial workers, in Russia it means the peasants. The future socialist society in Russia must grow out of the village communes. Contrary to the revolutionary theory of Ogarëv and Tkachëv, Lavrov did not see the task of the revolutionaries in Russia as utilizing the mass of the people in order to seize power, to replace one oppressive government by another, and to impose socialist measures from above. Instead of this, one should ascertain the real needs and interests of the people, make them realize what their needs are, and assist them in carrying out the revolution. For this purpose one should heed Herzen's appeal "to go among the people." A rather long process of propaganda and of training, from among "the people," a sufficient number of critically thinking persons—such was the prospect which Lavrov's teaching opened up to his followers.

The fate of Lavrovism in the history of the Russian revolutionary movement was checkered. It was enthusiastically greeted in the early 1870's as an alternative to Nechaev's amoralism as well as to Tkachëv's centralism and authoritarianism, which also appeared to be tainted with Nechaevism. The main Populist circle of the early 1870's—the Chaikovsky Circle in St. Petersburg—was solidly Lavrovist in its outlook, and it was, indeed, on the initiative of this circle that Lavrov published *Forward!*. But soon Bakunin's view—that there was no need for a long period of propaganda, that the peasants were ready to rise and only needed to be prompted—became dominant. The second Land and Freedom organization (1876–79) was predominantly Bakuninist, while the orthodox Lavrovists remained outside it and worked separately, concentrating mainly on propaganda among industrial workers in order to train them for future propaganda among the peasants. The leading members of the Workers' Unions in St. Petersburg and Odessa in the late 1870's were trained by Lavrovists. When, after the split of the second Land and Freedom organization, Lavrov himself joined the Tkachëvist-minded People's Will Party, orthodox Lavrovists did not follow his example; they continued their propaganda among the factory workers, giving its content an increasingly Marxist turn and thus preparing the ground for the emergence of revolutionary Social Democracy.

Whereas Lavrov remained a determined revolutionary until his death, revolutionism was never a prominent feature in the thought of the other main theorist of Populism, N. K. Mikhailovsky (1842–1904). Coming from a noble but impoverished family, Mikhailovsky received a technological training at the Mining

Institute in St. Petersburg, but because of his involvement in student disorders he was refused permission to take his final examinations and became a professional journalist. He was for many years the dominant personality on the editorial boards of the two main Populist journals—*Notes of the Fatherland,* in 1869–84, and *Russian Wealth,* from 1892 until his death—and exercised a profound influence on two generations of Populists. In his sociological and philosophical writings, Mikhailovsky was influenced by Comte, Darwin, Spencer, and Marx (perhaps also Proudhon), and in many respects he was a direct follower of Lavrov. Like Lavrov, he takes as his starting point the human personality, using for the elucidation of this and related concepts the data of contemporary natural sciences. Postulating that the main attribute of live matter is a tendency to grow more complex, Mikhailovsky pictures a series of organic "individualities" hierarchically subordinated to each other. Each "individuality" struggles to assert itself on two fronts: against the lower "individualities," its own component parts, trying to suppress their independence, and against the higher "individuality" of which it is itself a part, trying to prevent its own suppression. Hence the importance for human individuals of the struggle against society, the higher individuality. Here Mikhailovsky's notion of the "struggle for individuality" (as against Spencer's organicism in sociology) leads to his "formula of progress," which is an improvement—if only in the sense of greater precision—on Lavrov's rather vague idea of progress. The forms of cooperation between people for the satisfaction of the needs of society are different: the simpler and more uniform the society, the more many-sided is the man in it, and vice versa. Since the differentiation of society leads to one-sidedness of human beings, progress consists in achieving the highest possible degree of social uniformity, excluding extremes of social division of labor and thus ensuring the fuller development of human personality. The task of reasonable people is therefore to resist the "natural," "organic" development of society that leads to differentiation. A thinking person must oppose his "subjective" social ideal to "objective" social development, his desired aim to the "necessity" of evolution. Such an opposition is not futile, because people's subjective ideals are not entirely divorced from objective reality—e.g., different social groups come to desire certain things under the influence of the conditions of their lives and their often conflicting interests. Analyzing the position of different social classes, Mikhailovsky came to the conclusion that the intelligentsia, being in the possession of knowledge and at the same time not bound by any particular material interests, was the social group that was best suited to produce an ideal with the most universal validity. This ideal Mikhailovsky called Truth, in both the senses which this word has in Russian: truth as verity and truth as justice. Mikhailovsky's Truth, held to combine scientific knowledge and moral law, supplied the secularized substitute for religious certainty, which was so passionately desired by the radical intelligentsia. Developing further Lavrov's concept of "critically thinking personalities," Mikhailovsky demanded from young intellectuals that they dedicate themselves to the attainment of Truth, contrasting such dedicated "heroes" with the "crowd" of ordinary people. In concrete terms, seeking the Truth meant on the one hand adherence to Lavrov's and Mikhailovsky's "subjective method" of analyzing moral, social, and political problems, and on the other hand striving toward a socialist society. In Russia, in particular, socialism must be based on the existing village commune, not because of any Slavophile sentiment but because the village commune already presents a more progressive social structure, if measured by Mikhailovsky's criterion of progress, than the capitalist society with its advanced social division of labor. At first—like Lavrov—showing little interest in political (as opposed to social) problems, Mikhailovsky later—again like Lavrov—came to realize the importance of political power, approved of the activities of the People's Will Party, and even contributed to its journal; toward the end of his life he supported the efforts of the Liberal Populists aimed at social reforms through actions of the existing government. Though he did not join any of the factions into which the Populist movement was split, Mikhailovsky enjoyed great respect among practically all of them and was for a quarter of a century the recognized theoretical leader of the movement.

Populism in the Narrow Sense

A radically different concept of Populism was advanced in the early 1880's by I. I. Kablits (1848–93), a nobleman from Lithuania who had left Kiev University to "go among the people" and had lived for several years as an underground revolutionary. Life among the peasants convinced him that the approach adopted by the revolutionary intelligentsia was wrong, and he went on to develop his own theory, to which he gave the name Populism. In his *Russian Dissidents* (1881), Kablits (himself a Lutheran) argued that the seventeenth century schism in the Orthodox Church had been due to the antagonism between the people and the state power. It had been a protest of the Russian people against the innovations—partly of Tatar and partly of German origin—which neither fitted in with the character of the people nor corresponded to their interests. And a considerable part of the population still rejected the principles on which the social and political life of the country was based. Having thus asserted the position of the mass of the people as an independent and self-conscious agent, Kablits in his next book, *The Foundations of Populism* (1882), directly attacked the presumption of the intelligentsia that they are called upon to impose new forms of life on the people irrespective of the desires and opinions of the popular mass itself. Emotions are more important in the life of the people than knowledge and theoretical understanding, and as far as emotions are concerned, simple people are stronger and richer than the intelligentsia, they have a strong instinctive striving for truth and justice. Kablits further elaborated these basic views in *The Intelligentsia and the People in the Social Life of Russia* (1885). Kablits' attack on the views that had been universally held by the Populists, coming as it did immediately after the break-up of the People's Will Party following the assassination of Alexander II, was widely interpreted as a symptom of exhaustion and disillusionment. It undoubtedly was such a symptom, but it also performed a useful function as a check on the elitist tendency that was so strong in Populist thought. The Liberal Populism of the late nineteenth century and the Neo-

Populism of the early twentieth century profited from the impact of Kablits' attack.

Liberal Populism

The decade following the assassination of Alexander II in 1881 and the break-up by the police of the People's Will Party is usu·ally depicted by historians as an anticlimax, a period of dis-orientation and decay of public spirit. But this picture contains only a part of the truth. Certainly the high hopes and expecta-tions of immediate success, the reckless heroism and longing for self-sacrifice, so typical of the revolutionary Populists of the 1870's, had gone, and it was natural for the radical contempo-raries to feel that a glorious epoch had come to an end. But the feeling of helplessness in the face of a government that had turned out to be far stronger than they had expected was not universal among the Populists. Only a minority of them gave up hope and folded their hands. The majority, after the initial shock, adjusted themselves to the situation and found new ways of serving their ideals.

Kablits' sharp and passionate attacks made many wonder whether the road they had taken was the right one. And out of this re-examination was born the "theory of small deeds." It is usually associated with the name of Ya. V. Abramov (1858–1906), an ethnographer and journalist from the North Caucasus, who propagated it in Mikhailovsky's *Notes of the Fatherland* and in other radical journals. The idea was that instead of wasting their energies, sometimes their lives, in frontal attacks upon the gov-ernment, without even knowing exactly what to put in its place, the Populist intellectuals should work among the people whom they wanted to serve but of whom they knew so little. Not cam-paigns of "going among the people," but life and work in direct contact with them, learning their needs and trying to help them— this was the right path for a genuine friend of the people. Once the idea was conceived, it became obvious that there was ample opportunity for this kind of work. The new local government bodies in the provinces that were gradually set up after the re-form of 1864 were given charge of primary education, health

services, and to some extent the economic welfare of the peasantry. To perform these functions efficiently, large numbers of
professional people were required, especially doctors, statisticians,
and teachers. The majority of the Populist-minded intelligentsia
seized this chance with an enthusiasm and dedication which,
though less spectacular than the heroism of the People's Will,
was hardly less impressive and certainly more constructive. As a
result of the "small deeds" of this dedicated and determined army
of modest and moderate Populist intellectuals, Russia had, by
the end of the century, a free rural health service, a greatly ex-
panded network of primary schools (well on the way to achieving
universal primary education), and the practice of systematic social surveys probably unequaled anywhere in the world.

But the results of the decades of their work did not fill the
Liberal Populists with unqualified joy. The wealth of statistical
material on the conditions of the peasantry confirmed their direct
impression that not only was the standard of living of the peasants not improving as fast as they would have desired but that it
was frequently not improving at all, or even deteriorating. The
cause of this is clear to us now. The rapid industrialization that
Russia was undergoing was possible only at the cost of neglecting
the economic welfare of the peasants. But this connection was not
obvious at the time, and the state of economic theory then was
such that it was more likely to confuse than to enlighten those
who turned to it for an explanation. The theorists of Liberal
Populism were therefore faced with the problem of how to avoid
the undesirable social consequences of industrialization. True to
their Populist faith, they conceived this as a problem of industrialization without capitalism. Capitalist enterprise and governmental support for it were seen as the main causes of the misery
of the peasants. The task was therefore one of protecting the
peasant economy (and the artisans in the towns, who were in a
similar situation) from being destroyed by capitalism. The best
known and most penetrating of the theorists of Liberal Populism,
V. P. Vorontsov (1847–1918), who was himself active in local
government as a doctor and statistician, advanced the concept of
"peasant labor economy"—a peculiar type of economic unit consisting of a peasant household, self-sufficient and yet capable

of sustaining an expanding market, and therefore stimulating the expansion of the country's economy as a whole, provided it was not depressed by excessive taxation and was supported in its resistance to capitalism. The support should come both from the government and from the educated elements of the society, who should help the peasants to help themselves by introducing better methods of agriculture, improving marketing facilities, providing small-scale credit, and other similar measures.

One of the best ways in which the intellectuals could help was to promote cooperation among the peasants. The village commune was a natural framework for such cooperation, and support for it remained one of the main points in the Liberal Populists' program. But the commune was an unwieldy instrument and frequently too conservative to be efficient in competition with the enterprising capitalists. Other forms of cooperation were therefore often preferable, and the Liberal Populists supported agricultural cooperatives of the modern type. With their support, the cooperative movement made great strides in Russia beginning with the 1880's, mainly in the forms of agricultural marketing and credit cooperatives, which were so successful that shortly before World War I they entered the field of foreign trade (selling agricultural products and buying machinery and other equipment).

When, after the revival of revolutionary Populism around the turn of the century, the Party of Socialist Revolutionaries was formed, most Liberal Populists supported it as an organization that would give a better shape to the political side of the Populist movement. But the return of the Socialist Revolutionaries to the tactics of terror disgusted many Liberal Populists, who not only rejected it on moral grounds but also had become accustomed to more civilized ways of settling conflicts. The more thoughtful, moderate, and humane people left the Socialist Revolutionaries in 1905 and then formed the Popular Socialist Party, one of whose leaders was the veteran Populist N. V. Chaikovsky (1850–1926), who had returned from emigration. The party advocated socialization of all land with compensation to private owners and the gradual establishment of what one would now call a welfare state, laying stress upon cooperation between the government, social organizations such as cooperatives, and individual initiative on the part of both the peasants themselves and public-spirited intellectuals. The party did not aim at becoming a mass organization, but despite its small numbers it was able to put up active opposition to the Bolsheviks when the latter seized power in 1917. Chaikovsky himself took the initiative in forming the interparty Union for the Regeneration of Russia, and during the Civil War he headed an anti-Bolshevik government in Archangel.

Neo-Populism

From the late 1880's onward, when Marxism appeared on the Russian scene as a rival socialist theory (rather than, as before, a component part of the Populist theory itself), much of the Populists' theoretical efforts was devoted to polemics against the exclusive claims of the Russian Marxists. But it was not until after 1917 that anti-Marxism became the main theoretical orientation of Populist thought in its neo-Populist phase.

Neo-Populism had its roots in the Liberal Populism of the late nineteenth and early twentieth centuries. But the progressive erosion of the village commune after the Stolypin agricultural reforms of 1907, enabling the peasants to leave the commune and set up as individual farmers with consolidated plots of land owned by themselves, made it possible to change the approach and to look at the peasants not primarily as an object of care and protection but as independent agents. Vorontsov's concept of "peasant labor economy" served as the basis of the Neo-Populists' analysis, and it was further elaborated by the leading theorist of the school, Professor A. N. Chelintsev (born 1874). According to him, the future of Russia lay in the future of its largest social class—the peasants. The autonomous process of continuous change in the internal organization and functioning of individual peasant economies was an important aspect of the country's social evolution, no less important than industrialization. A continuous detailed study of this process, an elucidation of the needs of the peasants and assistance in solving their problems was therefore a task of great political moment. The place of the intelligentsia was side by side with the peasants, but if it was to fulfill its role it had to free itself from its preconceived ideas about the peasants,

ideas derived from abstract ideological schemes or from theories
based on the study of foreign or urban societies. Marxism was one
such theory, and it was—at best—useless to approach the peasant
economy with a Marxist yardstick. Like all Populists, the Neo-
Populists welcomed the nationalization of private land by the
Soviet government, but the economic and social policies of War
Communism, which undermined the peasant economy through
arbitrary requisitions of agricultural produce and were aimed at
the destruction of village solidarity with the help of the Committees of the Poor, brought them near the point of despair. The
New Economic Policy pursued after 1921, with its economic concessions to the peasants, appeared to the Neo-Populists as the
dawn of a new life, and the leading figure among them, N. D.
Kondrat'ev (1892–?), an economist of international standing
and an ex-Socialist Revolutionary, was for a time in charge of the
Soviet government's agricultural planning. Chelintsev, who had
been in emigration, where Neo-Populists formed a party of their
own called Peasant Russia and published a journal of the same
name in Prague, returned to Russia in 1927 and joined the
academic center of the Neo-Populists at the Moscow Agricultural
Academy. Other fields of Neo-Populist activities were the statistical service, which was largely staffed by former local government
statisticians, and the surviving agricultural cooperatives. Although it was increasingly difficult for the Neo-Populists, as it
was for all ideological opponents of the new regime, to express
their views in public—they could do no more than hint obliquely
at their position—they retained a certain cohesion as an ideological pressure group until 1929–30, when independent cooperatives were finally suppressed to make room for Communist-
managed collective farms and all the leading Neo-Populists were
arrested on charges of sabotage and plotting against the Soviet
regime. It is true that the Neo-Populists warned against the
dangers of forced collectivization (and history proved them right
on this point) and resisted it by all legal means at their disposal;
but the absence of available evidence makes it quite impossible
to assess the validity of the official charge that they had formed an
underground Peasant Labor Party and had cooperated politically
with the Peasant Russia group abroad.

Late Radical Populism

The decay of revolutionary Populism after 1881 lasted for almost two decades, but this does not mean that it had disappeared altogether. Theoretically, the People's Will Party continued to exist, and circles here and there often considered themselves as belonging to it. More important than others was the group of St. Petersburg students that made an attempt on the life of Alexander III in 1887. Other groups of People's Will adherents confined themselves to propagating revolution and socialism, or, at most, training people in underground techniques. There were also circles of former adherents of the Bakuninist Black Repartition, an organization of people who had not taken the Tkachëvist turn in 1879. The Black Repartition also disintegrated after 1881, with most of its leaders going over to Marxism, but many members and sympathizers retained their Populist outlook. Finally, there were also the remnants of the original Lavrovists who had not followed their ideological leader into the People's Will. Many of these diverse groups, unconnected or only loosely connected with each other, succumbed to the growing Marxist influence during the 1880's and 1890's and thus gave birth to Social Democracy. But others, partly in reaction to the appearance of the Social Democratic trend, clung to their Populist identity.

Toward the end of the 1890's there began to appear signs of a revival of revolutionary Populism: both the old theoretical leaders—Lavrov and Mikhailovsky—were still alive and active; some of the old underground fighters had returned from banishment; and some of those who in the 1880's had abandoned revolutionism for Liberal Populism or Tolstoyism had become disillusioned and now returned to the fold. A new generation of young radicals had grown up, people who had not experienced the defeat and humiliation of 1881. External conditions also were more favorable. The growth of the labor movement added a new element of mass unrest to the usual sporadic peasant disorders. And the weak and vacillating policy of Nicholas II emboldened many who had kept quiet under his father's regime of firm repression. Small circles coalesced into larger organizations until the underground Party of Socialist Revolutionaries was formally founded at a conference in 1902. The idea was to gather into the new party all socialists of Populist leanings, and the appeal proved sufficiently strong to attract, as we have seen, even many Liberal Populists, whose habits of thought and action were quite different from those of the revolutionaries and who left the Socialist Revolutionary Party a few years later. Made up of diverse elements, the new party remained a very loose organization. There was no attempt to subject members to strict party discipline, to evolve uniform tactics, or to impose an obligatory ideology, although there emerged a recognized theoretical leader in the person of Chernov.

V. M. Chernov (1873–1952) was the son of an official of peasant origin from the lower Volga area. For a short time he studied law and philosophy at Moscow and Berne universities, but, having taken part in the circles of the People's Will adherents from his earliest youth, he was soon too deeply involved in revolutionary activities to be able to continue systematic studies. He remained faithful to the tradition of the "ethical socialism" of Lavrov and Mikhailovsky, but wanted to combine this with the more "scientific" socialism of Marx. He was also influenced by the neo-Kantianism that had its vogue at the turn of the century and was certainly a more suitable philosophical basis for "ethical socialism" than the Positivism of Lavrov and Mikhailovsky. Finally, the propeasant trend among the "revisionists" in German Social Democracy attracted Chernov's attention as a welcome modification of Marxism, bringing it nearer to the Populist standpoint. Chernov was early recognized as the theoretical leader of the Party of Socialist Revolutionaries and enjoyed great popularity among its members. Occupying a central position in the party, he was its natural figurehead and in 1918, after a brief period of serving as Minister of Agriculture in Kerensky's Provisional Government the year before, he was elected President of the short-lived Constituent Assembly. Chernov took up an equivocal position during the Civil War, emigrated in 1920, and died in New York. He was a prolific writer, but the essence of his political views can be clearly gauged from the Program of the Socialist Revolutionary Party drafted by him in 1906, a collection of articles published under the title *Land and Law* (1919) and the book *Constructive Socialism* (1925).

Chernov's fundamental conviction was the traditional one of "Russian Socialism": The aim is the same as that of the West European Socialists, but Russia's path toward this aim must be different. The principal reason for the difference is that Russia is an overwhelmingly peasant country, and Russian peasants have a peculiar attitude toward land, one that Chernov called the consciousness of the right of toil. There are two aspects to this attitude. One is that the land cannot rightly be owned by anyone —it is nobody's property, or rather, it is God's. The other aspect is that every man who tills the land with his own hands has the right to use a suitable proportion of it. Roman law, Chernov argued, had only superficially touched Russia and the concept of property was still very weak in the minds of the people; the future socialist society should remove the veneer of Roman law and build a new socialist law on the basis of peasant consciousness. Faced with the orthodox Marxist contention that small producers were bound to be destroyed and eliminated by capitalism, Chernov pointed to the resilience shown by small producers in agriculture in many countries and maintained—following the Liberal Populists—that the peasant economy could compete in efficiency with large-scale agriculture because it could be much more labor-intensive. But whatever its economic effects, capitalism, if allowed to spread in agriculture, would have extremely adverse social and political consequences. It would establish the Roman-law notion of property, destroy the solidarity of the village, and produce a mass of landless laborers who would be as susceptible to reactionary as to revolutionary agitation. Fortunately for the prospects of socialism in Russia, capitalism is not an autonomous growth but has been artificially fostered by the government and continues to rely upon its support. It is therefore closely connected with the absolutist regime, and the overthrow of the regime would remove the main prop of capitalism. A political revolution would thus be a direct prelude to a social transformation. Urban workers belong essentially to the same broad class of toilers as do peasants, but the position of Russian workers differs from that of their fellows in Western Europe, for the Russian urban proletariat has developed in the absence of a strong and self-assertive bourgeoisie. On top of this, there exists in Russia a large and idealistic intelligentsia, which also belongs to the class of toilers and is able and eager to provide the leadership needed by the workers and the peasants for the success of revolution and of socialist reconstruction.

The Socialist Revolutionary program was based on these main theoretical propositions. Its central point was the socialization of all land through confiscation without compensation and its transfer to the control of local government bodies, which would ensure its equitable distribution among the peasants, who would cultivate the land either collectively or individually according to their own preference. Collective farming should triumph in the end, but no compulsion was permissible. Regular redistributions would ensure permanent equalization of land use by the peasants. Unlike socialization of the land, socialization of industry was not to take place immediately after the revolution, but, like the triumph of collective farming, was to be postponed to a more distant future; meanwhile the workers were promised far-reaching social benefits and a voice in factory management. In contrast to its indifference or direct hostility to civil rights, the program showed great concern for the political rights of citizens. It envisaged a democratic republic with proportional representation and such elements of direct democracy as referendum and the recall of deputies. In common with most socialist parties in Western Europe, the Socialist Revolutionaries wanted to replace the standing army by a people's militia, which in Russia would have entailed the revival of a pre-Petrine institution. In keeping with the traditional Populist interest and concern for local and national minorities, the Socialist Revolutionary program provided for a great degree of decentralization in administration and for a federal structure for the Russian state, the component parts of the federation being formed by those areas where the non-Russian majority of the population would not wish to exercise the right of secession.

The tradition of the People's Will Party asserted itself most strongly with Chernov and the Socialist Revolutionaries on two points. One was the acceptance in principle of a temporary revolutionary dictatorship, directed against the anti-Socialist minority, at the time of transition to full socialism; such a dictatorship was only to be established, however, if it turned out to be essential. The other—and more important—point where the People's Will tradition prevailed was the use of terror as a means of disrupting the government machinery. But whereas in the People's Will the political leadership and the direction of terroristic activities were in the hands of the same group of people, the Socialist Revolutionaries' "Fighting Organization," while subordinate to the Central Committee in matters of policy, was independent in tactics and built, unlike the rest of the party, on principles of centralization and total subordination to one person—the head of the organization. This arrangement proved disastrous when the post fell to E. F. Azef (1869–1918), who combined it with the duties of a police agent. Azef was disloyal to both sides, and, enjoying his power, played each against the other for five years, until his role was revealed to the revolutionaries by a high police official.

Subsidiary organizations of the Socialist Revolutionary Party were "peasant unions" or "peasant brotherhoods," which in 1906 were fused into the All-Russian Peasants' Union. Through these brotherhoods, through its fighting and military groups, its representatives on strike committees and in Soviets ("councils") of Workers' Deputies, the party actively participated in the revolution of 1905–7. The Socialist Revolutionaries rejected the semiconstitutional regime that was established in Russia following that revolution, but soon after the February revolution of 1917 they joined the Provisional Government, while at the same time again playing a prominent role in the revived Soviets. After the seizure of power by the Bolsheviks, the Socialist Revolutionaries won the majority of seats in the Constituent Assembly, and the Assembly was, significantly, debating a Socialist Revolutionary motion on socialization of the land when it was dispersed on Lenin's orders at the end of its one-day session. During the Civil War that ensued, the Socialist Revolutionaries were less united than ever, the right wing of the party siding with the Whites, the left wing with the Reds, while the center vacillated, unwilling to give up all hope of cooperating with the Bolsheviks in a Socialist coalition government. These hopes were finally dispelled when the Bolsheviks charged a number of Socialist Revolutionary leaders with sabotage at a show trial held in 1922, and the party was outlawed. As early as 1918, some right-wing Socialist Revolutionaries resumed the tactics of individual terror, directing it now against leading Communists (including an attempt on Lenin's life in 1918), and small underground circles of Socialist Revolutionary adherents continued to exist throughout the 1920's and early 1930's, the situation being somewhat similar to that of the 1880's and 1890's. In the absence of reliable information it is impossible to say to what extent the Communist charge that some of the peasant uprisings at the time of the collectivization of agriculture were inspired by former Socialist Revolutionaries corresponds to the facts.

The program worked out by Chernov for the Socialist Revolutionaries in the end benefited not them but their rivals for the support of the peasantry, the Bolsheviks. Aware of the popularity of the Socialist Revolutionaries' demand for confiscation and partition of the landlords' estates, Lenin in 1917 openly abandoned the Social Democratic agrarian program and adopted the Socialist Revolutionaries' plank. There were also other Populist elements in Lenin's thought and tactics, which will be discussed in the chapter on Communism.

Besides the Party of Socialist Revolutionaries, there existed several radical Populist groups which had at one time or another split off from the main party and all of which cooperated with the Bolsheviks in 1917–20. The most important of these groups was the Party of Left Socialist Revolutionaries, which broke off in the autumn of 1917 and allied itself with the Bolsheviks. They took an active part in the seizure of power and a few days after the coup entered the Soviet Government as a junior partner. The cooperation of the Left Socialist Revolutionaries ensured to the Bolsheviks the support of the more radical elements among the peasants, who looked to the Left Socialist Revolutionaries for leadership. The main concern of the Left Socialist Revolutionaries was to effect the partition of the landlords' estates as soon as possible, and this was the main point they had in common with the Bolsheviks. The other policies they advocated were also very similar. The Left Socialist Revolutionaries were in favor of abandoning democratic procedures, and they actively participated in operating the dictatorial regime established by the October coup. They left the government in 1918, rejecting Lenin's opportunist stand on the peace treaty with Germany and wanting to continue a revolutionary war. But even then they continued to occupy high positions in the Extraordinary Commission for Combating the Counterrevolution (the Cheka), i.e., the political police. Cooperation ended in the same year after the assassination by a Left Socialist Revolutionary of the German Ambassador in Moscow and an armed clash between the Left Socialist Revolutionaries and the Bolsheviks (also in Moscow), which is usually referred to as the Left Socialist Revolutionary uprising. Although recent research (by Dr. George Katkov) has cast some doubt on the Left Socialist Revolutionaries' initiative in these events, it is the official version, accepted by both sides at the time, that had political significance. After a short break, the party again functioned openly from 1920 to 1922, had its own journal, and advocated a "dictatorship of the masses instead of the dictatorship of a party" and the formation of a semi-trade-union, semi-cooperative organization for the peasants. The Party of Left Socialist Revolutionaries counted among its adherents some of the leading intellectuals, such as the poets Blok and Esenin and the literary critic and publicist R. V. Ivanov-Razumnik, who had earlier written a history of Russian political thought in the nineteenth and early twentieth centuries in terms of a struggle between intelligentsia and philistinism. Another radical Populist group cooperating with the Communists was the Party of Revolutionary Communism, which broke off from the Left Socialist Revolutionary Party in 1918 over the German peace-treaty question. It counted among its members some of the veterans of revolutionary Populism, including one of its most revered figures, M. A. Natanson (1850–1919), who had set up the Chaikovsky circle and the second Land and Freedom organization in the 1870's. The group accused the Bolsheviks of disregard for human personality, of "being interested in the people's bellies rather than in their spirit," and of Taylorism in industry. They opposed the use of armed detachments for food procurement and advocated the formation of agrarian and factory communes. But in other respects they tried to cooperate with the Communist Party as closely as possible, and in 1920 most of them joined it.

This survey of Populism over the half century during which it was of primary importance in Russian political thought and practice shows that all the different Populist trends had, among other things, adhered to two propositions: that Russia was different from Western Europe in her past and in her foreseeable future, and that one of the main differences was the communal spirit of the Russian peasants. Both these propositions were clearly of Slavophile provenance, and since they occupied a very important place in the Populist thought, we can agree with the Populists' opponents that Populism was a quasi-Slavophile movement.

But it was also a pro-peasant movement, much more so than any other intellectual movement in modern Russian history. This pro-peasant aspect of Populism attracted like-minded people in other countries of eastern and southeastern Europe, and, as Professor D. Mitrany has recently shown, the Populist doctrine has exercised a considerable influence on a number of thinkers and on several political parties there.

Looking back from the vantage point of the mid-twentieth century at the problems the Russian Populists were trying to solve and at the solutions they suggested, we recognize that what appeared to them as a peculiarly Russian situation has since arisen and continues to arise in our own days in other "underdeveloped" countries, and that the Populist theory and practice could often serve as useful precedents.

8. Regionalism, Anarchism, and Syndicalism

PARALLEL with the Populist movement, and having many points of contact with it, there developed in Russia from the 1860's onward three vigorous radical political trends—regionalism, anarchism, and syndicalism.

Regionalism

Regionalist tendencies were by no means new in Russia. They had appeared almost as soon as the centralized Muscovite state had been consolidated, and they had often been successful. Thus when the central part of the Ukraine was united with Muscovy in 1654, it retained almost complete internal autonomy, which was only gradually whittled down during the eighteenth century. The Baltic provinces, annexed by Peter the Great from Sweden, retained their old legal system and administrative autonomy. The Cossack communities, especially the Don Cossacks, also enjoyed autonomy and (until 1714) republican constitutions. Even at the height of the centralizing tendencies in the eighteenth century, Desnitsky defended internal autonomy for the Cossack regions and for areas inhabited by nomadic peoples on grounds of their different traditions and ways of life.

Modern regionalism, however, dates from the Decembrists. Murav'ëv, as we have seen, envisaged a federal structure for Russia, while a branch of the Decembrist movement in the Ukraine—the Society of United Slavs—aimed at extending the federation to include the other Slavic peoples as well. The tradition of the Society of United Slavs was picked up by another secret society, the Society of SS. Cyril and Methodius, which existed in the Ukraine in 1846–47 and among whose members were the historian N. P. Kostomarov (1817–85) and the famous Ukrainian poet T. G. Shevchenko (1814–61). They also aimed at a Slavic federation, thinking that Russia would not be one of the constituent states but would be broken up into a number of states formed out of its natural and historical regions: central, northern, northeastern, southeastern, Upper Volga, Lower Volga, two Ukrainian states, two southern states, two in Siberia, the Caucasus, etc. As a professor of St. Petersburg University in the 1860's, Kostomarov studied regionalist tendencies in the history of Russia and propagated them in his writings and lectures. His influence played an important role in the intellectual development of the two most outstanding regionalist thinkers, Dragomanov and Yadrintsev.

M. P. Dragomanov (1841–95) was a nobleman of Cossack descent from the heart of the Ukraine—the Poltava province. Educated at Kiev, Berlin, and Heidelberg universities, he taught Roman history in Kiev until 1876, when he was dismissed for alleged Ukrainian separatism. He emigrated and lived in Geneva until 1889, when he accepted the chair of history in Sofia, which he occupied until his death. While in Kiev, Dragomanov had already established his reputation as the foremost theorist of the Ukrainian regionalist movement, known at the time as Ukrainophilism. His influence was perhaps even stronger in Galicia (more precisely, its eastern part, inhabited by Ukrainians), which then belonged to Austria, where he converted the leaders of the Moscowphile trend, who had previously been under the influence of Russian Pan-Slavists, to Ukrainophilism. However, Dragomanov did not confine his interests to the Ukraine, taking an active interest in the political life of Russia as a whole and publishing the journals *Free Word* (in Russian) and *Commune* (in Ukrainian) in Geneva.

Like the Populists, Dragomanov was primarily concerned with the well-being of the mass of the people rather than with politics in the narrower sense. And well-being, he thought, was only possible when the people had reached a high cultural level. Culture for him was synonymous with the perfect organization of the life of the whole people in all its aspects—economic, social, and spiritual—and, rather like Mikhailovsky, he saw the full development of individuality as the highest cultural achievement. But while Mikhailovsky was mainly concerned with the individual human person and with the village commune, Dragomanov added the ethnic group as an entity the individuality of which deserved furthering. Considering himself a pupil of Herzen, Dragomanov argued on the one hand against autocracy and on the other against the tendencies prevalent in the Russian revolutionary movement of the 1870's–80's—Bakunin's anarchism and Tkachëv's centralism. He was the only political writer among his contemporaries to advocate firm constitutional guarantees as a necessary safeguard for civil and political rights. But a centralistic constitution would not be a suitable means of furthering all those types of individuality that should be furthered. In his draft of a constitution for Russia, Dragomanov, following the example of the Society of SS. Cyril and Methodius, envisaged a federal structure with natural and historical regions as the component units of the federation. The regions were to enjoy far-reaching autonomy in the manner of the Swiss cantons. Like them, too, the regions were not intended to be ethnically homogeneous, and the Ukraine, for example, was to be divided between several regions. The ethnic individuality of a nation was to be furthered by means of complete freedom of national culture and a national-cultural autonomy, and it seems likely that Dragomanov's teaching contributed to the elaboration of the concept of national-cultural autonomy which later was so prominent in the program of the Austrian Social Democrats and which, mainly via the "Austro-Marxists," was accepted by most democratic and socialist parties in Russia, including the Constitutional Democrats, the Socialist Revolutionaries, and the Menshevik wing of the Social Democratic Party. Dragomanov shared a belief in the socialist ideal with the Populists, but at the same time he was as emphatic as the Liberals were in arguing against intolerance and in advocating freedom from any kind of absolute dogma, whether originating from the despotic state power, the established church, or a revolutionary sect. Socialism, the community of goods, was to be achieved through a gradual evolution based on persuasion.

Dragomanov firmly believed that a clean cause demands clean hands. He condemned violence of any kind and opposed the resort to political terror, predicting (correctly) that it would only result in harsher measures of repression, with the government feeling that such measures were justified by the revolutionaries' own conduct.

The federal idea persuasively advocated by Dragomanov was fairly popular among the Populists, was included into the program of the Party of Socialist Revolutionaries, and after the February revolution of 1917 it was proclaimed by all the main non-Great Russian political movements in Russia, including the Ukrainian Central Council and the All-Russian Muslim Union, and the Provisional Government took the first practical steps toward its implementation. It was traditionally rejected by Social Democrats, who followed Marx in his preference for centralized states, but after 1917, Lenin accepted the term and some of the outward forms of federation, without, however, tolerating any genuine division of political sovereignty.

While some of the regionalists advocated a reconstruction of the whole of Russia on federal lines, others concentrated on the interests of particular areas and the need for autonomy to safeguard them. The most outspoken and most interesting of these movements was Siberian regionalism, the main theorist of which was Dragomanov's contemporary N. M. Yadrintsev (1842–94). The son of a merchant from Perm' in the Urals who had settled in Siberia, Yadrintsev lived as a child in several towns of western Siberia and early conceived a strong regional patriotism. While studying at St. Petersburg University, this was reinforced by the influence of Kostomarov, and Yadrintsev devoted his life to the study of Siberia and to championing its interests. The geography, archeology, and ethnography of Siberia, its economic, social, intellectual, and cultural life—all of these attracted the attention of this dedicated Siberian patriot. As a scholar, he acquired international fame by the discovery of the ruins of Karakorum, Genghis Khan's capital in Mongolia, and of the Orkhon inscriptions, the oldest specimen of a Turkic language. As a politician, he wrote *Siberia as a Colony* (1882), the main work of Siberian regionalism, and founded and edited, first in St. Petersburg and later in Irkutsk, the organ of the movement, the newspaper *Eastern Review*. Yadrintsev's demands were comparatively moderate. As a first stage on the path to autonomy, he advocated the extension to Siberia of conditions prevailing in European Russia, in particular of local government in rural areas in accordance with the reform of 1864 (the municipal reform of 1870 had been extended to Siberia) and of the new judiciary, the founding of a university, stopping the deportation of criminals to the territory and opening it up to free settlement, and measures to protect the native peoples from exploitation and degradation. As their final aim, the regionalists envisaged a kind of dominion status for Siberia.

The movement for Siberian autonomy influenced political thinking in the adjacent areas, and in the early twentieth century similar movements arose in the Russian Far East and in Turkestan. Regionalist tendencies manifested themselves particularly strongly after the fall of the monarchy in February, 1917, and when the Bolsheviks seized power later in the year, rejection of the Bolshevik regime often took regionalist forms, regional governments being proclaimed in the Ukraine, the Cossack areas, Transcaucasia, Siberia, and Turkestan; all these, however, were suppressed either by the Whites or by the Bolsheviks during the Civil War.

Anarchism

The advocacy by the regionalists—especially the trend that was represented by Dragomanov—of far-reaching autonomy for small communities and of a federal union of such autonomous communities, brought them near to the standpoint of the anarchists, and there were cases, especially in the 1870's and 1880's, where it would be difficult to decide whether to classify someone as a regionalist or as an anarchist.

The father of Russian anarchism was M. A. Bakunin (1814–76). A nobleman by birth, he had belonged to the Stankevich Circle in the late thirties and early forties, where he was one of the most ardent Hegelians. Living in Berlin and Paris after 1842, and taking an active part in the life of the radical circles there, he was at first the most radical of the Left-Hegelians and then, under the influence of the French socialists (especially Proudhon), he became himself a socialist with noticeable anarchist tendencies. During the 1848 revolution in Western Europe, he advocated an uprising of the Slavs in Austria, the destruction of the Austrian Empire, and the establishment of a Slavic federation as a first step to the revolutionary transformation of the whole of Europe on republican and socialist lines. A former artillery officer, he took the leadership in the defense of Dresden, the capital of Saxony, whose population had joined the revolution, against the Prussian counterrevolutionary forces. After the fall of the city, Bakunin was captured, sentenced to death, reprieved, extradited to Austria, and finally, in 1849, to Russia. He spent seven years in a fortress and was then banished to Siberia, but in 1861 he fled abroad. The last years of his life were again spent in Western Europe, where he became the leading figure in the revolutionary anarchist movement. He was involved in the propaganda of anarchism and revolution and in practical agitation and plotting in several countries of Europe, finding most of his supporters in the Latin countries. He headed the International Alliance of Socialist Democracy (1868) and was Marx's rival in the leadership of the International Workingmen's Association. With the victory of Marx and his state-socialist trend, Bakunin and his followers were expelled from the International, but they were the main inspirers and leaders of the Paris Commune in 1871. Deeply involved in Western Europe, Bakunin only occasionally took an active part in Russian developments. He joined the first Land and Freedom group in 1862, supported the Polish uprising in the following year, and assisted Nechaev in 1869–70, but his influence was most strongly felt during the second half of the 1870's, when active Populists, who until then had mainly adhered to Lavrov's views on the need for socialist propaganda among the people, became impatient and turned their ear to Bakunin's appeals for direct agitation among the peasants. The peasants, Bakunin thought, did not need theoretical propaganda—they were ready at all times to rise against the landlords and the state that was supporting the landlords, and all the revolutionaries needed to do was to arouse this passion. The second Land and Freedom organization, gradually formed in 1876–78, among whose leaders were Natanson and Plekhanov, was predominantly Bakuninist in its outlook. Their acceptance of Bakuninism was not confined to his revolutionary strategy and tactics, but included Bakunin's views on the organization of society after the successful revolution.

Bakunin developed his theory of anarchism in many articles, pamphlets, and letters during the 1860's and 1870's, but most systematically in the pamphlets *God and the State* and *Statehood and Anarchy*. His argument was primarily directed against the social-contract theory of the state, both in its liberal and in its radical, "Jacobin" interpretation. The theory of social contract, Bakunin thought, left society out of account. Both the liberals and the Jacobins were considering only individuals on the one hand and society organized in the state on the other. The liberals knew perfectly well that actual states everywhere had been founded by violence and conquest, but they needed the fiction of a free contract to justify the existence of the state. The liberal view of the individuals who constituted the state was highly inconsistent and self-contradictory. On the one hand, they are self-contained and self-sufficient beings who have no need for society and for whom society is an obstacle to perfect freedom. On the other hand, the same people appear as weak and imperfect, utterly dependent on the forces of nature and in need of protection. But in order to secure protection, they abandon their freedom. The usual liberal definition of the limits of personal freedom— the freedom of one individual being limited by the freedom of others—contains in an embryonic form all the theories of despotism, since the essence of the state, according to this formula, is the negation of freedom. To this formula of freedom, Bakunin opposes his own, which he calls materialist, realist, and collectivist. Man becomes man, reaches an awareness of his humanity and its realization, only in society and only through collective action of the whole society; he frees himself from the yoke of external nature only through collective work, which alone can transform the earth into a place suitable for human existence; and without his material liberation there can be no intellectual or moral liberation. Man cannot free himself from the yoke of his own nature, his instincts, except through education, which is necessarily a social process. Finally, an isolated man cannot be aware of his freedom. Freedom is the fruit of interaction, because the freedom of each individual is the reflection of his humanity in the consciousness of all his fellow men. The freedom of others is therefore not a limitation, a negation of my freedom, but, on the contrary, is a necessary condition of my freedom. The greater the freedom of everyone else, the greater is my freedom, and, conversely, the slavery of another limits my freedom.

Thus the first aspect of Bakunin's conception of freedom is, as he puts it, positive. The second aspect is negative. It is rebellion, a rebellion of the human personality against all authority, divine and human, collective and individual. The fiction of God serves to sanctify intellectual and moral slavery on earth, and human freedom will be complete only when the harmful fable of the Heavenly Lord is destroyed. Rebellion against the state is also necessary, because the state is only a particular historical form of the existence of society, and being essentially a negation of freedom it must be fought in order to attain full freedom. But if the state is an evil, this cannot be said of society. Society is neither good nor evil—it is necessary and inevitable. Particular forces, however, which are active in society—customs, habits, opinions—can be either good or evil. The pressure of society upon an individual is good if it is directed towards the development of science, material well-being, freedom, equality and brotherly solidarity among men; it is harmful and must be resisted if it has the opposite tendencies. But rebellion against society is far more difficult than rebellion against the Church and the state, because society is not something external, it exists through the individual and in the individual, who is subject to a continuous process of conditioning. In every section of society, however, there are usually people who nevertheless manage to break through their conditioning and to rebel against the harmful aspects of social existence. Turning to the society of his time, Bakunin found that in bourgeois society every individual is of necessity a potential exploiter of others, because, according to the prevailing view of man, he has need of every other individual from the material point of view but does not need anyone morally: Everyone avoids social solidarity as being an obstacle to the freedom of his soul, but seeks it as a means of satisfying the needs of his body. But although everyone is an exploiter as a matter of principle, in reality some are exploiters and some the exploited. Government exists to perpetuate this situation. Exploitation is the visible body of the bourgeois regime, while government is its soul. Both are necessary consequences of the bourgeois doctrine that seeks the freedom and morality of individuals outside social solidarity. The task of the revolution is to overthrow all three forms of oppression—theological, governmental, and social.

But what should happen after the revolution? As far as Russia is concerned, Bakunin drew up a positive program in 1868. The aim was to achieve the complete intellectual, socio-economic, and political liberation of the people. To achieve intellectual freedom, it would be necessary to spread atheism and materialism. To achieve social freedom it would be necessary (1) to abolish the right of inheritance; (2) to achieve full equality for women, i.e., to abolish family law and the institution of marriage; (3) to transfer the responsibility for the maintenance and education of children to society. To achieve economic justice, all land must belong to those who till it—i.e., to agricultural communes—while capital and tools in industry must belong to the workers—i.e., to workers' associations. The future political organization of society must not be anything but a free federation of free agricultural or industrial associations. Statehood must be rooted out "with all its ecclesiastical, political, bureaucratic (military and civilian), juridical, learned, as well as financial and economic institutions." There must be full freedom for all peoples oppressed by the Russian Empire, with the right of full self-determination according to their own instincts, needs, and will: those who wished to be members of the Russian people would, in the process of upward federation, create a free and happy society, which would in turn enter into federal relationships with similar societies in Europe and throughout the world.

The members and sympathizers of the second Land and Freedom organization who accepted Bakunin's thesis of the readiness of the peasants for a rebellion soon realized that this was too optimistic and that there was scarcely any positive response to their agitation. Some of them, as we have seen, disappointed in

Bakunin, turned to Tkachëv's "Jacobin" solution of the problem of a communist revolution and in 1879 formed the People's Will Party. The more faithful Bakuninists, headed by Plekhanov and Aksel'rod, formed the Black Repartition organization, but soon afterward most of its leaders emigrated and the organization itself disintegrated. Some local groups of its adherents reverted to Lavrov's earlier view that a long period of socialist propaganda was necessary before a revolution would be possible, and some of these semi-Bakuninist, semi-Lavrovist Populist groups developed toward Social Democracy during the 1880's. But there were also people who saw the essence of Bakunin's teaching not in its strategic and tactical precepts but in the anarchist ideal, and from among these there emerged another outstanding theorist of anarchism, Kropotkin.

Prince P. A. Kropotkin (1842–1921), descendant of a minor branch of the Rurikid clan, was educated in the Corps of Pages at the Imperial Court but volunteered to serve as an army officer in Siberia. While in Siberia, he engaged in research in physical geography and on his return to the capital became secretary of the Imperial Geographical Society. During a trip to Western Europe in 1872, he joined the International Workingmen's Association, adhering to its Bakuninist wing. In the following two years he was an active member of the Chaikovsky Circle in St. Petersburg, was arrested, simulated insanity, and managed to flee to Western Europe. Sentenced by a French court to five years' imprisonment in 1883, he was released three years later, settled in London, and soon became the recognized theorist of the anarchist movement in Europe. Continuing Bakunin's tradition, Kropotkin called his theory communist anarchism. He elaborated it in many books and pamphlets, including *The State, Its Part in History; Fields, Factories and Workshops;* and *Ethics: Origin and Development.*

Kropotkin's doctrine was based on the idea of mutual aid, which he conceived as a phenomenon characteristic of all living creatures: In his *Mutual Aid, a Factor of Evolution,* he argued against the one-sided Darwinian stress on struggle for survival and demonstrated the role of mutual aid in the lives of animals. Tracing its role in human history, Kropotkin found that mutual-aid associations of various kinds (peasant communes, guilds, city corporations) had flourished in Europe from the ninth to the fifteenth century, and that only with the beginning of the sixteenth century had they been destroyed by the state. The state was thus a comparatively new institution in Europe, but it had entrenched itself strongly thanks to its alliance with the Church and with the institution of private property. Yet the injustice of both—private ownership of the means of production and the state—was obvious to the oppressed and exploited majority, and a revolution was inevitable. Kropotkin opposed the resort to violence and thought that it would not in fact be necessary, since even the oppressors themselves had come to realize the injustice of their position and knew in their hearts that a revolution was coming. Unlike most Russian socialists, Kropotkin drew in considerable detail a picture of the society which was to emerge from the revolution, a society which he called anarchic communism and opposed both to a system of Fourier's *phalansteries* and to Marx's state communism. It is a society from which nobody is excluded, and it therefore includes an infinite variety of personal abilities, temperaments, and forces. Society desires a contest between these varied forces, because the greatest achievements of the human intellect have always been made in times of unfettered debate and contest. The anarchic communist society recognizes in practice the right of every one of its members to all the riches accumulated in the past. It knows no division into exploiters and exploited, rulers and ruled, superiors and subordinates, and seeks to establish harmonic relationships between its members—not by subordinating them all to some authority deemed to be representative of the society as a whole, nor by attempts to establish uniformity, but by calling on the people to develop freely, to exercise free initiative, to act freely, and to unite freely. Such a society inevitably aims at the fullest possible development of individual personality, as well as at the maximum development of voluntary associations of every kind. These associations change constantly, are of no definite duration, and at any given moment assume such forms as are best suited to the manifold desires of all. The anarchic communist society rejects any kind of immutable form in the shape of a law: It seeks harmony in the constantly changing equilibrium of manifold forces and influences, each going its own way. The totality of such freely developing forces is the best guarantee of progress. Greatly influenced by the Positivism and scientism of his time, Kropotkin thought that such a view of society was in accordance with the atomistic and energetic picture of the world arrived at by modern science, and that anarchism was, therefore, a branch of modern science. The aim of the ideal society was universal well-being, and the practical measures necessary for its establishment and functioning were expropriation of all privately owned means of production and distribution of excessive consumer goods—in short, of everything that now makes it possible for the owners to appropriate the fruits of other people's labor; the abolition of the division of labor, the training of everyone in some kind of productive trade, and the assurance that all have free access to the facilities that are required for productive effort.

Communist anarchism as propagated by Kropotkin was the most influential trend among anarchists in Russia in the late nineteenth and early twentieth centuries, but there were also groups under the influence of contemporary West European ideas who were professing individualist anarchism and anarcho-syndicalism. After the fall of the monarchy in 1917, all the main anarchist organizations combined for the first time to form the Federation of Anarchist Groups. Anarchists were very active during the revolutionary year of 1917, joining several Soviets and exercising a strong influence in one of the most important of them—in Kronstadt, the naval base on the sea approaches to St. Petersburg. The Bolshevik slogan "All power to the Soviets" appeared to the anarchists as a promise to abolish the central state power, and they usually cooperated with the Bolsheviks in undermining the authority of the Provisional Government. They formally allied themselves with the Bolsheviks at the time of the October coup, when four anarchists were included into the Petrograd Military Revolutionary Committee, which directed the seizure of power. The squad of sailors that, on Lenin's orders, dispersed the Constituent Assembly in January, 1918, was commanded by an anarchist. Some anarchists went further and worked in the organs of the new regime, including the Extraordinary Commission for Combating Counterrevolution. Anarcho-syndicalists, in particular, tried—like the radical Populists—to cooperate with the Bolsheviks as closely as possible, at the same time offering ideological opposition. Kropotkin, who returned to Russia in 1917, differed from the majority of his fellows. Having inherited Bakunin's antipathy to the Germans, he saw the German Empire as the bulwark of statehood in Europe and took an anti-German line during the war; in 1917, he advocated the defense of revolutionary Russia, in contrast to Lenin's advocacy of defeat for one's own government. Kropotkin continued to regard Bolsheviks as Jacobins and did not directly support the Bolshevik regime in Russia, although he did appeal to foreign workers to stop their governments' anti-Red intervention in the Russian Civil War. Many of the early measures of the new rulers—the slogan of "local power," the confiscations of the land, of food, houses, and clothes, "workers' control" in industry—seemed to the anarchists to have been taken directly from Kropotkin's program. But the anarchists' attitude toward the Bolshevik dictatorship was of necessity ambivalent, and as early as 1918, some of them turned against it; the leader of the anarchist peasant bands in southern Ukraine, N. I. Makhno, while allying himself with Bolsheviks against the Whites, fought back when the Bolsheviks attacked him. Anarchist organizations in the main political centers had already been subject to persecution in 1918, and they were suppressed after the Kronstadt uprising against the Bolshevik regime in 1921, but some leading anarchist theorists were allowed to carry on their theoretical work until the early 1930's. One of them claimed in a book on the history of the anarchist movement in Russia, published in 1926 with an enthusiastic dedication to Bakunin, that the October revolution had given new impetus to the movement and that a number of interesting new trends and ideas had appeared.

Syndicalism

Anarcho-syndicalists were not the only syndicalist trend that existed in Russia in the late nineteenth and early twentieth centuries. Syndicalist tendencies were widespread in the labor movement, and already in the late 1870's, E. O. Zaslavsky, the leader of the Workers' Union of Southern Russia (which existed as a secret organization in Odessa), proposed to expel all nonworkers from the Union, despite the fact that he was an intellectual himself. Mistrust for the intelligentsia remained a typical feature of syndicalist thought. It manifested itself again in the Fellowship of St. Petersburg Workingmen in the 1880's and in the Group of Self-Emancipation of the Working Class in the late 1890's. The syndicalist-minded Workers' Organization in St. Petersburg was the most determined opponent of Lenin within the Russian Social Democratic Labor Party in 1900–1903.

A systematic anti-intellectual syndicalist theory was worked out in 1898–1900 by J. W. Machajski (1867–1927), a former Polish Social Democrat who was at that time living in banishment in Siberia; his book *The Brain Worker,* in which the theory is elaborated, appeared in Geneva in 1905.

Machajski's theory was an attempt, starting from the basic conceptions of orthodox Marxism, to find an answer to the question of the place occupied in the social organism by the intelligentsia. In Machajski's view, knowledge is a kind of means of production, and its possession by the intelligentsia means that the latter is a separate social class. In the process of production and distribution, the intelligentsia appropriates a part of the surplus value; hence it is an exploiting class. This is the main thesis of the Machajski-ist theory. The interests of the intelligentsia are therefore opposed to the interests of the proletariat, and the "socialist" phraseology used by the intelligentsia is merely a device in the struggle for its own interests. It wants to use the proletariat for the socialization of the means of material production, which would then be managed by the intelligentsia without interference from the capitalists. But the intelligentsia does not want to "socialize knowledge"—the means of intellectual production; rather, they want to preserve it in their own monopolistic possession. Thus socialism is the "class ideal" of the intelligentsia, which wants to replace capitalists and to concentrate in its hands all means of domination over the proletariat. The proletariat, on the other hand, must strive to "socialize knowledge" by removing the inequality of opportunity for acquiring it, and the practical way to this is the abolition of inheritance of any property. The proletariat must also make it impossible for the intelligentsia to appropriate surplus value—by a leveling of incomes. Everybody must receive the same remuneration for his work.

Machajski-ist views on the organization and tactics that the proletariat should adopt in order to achieve a revolution are basically syndicalist, with the general strike as the chief weapon. It is interesting to note that, until such a revolution, he expected the "hungry masses" to be tempted to use every opportunity to destroy as much as possible of "those cursed goods which they endlessly create and which are always taken away by the masters," and approved of such destruction. And the seizure of power by the proletariat would be used for seizing the property of the educated society, of the "learned world."

Syndicalist tendencies were very much in evidence during the 1905 revolution, and syndicalist-minded people were prominent in forming trade unions and Soviets of Workers' Deputies and in organizing the general strike in October that forced Emperor Nicholas II to grant a constitution. A specifically Machajski-ist organization was the Union of Unemployed in St. Petersburg. The flooding in 1917 and after of the ranks of the Bolshevik Party with large numbers of unskilled workers, soldiers, agricultural laborers, and urban *déclassés* greatly strengthened Machajski-ism. Its ideas exercised influence on the thinking and behavior of a large section of the Bolshevik Party after 1917, though it is not easy to disentangle the purely Machajski-ist tendencies from the anarchist. Machajski-ism was at the root of all the "intellectual-baiting" tendencies. Moreover, it greatly influenced early Bolshevik legislation and party policy, whatever the explanations given at the time for various measures may have been. The first law on inheritance abolished inheritance altogether and merely provided (as a temporary measure until the full development of social-security schemes) for a limited use of an estate for the maintenance of the unemployed relatives of the deceased. The attempts to introduce a maximum salary for party members not exceeding the earnings of a skilled worker were also, at least partly, due to the influence of Machajski-ism, as was the policy of the resettlement of workers into the houses and flats of the bourgeoisie and intellectuals, and vice versa. The Machajski-ist cultural vandalism and nihilism were also characteristic of the outlook of many party members.

The Machajski-ist trend was fashionable in the party, despite halfhearted reproofs from the party authorities, until 1936, when Stalin declared that the intellectual-baiting by the Machajski-ists must no longer be applied to the new Soviet intelligentsia.

9. Religious Thinkers of the Late Nineteenth and Early Twentieth Centuries

In the last quarter of the nineteenth century there appeared, partly under the influence of the Slavophiles and of Dostoevsky, a number of thinkers who did not fit into any of the main ideological and political schools of the time. Common to them all was the clearly realized and strongly emphasized religious basis of their thought. But beyond this they bore little relation to each other and went different ways. In terms of nineteenth-century political divisions they can be classified as representing, from Right to Left, Conservatism (Leont'ev, Rozanov), Liberalism (Solov'ëv), Socialism (Fëdorov), and Anarchism (Tolstoy).

Non-Westernist Conservatives

K. N. Leont'ev (1831–91), another of those impecunious noblemen whom we have met with so frequently among the Russian intellectuals of the second half of the nineteenth century, studied medicine at Moscow University, volunteered as a surgeon in the Crimean War, and after a short period of medical practice entered government service and spent ten years as Russian Consul in different parts of the Ottoman Empire. He resigned from the service because he disagreed with the government's foreign policy, became a professional journalist and essayist, but in the 1880's was again in government employ for a time as a censor in Moscow. The last years of his life Leont'ev spent in retirement near the Optina Pustyn' monastery, famous at the time for its intensive spiritual and intellectual life, and shortly before his death he secretly became a monk.

Leont'ev was an independent and rather lonely figure among the politicians and men of letters in Russia, though he acknowledged his indebtedness to the Slavophiles and to Danilevsky and usually contributed to right-wing periodicals. At the basis of his political philosophy lay his attachment to Orthodox Christianity, his intensely aesthetic approach to the world, and his belief that nature and human history were governed by essentially identical laws. At first, attachment to Orthodoxy and aestheticism combined in Leont'ev's mind into a kind of aesthetic Orthodoxy—a familiar phenomenon in the history of Russian spirituality since its very inception. But later, when Leont'ev's religiosity acquired an ascetic character, he condemned aestheticism as "the poetry of graceful immorality," though he never succeeded in abandoning the aesthetic approach altogether. The general law that, according to Leont'ev, governed the development of inanimate nature, of organisms, and of human societies (whether tribes, states, or whole civilizations), was the "cosmic law of disintegration." Universal stages of development were those of initial simplicity, "flourishing complexity," and secondary simplification or "equalizing mixture." Leont'ev saw Western Europe as having reached the third stage. Simplification and equalization expressed themselves in what Leont'ev called the "anthropolatry" typical of modern Europe—concern for man simply because he is man, irrespective of his qualities. Liberalism, democracy, socialism, cosmopolitanism, and nationalism were all manifestations of this anthropolatry. The aim of European progress was the average man, the bourgeois, living a calm and satisfied life among millions of others like himself. This prospect repelled Leont'ev as un-Christian and ugly. It was un-Christian because it presumed salvation on earth, which was in fact unattainable. It was childish to indulge in shortsighted optimism or in what Leont'ev called the "rosy Christianity" of Dostoevsky or Solov'ëv. Life on earth was incorrigible, and the only sense in which Leont'ev would accept the notion of progress was that of progressive disillusionment and acceptance of earthly reality. Not all reality was grim, however, and above all, it was not always gray and uniform. Europe had

had its long history of cultural greatness; so had Byzantium and, in its footsteps, Russia. Great cultures were characterized by recognition of the principle of harmony, i.e., unity in diversity, not of unison. They were evaluative and hierarchical, with an "inner despotism of form" that prevented the whole structure from disintegrating. Having lost this inner force, Europe was rapidly tumbling down, dragging imitative Russia with it. Even if Russia stopped imitating, it might not be able to survive much longer, because Russia was little younger than the Western Europe whose social history could properly be regarded as having begun at the time of Charlemagne: a thousand years was about as long as a state could reasonably hope to survive. Yet there was, perhaps, a way out for Russia. Since she had not yet completely dissipated her main constructive qualities—vigor, thirst for learning, fear of sin, love for coercive power—Russia might obtain a new lease of life if she turned away from Europe and devoted her energies to establishing a new Orthodox Russo-Byzantine empire. This notion of Leont'ev's was not identical with the Pan-Slavists', but was a new version of the old idea of the Third Rome. Unlike Philotheus, however, who had stressed the decay of Byzantium and had wanted to base the Third Rome upon Moscow, Leont'ev stressed the danger of decay facing Russia and wanted Russia to return, so to speak, to Byzantium.

Leont'ev's view on the political problems of his day followed from his general conceptions. He was bitterly disappointed when Russia, at the Berlin Congress, threw away the fruits of its 1877–78 war against Turkey. In internal politics he was thoroughly reactionary: He welcomed Alexander III's manifesto after his accession in which the principle of autocracy was reaffirmed; he thought that it was wrong to spread education among the popular masses before the educated classes themselves had shed their European veneer and become much more Russian in outlook; the social position of the nobility he believed should be strengthened rather than undermined, both for general reasons—in order to preserve hierarchical elements and to resist egalitarianism—and because there was a higher proportion of men of taste, intelligence, and generosity among the nobility than in any other class.

The other outstanding religious thinker who may be classified as a conservative was V. V. Rozanov (1856–1919). Born into a poor family, he had an unhappy childhood. After studying at Moscow University, he taught history in a provincial school until 1893. He started writing early, but his first large philosophical work, *On Understanding,* passed unnoticed. However, soon after he had moved to St. Petersburg and become a regular contributor to the right-wing paper *The New Time,* Rozanov was recognized as one of the foremost journalists. He was a highly controversial figure and was expelled from .the St. Petersburg Religious and Philosophical Society for encouraging anti-Semitism (he had published a book on the strange subject of Jewish attitudes toward blood). Rozanov was an original thinker, though he stressed the merits of his elder contemporaries and friends N. N. Strakhov (one of the leaders of the "soil-bound" school) and Leont'ev. He died, like Tikhomirov, under the walls of the Trinity Monastery of St. Sergius near Moscow, where he had moved after the 1917 revolution.

Rozanov published a number of books, chiefly collections of articles or aphorisms, most of which touch on problems of political philosophy: *The Legend of the Grand Inquisitor* (on Dostoevsky); *In the World of the Unclear and Undecided; Religion and Culture; Nature and History; The Family Question in Russia; Near the Church Walls; Metaphysics of Christianity.* More directly political are *The Twilight of Enlightenment; The Weakened Fetish; About the Supposed Sense of Our Monarchy;* and, his last book, *The Apocalypse of Our Time,* written in 1917. Rozanov remained a religious thinker throughout his life, but his religiosity gradually acquired a peculiar "biological" turn. At first he was devoted to Orthodoxy and sharply opposed it to Western Christianity. Everything was brighter and more joyful in Orthodoxy; its spirit was that of the Gospel, while the West's was that of the Old Testament. True Christianity was for Rozanov a complete joy, with no gloom of any kind. Not surprisingly, all historic Christianity soon began to appear to him as unreal, as merely a doctrine, a rhetoric, the product of a great "misunderstanding." Historic Christianity had been dominated by Golgotha, it had tried to imitate the suffering Christ; the great ideal of the Church was to imitate death, and, as a result, Chris-

tianity had become a religion of death—the act of redemption
was wasted on humanity. For a time Rozanov thought that it
might be a task for the Russian genius to realize the true Christianity of Bethlehem, so full of joy and the sweetness of life that
compared to the ascetic, Golgothian phase of Christianity it would
appear as if it was a new religion. Yet Rozanov soon abandoned
this halfway position. The whole of the Gospel now appeared to
him to point toward the abandonment of life, toward the monastery, and it was not surprising that the Church had "no sense of
children." The world had gone bitter in Christ, who had made
human life unbearably difficult—His coming was an evil. Rozanov turned to the Old Testament, the religion of the Father
and of life in its real, fleshy sense. Life was the greatest divine
mystery, and in creating life man was closest to God, closer than
in his intellect or in his conscience. Children and family were
therefore the greatest treasures, and the disintegration of the
family was at the root of the decline of European civilization.

Rozanov's political views reflected his preoccupation with the
phenomenon of life. He strongly criticized the educational system
that substituted lifeless cramming for the stimulation of initiative
and independent judgement: The fault was the government's,
which tried to regulate in minutest details a sphere in which it
should limit its role to supervision. The machinery of the state
which drained life from the country's young generation had
done the same to the Russian autocracy, to the extent that the
person of the monarch had been completely obliterated: Identified with the bureaucracy, he would in the end be hated by the
oppressed population. Although in general Rozanov favored
monarchy, as a more personal form of government, he would have
preferred even a republic to the post-1905 Russian monarchy, for
a republic, he thought, would be more youthful and creative.
But Rozanov was pessimistic about the ability of any government
in Russia, consisting as she did of many diverse ethnic groups, to
maintain the unity of the state by other than despotic means.
Toward the end of his life, he came to reject politics altogether:
"God will wish to annihilate politics altogether after it has cov-
ered the earth with blood, deception, and cruelty," he wrote in
1912. And in his *Apocalypse* he wrote of the 1917 revolution:

"We are dying like clowns because we cannot respect ourselves any longer, we are committing suicide. . . . We Russians were made for ideas and feelings, for prayer and music, but not to rule over people. Unluckily we have been ruling over one sixth of the earth's surface and we have ruined it. . . . Enough talking about our stinking Revolution and our mouldy Empire, rotten to the core—they are worthy of each other . . ."

This is hardly the language of a Conservative, though Tikhomirov's feelings toward the end of his life were not very different. The leaders of Conservative thought, both Westernist and non-Westernist, had, by 1917, lost faith in the Russian monarchy.

Solov'ëv

V. S. Solov'ëv (1853–1900) was widely regarded even in his own lifetime as the most outstanding Russian philosopher, combining great power of thought with the rigorous discipline of academic philosophy. He was the son of S. M. Solov'ëv, the famous Russian historian, while on his mother's side he was descended from the remarkable eighteenth-century Ukrainian itinerant philosopher G. S. Skovoroda. He studied natural sciences and philosophy at Moscow University, at the same time attending lectures at the Moscow Theological Academy, and at the age of twenty-two began to teach philosophy at the university. However, he resigned two years later because he disapproved of the ostracism to which liberal-minded professors had subjected one of their colleagues—a reactionary in politics—who had submitted proposals for limiting the autonomy of the universities; Solov'ëv did not share his views, but was repelled by the intolerance of the liberals. This episode is revealing: Tolerance and a sense of justice were among the most pronounced features of Solov'ëv's character and mental make-up. In 1881, he again resigned his official position (this time as a member of the Learned Council at the Ministry of Education) because, having declared in a public speech after the assassination of Alexander II that the new emperor should pardon the regicides, he felt that he should no longer remain a government official. From 1882 until his death, Solov'ëv lived as a free-lance journalist, though during the 1890's he had a small regular income as the editor of the philosophical section of the Brockhaus-Efron *Encyclopaedic Dictionary,* the Russian equivalent of *Encyclopaedia Britannica.* Theologian, philosopher, political writer, and poet—Solov'ëv excelled in all these fields and exercised a strong influence on most subsequent Russian thought, while his saintly and selfless personality was an embodiment of the lofty ideals he preached.

Solov'ëv twice gave a brief systematic exposition of his political philosophy—in the second part of *The Spiritual Foundations of Life* (1884) and in the third part of *The Justification of the Good* (1897). Three speeches in memory of Dostoevsky (1881–83) and *Three Conversations* (1899–1900) complete his treatment of the subject. His more directly political writings, most of which appeared during the decade 1883–93 in the liberal monthly *Messenger of Europe,* dealt chiefly with the problems of national minorities in Russia and were directed against the Pan-Slavists.

The state, according to Solov'ëv, is the pillar of humanity against the external elemental forces that act upon it and in it. Such a pillar necessitates the unification of human forces, and unification presupposes subordination. The state, therefore, while in general it gives expression to human independence, at the same time demands strict subordination of particular forces. It has always been so and always will be so; differences exist only in the nature and form of this subordination.

Pre-Christian history demonstrated two types of states: the Eastern, based on slavery, and the Western (Greco-Roman), conditioned—apart from slavery—by constant struggle among the masters themselves. In the East, the state meant only domination, either patriarchal or based on conquest. In both cases the power of the sovereign and the subordination of the subjects were absolute and limitless—just as children could not seek to establish their rights against their fathers in court, captives could not so seek against the victor. The clan principle and the conquests were operative in the West also, but the main formative factor there was the constant struggle between political forces. In the East, political struggle could only be an accidental phenomenon, because of the mental make-up and the world view of the peoples living there. Oriental man, a quietist and fatalist by nature and conviction, interested chiefly in the eternal and unchangeable aspect of existence, is incapable of standing on his rights and stubbornly fighting for his private interests. He who is strong has the right, and it is madness to oppose the strong. Oriental potentates may rival each other and struggle against each other, but this struggle is of short duration and does not change the general situation. The issue is decided at the first sign that one side has superior strength, and the subjects hasten to subordinate themselves to the stronger side, seeing in it an instrument of fate or of the higher will. Hence the frequent change of despotic regimes, with the despotism itself remaining unaltered.

But the "daring clan of Japhet," who challenged the gods, based their political system also on struggle, and hence there is a completely different type of state in the West. With a contest of more or less equal political forces, none of which can gain absolute predominance, the state cannot be domination but must appear as an equilibrium of many forces. This equilibrium finds its expression in the law. Each of the contending forces advances its right, but these rights—indefinite and unlimited by themselves, and therefore mutually exclusive—can be challenged and balanced only if there is a limit common to them all. This common limit of all rights, before which all are equal, is the law. Western states, being an equilibrium of contending rights, are legal states *par excellence.*

The pre-Christian state of the West found its full expression in Rome. Roman statehood developed in a centuries-long unceasing struggle for rights between patricians and plebeians, and it always took the form of precise and strict legislation. But this legal state found its completion at a moment when the contending parties had arrived at a final equilibrium through full equalization of rights. At that moment the empire was created. If the state is an equilibrium of real, live forces, it cannot be represented by the abstract, dead formula of the law alone. The law must be embodied, and the embodiment of the law is authority. Authority, as a live and active force, holding the balance between everybody, must be concentrated in a single live person. Authority, or *imperium,* has its real practical meaning only in the emperor.

Thus the Western state came, at the end of its development, to the same form to which the East had adhered from the beginning. But there was a great difference between the Western empire and the oriental despoties, a difference that was fateful for the West. Their despotic state appeared to Oriental peoples as an unavoidable evil, as one of the burdensome but inevitable conditions of earthly existence. But for Western paganism with its purely human religion, the state, as the embodiment of human reason and human justice, was everything, was the highest norm and the highest aim of life. And now the aim was fully achieved with the creation of a complete, all-embracing, invincible state, the state *par excellence*—the universal Roman Empire. As soon as it was created, however, the complete emptiness of this formal greatness, the helpless barrenness of this embodied reason, became apparent.

When the embodiment of human reason—the empire—proved completely bankrupt, the time came for the embodiment of divine reason. Christianity came into the world in order to save it, and it saved the highest manifestation of the world—the state—by revealing its true aim and the purpose of its existence. The difference between the Christian and the pagan state is that the latter intended to have its aim in itself and therefore turned out to be aimless and senseless; whereas the Christian state recognizes above itself the higher aim which is set by religion and represented by the Church—the Kingdom of God—and the Christian state finds its higher meaning and purpose in free service to this aim. The Christian state combines the features of the Eastern and the Western state. In accordance with the Eastern view, Christianity removes state life to a secondary place, putting above it the spiritual or religious life; but on the other hand, together with the West, Christianity recognizes that the state has a positive task and an active, progressive character: not only does it call upon the state to wage war under the banner of the Church against the evil forces of the world, but it also demands that the state should implement moral principles in political and international life, that it should gradually raise worldly society to the level of the Church ideal, should re-create it after the image and likeness of the Church of Christ.

Everything that had been in the pagan state, both Eastern and

Western, is found in the Christian state, but it all receives a new meaning. There is domination in the Christian state, yet it is domination not for the sake of its own power but for the common good and in accordance with the directions of the authority of the Church. There is subordination in the Christian state, not out of servile fear but voluntarily, out of conscience, for the sake of that common cause which is served equally by the ruler and by the subjects. Rights existing in the Christian state do not flow from the limitless human egoism but from the moral endlessness of man as a godlike being. There is law in the Christian state, not in the sense of simple legalization of actual relationships but in the sense of their correction according to the ideas of higher justice. There is a supreme power in the Christian state, not as the deification of human arbitrariness but as a special kind of service to God's will: the holder of power in the Christian state is not merely the possessor of all rights, as is a pagan caesar; he is principally the bearer of all the obligations of Christian society toward the Church, i.e., toward God's cause on earth.

State power, in its functions and in its origin, is completely independent from spiritual power. Their relationship can therefore only be free—according to faith and conscience. The main question is whether the secular government believes in the Church or not. The government of a Christian state must believe in the Church. On the strength of this purely moral, not juridical, obligation, it must voluntarily subordinate its activities to the higher authority of the Church, not in the sense that this authority should interfere in the worldly affairs of the state, but in the sense that the state itself should subordinate its activities to the higher religious interests, should not lose sight of the Kingdom of God.

There was a time in the Christian West when the Church sought to embody itself in state forms, whereas in the Christian East, state power concentrated in its hands not only the temporal but very often also the supreme ecclesiastical administration. In the ideal free theocracy, both tendencies merge in a new moral sense: Here the Church embodies itself in the state only to the extent that the state itself is spiritualized by Christian principles; the Church descends the same steps toward worldly reality as the state ascends toward the Church ideal.

The state is idealized and spiritualized through free service to the higher religious interests, which can be reduced to the following: (1) spreading Christianity in the world, (2) peacefully bringing peoples together within Christianity itself, and (3) ordering the social relations within each people according to the Christian ideal. Spreading Christian culture to barbarous and savage peoples, introducing the principle of Christian solidarity in international relations instead of the national rivalry and enmity, taming the proud, disarming the rapacious, helping the oppressed—in all this the Christian state serves the Church.

In giving a meaning to the state, Christianity at the same time creates society. As long as the state was everything, society was nothing. By raising religion above the state and by creating the Church, Christianity frees society from the omnipotent state, creates a free and independent society. On the one hand, it creates the people in the narrow sense of the word—that is, the lower, and at the same time the basic, class of society. Without a formal abolition of slavery, simply through recognizing slaves as members of the Church with full religious rights, Christianity introduces them into society and gives to society itself its proper base —former slaves become peasants. On the other hand, the free citizens (free in relation to their slaves, but themselves slaves of the state), in becoming members of the Church, cease to be exclusively members of the state and, developing their individuality— which had been suppressed by the state—form the higher social class.

True human society consists only of free persons. There was no genuine society in antiquity because there was no real personality. It is true that the ancient West, in its philosophy, art, and politics, tended toward the idea of man, but it could only reach the *form* of humanity. Fullness of the human being demands absolute freedom, but man cannot have absolute freedom outside God. With the coming of God-man, humanity receives a fulcrum above the world, in the truly absolute sphere, and thus frees itself from the world. There appears free man and the possibility of a free divine-human society. This possibility, given in Christianity, must be realized by humanity itself. Personality that has been innerly freed by the grace of Christ must apply this freedom to the cause of building Christian society.

Human society is not a simple mechanical agglomeration of individuals. It is an independent whole with its own life and organization, and the task of Christianity in this respect consists in bringing into the life and organization of social forces the Christian principle of moral solidarity and true brotherhood. The structure of human society is essentially very simple and very sensible. It must first of all safeguard its own material existence, must live a natural life. But since the natural life of humanity is not perfect and does not contain its aim in itself, society must, secondly, have the means to change its life, to move and to develop its forces. The conditions for such development and progress are created by civilization, which makes up the artificial life of society. But changes and movements of civilized life must not be aimless and senseless. Social progress must lead society toward a definite aim, and this aim must be absolutely worthy, ideally perfect. Society must perfect itself: It must therefore also live a third, spiritual life, its best forces must create those higher goods for the sake of which it is worth living.

To these three aspects of life correspond the three classes of which society consists: people in the narrow sense, chiefly a rural or agricultural class; the urban class; and finally, the class of the best people, public figures and leaders. These three main elements of society were fettered in antiquity by the absolutism of the state; Christianity has freed them, and the task of Christian politics is to place them into the right positive relationships with the Church, the state, and each other. This depends directly on the class of the best people, the ruling class, which leads society and has all the initiative. For the people itself has always had the right attitude to the Church, the state, and the other classes: It has always fulfilled its function, cultivated land for the common benefit, fully maintaining its solidarity with the higher religious and civil interests, while the urban class, essentially intermediary and secondary, has always been guided by the example of the upper class, and it is not its fault if it has not always been given a good example. Generally speaking, the best people in Christian society have hitherto fallen far short of their destiny, have often on the one hand oppressed the people and on the other engaged in a criminal rivalry with the state and Church authorities. Instead of being leaders of the people, free servants of state and Church, they too frequently wanted to be masters in everything and over everything.

In the task of creating a free theocracy, the most important and honorable, but also the most responsible, role falls to the "best people." Freely deferring to the authority of the Church, receiving from the Church the immutable principles of justice and righteousness, they must, in accordance with these principles and being guarded and protected by the state, guide all social forces toward their supreme aim. The aim itself is not arbitrary or accidental, not set by people. It is the realization of what Christians believe in—the transfiguration of all human and worldly reality after the image and likeness of the Christian truth, the realization of God-manhood.

This exposition, taken from *The Spiritual Foundations of Life,* is typical of Solov'ëv's views in the 1880's, when he was most interested in political matters. Solov'ëv did not always assign to the state the role of guard and protector of positive social forces. Earlier (in the *Critique of Abstract Principles*), he had maintained that the common good was a phantom, that the state could only delimit mutually contradictory interests and not assist in their realization. In *The Justification of the Good,* on the other hand, he went further than in *The Spiritual Foundations* in asserting a positive role for the state. The state now appeared as "organized pity": "Full realization of the good presupposes the organization of just pity in the state, in which justice and mercy rule instead of arbitrariness and violence." A similar evolution can be detected in Solov'ëv's views of society. In the first lecture on God-manhood (1877), he described the West European society of his time in almost Marxist terms, while in *The Justification of the Good* he takes up a personalist position, saying that "society is only a completed and extended personality" and "personality is compressed and concentrated society." The ideal of "free theocracy" embracing the whole Christian world permeates most of Solov'ëv's writings. It was not meant to be something new, but simply a restatement and a philosophical justification of the Christian position, and in fact it is essentially identical with the ideal of St. Augustine and St. Vladimir. Solov'ëv believed in the realization of his ideal in the near future, and for a time thought that it could be achieved through a unification of Christian Churches and an alliance between the Pope and the Russian Emperor. At the end of his life, in *Three Conversations,* he conjured up a vision of the imminent conquest by the Mongol race of a Western world that had lost its spiritual foundations, followed by the coming of Antichrist in the shape of a benevolent and efficient World President. But he also had less eschatological perspectives. In the first lecture on God-manhood, he maintained (under the influence of Lassalle) that socialism was historically justified and about to be established in Western Europe, though he denied it any moral value or significance. In his numerous articles on the treatment of Russia's ethnic minorities, Solov'ëv advocated a humane and practical approach to the problem, based on the idea of complete freedom of cultural self-determination and development.

Solov'ëv owed much in his understanding of Christian dogma, of the human spirit and of the problems facing contemporary civilization, to the early Slavophiles and to Dostoevsky. But, having freed himself from the notion of a peculiar Russian mission in the world, and having further developed the liberal tendencies of the classical Slavophiles, he had established a foundation for a liberal Christian approach to politics and strongly influenced a number of prominent Russian political thinkers of the first half of the twentieth century, ranging from the liberal conservative P. B. Struve (in his later years) to the moderate socialist N. A. Berdyaev.

Fëdorov

A peculiar theory of a kind of religious socialism (though its propounder himself never called it socialist) was advanced by N. F. Fëdorov (1828–1903), illegitimate son of an aristocrat and a serf girl, who, having started his career as a school teacher, was later for many years librarian at the Rumyantsev Museum in Moscow (the Russian equivalent of the British Museum or the

Library of Congress). A kind and selfless person, like Solov'ëv, Fëdorov usually published his articles anonymously or under varying pseudonyms, so that the reading public, assimilating his ideas, was for the most part unaware of the author's identity. He was, however, on friendly terms with most of the other religious thinkers of the time, including Dostoevsky, Solov'ëv, and Tolstoy. Only after his death were two volumes of his articles, notes, and letters published under his own name (*Philosophy of the Common Cause,* 1906 and 1913).

The mainspring of Fëdorov's thinking, which permeated all his writings, was an irreconcilable attitude toward death, and he developed a consistent all-embracing theory of the conquest of death, beginning with a liturgic theology, through a "projectivist" system of philosophy, to practical suggestions for a course of action. Fëdorov held that the hostile attitude of men and nations toward one another is a result of the pressure upon man of the menacing, death-bearing forces of nature; that every man is chiefly concerned with his own preservation, and that as a result, men's energies are divided and therefore insufficient to solve the great problem of ruling nature. The social order arising out of this egoism is founded upon the separation of the conscious and directing functions from the executive ones, and thus arise the distinctions of class and social standing. Fëdorov bitterly criticized the capitalist society of his day, based on greed and permeated by mutual distrust. Its state forms, whether constitutional monarchy or republic, reflected the same spirit of commercial contract. The multiplication of laws and institutions merely legalized and formalized the division and strife. For Fëdorov, the ideal social order should rest upon a unity of consciousness and action; there should be no class distinctions, no coercion by military or police. In such an ideal regime every man would do his duty fully aware of the tasks with which he is faced. Fëdorov believed that the special task of scientific activity under such a regime would be to study the deadly forces of nature with the aim of turning them to the benefit of man. Once man has learned to rule nature and so to do away with hunger and all other wants, the causes of discord between men will automatically disappear. Mankind could then concentrate all its forces upon the common task of regulating the nature of the earth and even of the cosmos. Fëdorov believed that in the ideal regime armies should still exist, but for the purpose of regulating the forces of nature rather than for the destruction of man by man.

This belief in the aims of science leads Fëdorov to what he considers to be mankind's supreme task—the resurrection of all ancestors. He regarded as immoral the Positivist theory of progress, which builds the welfare of the future generations upon the sufferings of the past. "One must live not for oneself (egoism) and not for others (altruism), but with everyone and for everyone; this is the union of the living (sons) for the resurrection of the dead (fathers)." Fëdorov contended that even the materialists cannot prove it is impossible to resurrect the dead, and therefore they have no right to shirk the task. "Put the engine together, and consciousness will return to it," he says. According to him, the disintegration of the body and the dispersal of its particles are not an obstacle to its reconstitution, since it is impossible for the particles of the body to go beyond the limits of space.

Fëdorov's views appealed to the enthusiasts both of revolution and of science. They were very widely shared, and even Marxists could accept many of his ideas as a logical development of some remarks in Marxist literature on the proper purpose of philosophy and on life in a classless society. Fëdorov was against the socialist doctrines based on the greed of the proletariat contaminated by the capitalists, and he deeply mistrusted state socialism, which he thought was bound to transform humanity into a herd and deadly to any form of higher culture. Ironically, many of Fëdorov's ideas were taken up under the Communist government in the 1920's, for instance, his idea of bringing together knowledge and action, and various technical plans. Labor armies, too, were in fact created by Trotsky after the Civil War. Even Fëdorov's central and most exalted idea—that of conquering death and resurrecting the dead—found followers, among whom were the famous writers Mayakovsky and Gorky. Finally, in the 1930's, many Fëdorovist ideas on the control of nature as the proper task of government were incorporated into the official Stalinist doctrine.

Tolstoy

At the beginning of the 1880's (with the publication of his *Confession* in 1882), the great novelist Count L. N. Tolstoy (1828–1910), unexpectedly for the reading public, emerged as a religious and moral preacher. From then until the end of his life, he largely devoted himself to preaching, by way of innumerable pamphlets, his own religious and moral doctrine, which soon acquired the name Tolstoyism and, especially in the 1880's, won many adherents in Russia. In its social and political aspects, Tolstoyism was a kind of Christian anarchism. Tolstoy had come to believe that the essence of Christ's message lay in the words "that ye resist not evil." This interpretation of the Gospel, combined with the influences of Henry George and Ruskin, produced Tolstoy's version of the ideal of "God's Kingdom on earth." He rejected the state as "organized brigandage," argued that love for one's country was incompatible with Christianity (*L'ésprit chrétien et le patriotisme*, 1894), as were wars and military service. This attitude to the state was not in fact new; in 1857, having witnessed a public execution in France, Tolstoy had written in a private letter: "Human law is nonsense! Truly, the state is a conspiracy not only for the exploitation, but chiefly for the corruption of the citizens." Forms of government were irrelevant, and American Presidents were regarded by Tolstoy merely as representatives of the interests of different capitalist groups (*On the Meaning of the Russian Revolution*, 1906). Social legislation and social reforms were nothing but cunning devices on the part of the exploiters to enable the "slaves" to work for them (*The Kingdom of God is Within You*, 1896; *Where is the Way Out?*, 1900). Industrialism and capitalism had always been repulsive to Tolstoy—unlike the other aristocratic anarchist, Kropotkin, he did not draw a distinction between the two. From the 1880's, Tolstoy condemned all higher forms and manifestations of civilization as being directly or indirectly based on exploitation and oppression. Everyone should live a simple rural life and feed himself with the fruits of his own labors. But the doctrine of non-resistance to evil precluded a revolutionary way of attaining the

ideal. There was even a quietist streak in Tolstoy's preaching
(*On Non-Activity*, 1893).

A similar doctrine had already been advanced by Malikov, a
lay preacher, in the early 1870's, and it had been accepted by
some of the members of the Chaikovsky Circle, including Chaikovsky himself; but these had emigrated to America to try and
live up to their ideal there. With the failure of revolutionary
Populism to achieve practical results, many Populist-minded
intellectuals took to Tolstoy's teaching. There were several other
points of contact between Populism and Tolstoyism. Tolstoy's
rejection of culture was reminiscent of Chernyshevsky's utilitarian
approach, which was shared by many Populists; his anarchist
ideal appealed to the Bakuninist-minded former members of the
second Land and Freedom organization (many of whom had already independently decided to settle among peasants). Kablits's
advocacy of an acceptance of peasant opinions and values was also
similar to Tolstoy's preaching.

In the decades following the 1880's, after a period of great
popularity, Tolstoyism lost some of its appeal with the renewed
popularity of revolutionary ideas among the radical intelligentsia.
During the last years of his life, Tolstoy gained great fame
throughout the world as a moral preacher and social thinker.
This influence was not lasting, however, and his only outstanding disciple was Gandhi.

10. Late Nineteenth and Early Twentieth Century Reformist Trends

THE LAST quarter of the nineteenth century and the beginning of the twentieth witnessed the appearance of several new reformist trends, some of which had a strong influence on practical policies, while the others contributed to the political controversies of the time.

Technocratism

The swift progress of industrialization during the 1880's and 1890's created a large category of industrial specialists—technical and commercial managers of big capitalist concerns. These soon acquired an influential position in the business world, and played an active, often a leading, role in the organizations of various branches of industry (the mining industry of southern Russia, oil, steel, etc.). Their main central organization was the Council of the Congresses of Industry and Commerce; the various voluntary societies for the promotion of industry and trade were another important form of organization of industrial specialists.

The most brilliant spokesman of the technical intelligentsia was the great scientist D. I. Mendeleev (1834–1907). The youngest son in the large family of the headmaster of the secondary school in Tobol'sk, the former administrative and cultural center of Siberia, he was educated in St. Petersburg and Heidelberg, and was for more than thirty years a professor at St. Petersburg University. He resigned this post in 1890, because of a disagreement with the Minister of Education. After his resignation, he was the head of the Chamber of Measures and Weights and served on a number of official committees, including the commission which drew up a new customs tariff. Himself a successful industrialist, Mendeleev was a determined protagonist of rapid industrial development for Russia through the utilization of her rich mineral resources, advanced technology, protectionist tariffs, and the spread of education (*The Tariff Explained*, 1892; *Thoughts on the Development of Agriculture*, 1899). In his later works he developed a political ideology—the Russian brand of Technocratism—which he called "gradualism" (*Cherished Thoughts*, 1903–5; *On Knowing Russia*, 1906; *Thoughts on the Theory of Knowledge*, 1909). Basing his political ideas on the philosophical position which he called realism (in contradistinction to both idealism and materialism), Mendeleev thought that forms of government were relatively unimportant. He urged like-minded people to abstain from "politics-mongering" and to concentrate on concrete practical work, making use of existing opportunities. The advance of science and technology, training scientifically minded and patriotic public figures, and organizing and expanding Russian industry were for Mendeleev the tasks worth undertaking.

World War I marked a new stage in the development of the technocratic trend. As in the other belligerent countries, it came to be realized in Russia in 1915 that the war could not be conducted successfully unless measures were taken to adjust the country's economy to the abnormal conditions. As a result, special councils and committees for the state control of economic life were created in 1915–16, as were institutions of an unofficial character—the War Industries Committees. All these institutions employed a great number of various specialists in their headquarters and regional and local branches. Invested with wide powers (as were the officials of the special councils and their branches), or anticipating for themselves and for the social groups they represented a great increase in influence and social importance after the war (as did the personnel of the unofficial bodies), they engaged not only in the immediate work of mobilizing resources for the war effort, but also in deliberation on the future course of the Russian economy and on long-term economic planning: "And it is here," wrote one of them, "that the whole might of the industrial public initiative has displayed itself; it is here that they have touched upon issues of enormous state importance." Another active member of the Moscow War Industries Committee, Professor V. I. Grinevetsky, wrote a book, *The Postwar Prospects of Russian Industry* (1919), which served as the basis for all subsequent economic planning.

The impact of the February revolution of 1917 on both the official and the unofficial bodies was twofold: On the one hand, wherever possible they were called upon to replace the old bureaucratic machinery, which had, to a considerable extent, disintegrated; on the other hand, all these institutions, as well as new combinations of them—the Economic Council and the Supreme Economic Committee in Petrograd, supply committees in the provinces and districts—were flooded by representatives of the so-called "revolutionary democracy" (i.e., representatives of socialist parties) whose interests were directed toward "deepening revolution" rather than toward the positive work of guiding the Russian economy. Any productive work was made all but impossible by this "revolutionary democratic" majority. The democratic idea was never particularly attractive to the technical intelligentsia, and the failure of democracy in 1917 must have made even those who had tended toward it doubt the validity of democratic premises and strengthened the elitist tendencies in their thinking.

Such were the views held by the majority of these "bourgeois specialists" as they entered into the service of the Bolshevik state. With his usual acute sense of reality, Lenin advanced the theory that the capitalist economy, in its monopolistic stage, creates forms of economic management that precipitate socialist practice; it was therefore unnecessary to destroy the apparatus of the economic management of the country: It could simply be taken over. Ministries, together with their experts, were subordinated to the People's Commissariats. Wartime institutions for the regulation of the national economy were transformed into Chief Administrations of the respective branches. Some of the Chief Administrations were created out of former monopolistic associations of industrialists. In those branches where there had been no monopolistic development, or where it was incomplete, it was made compulsory. Instead of the expected increased prestige and influence in public affairs, which would have corresponded to the importance of their function as managers of the national economy, the technical intelligentsia found that they were merely tolerated as a necessary evil under the new regime. Yet the very fact that their declared political enemies could not do without them must have further strengthened their belief in the social value of their class. Isolation from the political life of the country was another factor that stimulated the development of their class consciousness. The official Leninist policy of suspicion, and the open hostility of the syndicalist elements, made it extremely difficult for them to reconcile themselves to the Bolshevik regime. Hence their hopes that it might be succeeded by a system under which they would not have to fear interference with their work either from the Party committee or from the Works' Council—though they heeded Mendeleev's words that in Russia it was often preferable not to be too outspoken, indeed, not to talk about one's views at all unless there was compelling reason to do so. The old technocratic ideas were thus strengthened by the conditions of life and work under the Soviet regime.

The main organizational centers of technocratically minded specialists were the State Planning Commission and the Supreme Council of the National Economy, as well as the various societies of engineers and technicians; the main academic centers were the Moscow Higher Technical School (of which Grinevetsky had been the director) and the Thermo-Technical Institute set up in 1921. The most outstanding individual representatives of the group were specialists in fuel and power: P. I. Pal'chinsky (who had been the virtual head of the Central War Industries Committee and the Deputy Minister of Trade and Industry in Kerensky's government), L. K. Ramzin (who organized and headed the Thermo-Technical Institute), and I. G. Aleksandrov (the builder of the large hydroelectric station on the Dnieper). They took the leading part in working out the plan of electrification at the beginning of the 1920's and in the subsequent economic planning and management, developing further the ideas put forward by Mendeleev and Grinevetsky. Organized technocratism was eliminated in 1928–30 in the course of a large-scale purge of the old intelligentsia, in which many leading persons were shot or imprisoned and others reduced to purely technical functions. Pal'chinsky (who had been the most left-wing of the leading technical specialists and a great admirer of Kropotkin) was accused of sabotage at the beginning of the campaign and shot in 1929; at the Industrial Party trial in 1930, he was said to have established an underground League of Engineering Organizations which subsequently developed into the Industrial Party. Ramzin confessed to having headed the Industrial Party after Pal'chinsky's arrest and was sentenced to death but reprieved; he was released from imprisonment during World War II and continued to act as a technical expert. Aleksandrov, who had laid the theoretical foundations for the territorial aspect of Soviet economic planning, escaped the fate of his colleagues, though he was repeatedly accused of holding "bourgeois" views.

Technocratic ideas to some extent affected the next generation of technical experts, trained during the 1920's and early 1930's. They were latent during the greater part of the period of Stalin's rule, but remained a potential source of opposition to the Communist Party's claim to exclusive authority. With the revival of political thought after Stalin's death, the technocratic tendency has again appeared on the scene: It largely inspires the efforts to rationalize economic planning and management (which in Stalin's time were based on a mixture of routine and arbitrariness), and some of its adherents even suggest that economic administration should be entirely entrusted to local and regional councils made up of factory managers. The new vogue for cybernetics further strengthens technocratic tendencies.

Social Reformism

Simultaneously with the growth of technocratic tendencies, and similarly prompted by the progress of industrialization, there developed a trend of thought that can be described as Social Reformism. The hardships which the new industrial proletariat had to endure soon began to trouble the consciences of some people. Modern factory legislation began in the 1880's, one of the first measures being the institution of factory inspection. Among the active participants in the committees that prepared the factory

and labor legislation, and among the first factory inspectors, was
I. I. Yanzhul (1846–1914), the most prominent representative of
undogmatic social reformism in Russia. A Ukrainian of Molda-
vian descent, he was educated at Moscow University, where
Chicherin was one of his teachers, was later professor of public
finance there, and in 1882–87 the factory inspector of the Moscow
province. Among his chief works are *English Free Trade*, 2 vols.,
1876 and 1882; *Factory Life in the Moscow Province*, 1884; *Essays
and Studies: a Collection of Articles on National Economy,
Politics and Legislation*, 2 vols., 1884; *In Search of a Better
Future. Social Essays*, 1893; *Industrial Syndicates or Entrepre-
neurs' Associations for Regulating Production, Especially in the
U.S.A.*, 1895; and three volumes of reminiscences, 1907–11.

Yanzhul was greatly influenced by English thought and practice, which he studied at first hand during his frequent visits to
England. He rejected socialist utopias (e.g., that of Bellamy
among his contemporaries) and such simple panaceas for all ills
as neo-Malthusianism or Henry George's "single land tax," advocating instead a combination of humane social policies by the
government, which must maintain an equilibrium between various classes and parties, with social work by private individuals
and voluntary associations. *In Search of a Better Future* is devoted to a description of examples of such social work in England
and America: the People's Palace in London, the activities of
Ruskin and the Toynbee Hall, the University Extension movement, the Salvation Army, the Neighbourhood Guilds, the Y.W.
C.A., Carnegie and his philanthropic work, etc. These, Yanzhul
said, were without doubt the most remarkable phenomena of the
time.

While Yanzhul and his followers (who were not very numerous)
rejected projects of social reform based on a belief in salvation
through the exclusive application of a particular idea, there were
people, besides dogmatic socialists and anarchists, who believed
in some such idea. Perhaps the most noteworthy of them was
V. F. Totomiants (born 1874), an ardent and untiring advocate of
Cooperative Socialism after the fashion of Charles Gide.

"Police Socialism," initiated by S. V. Zubatov (1864–1917), the
head of the Moscow branch of the political police, was also a pecul-

iar kind of social reformism. Himself a former revolutionary, Zubatov thought that it would be possible to prevent workers from being influenced by revolutionary socialism if a legal workers' movement were developed that would be largely controlled by police agents. With the help of some former Social Democratic workers whom he had converted to his ideas and some Moscow University professors (including I. Kh. Ozerov, a pupil of Yanzhul and his successor in the chair of public finance), Zubatov in 1901 founded the Society of Mutual Help of Workers in Mechanical Production, which was in fact the first legal trade union in Russia. This society flourished under police protection and was imitated in Minsk and Odessa. Zubatov was able to control the movement in Moscow, but in the other two towns it got out of hand and he was forced to resign in 1903. The movement seemed to have come to an end, but it was resurrected in the same year in St. Petersburg by G. A. Gapon, an Orthodox priest who was in touch with the police. He founded the Assembly of Russian Workers which, however, soon became penetrated by Social Democrats who used it as a "front" organization for revolutionary agitation. The procession of workers led by Gapon on January 9, 1905 (known as "Bloody Sunday") with the intention of presenting a somewhat provocative petition to Nicholas II was fired upon by the police, and this was the start of the 1905 revolution.

The "Landmarks" Movement

The third principal new reformist movement among the intellectuals of the late nineteenth and early twentieth centuries is commonly known as the "Landmarks" Movement, after the title of a collection of essays that appeared in 1909 and received wide publicity. Its beginnings can be traced to a philosophical trend of the 1890's that attempted to combine Kantian and Hegelian Idealism (the latter as represented in Russia by Chicherin) with the religious philosophy of Solov'ëv. One of the first writers to extend this approach to the field of political theory was P. I. Novgorodtsev (1866–1924). Educated at the universities of Moscow, Berlin and Paris, he was a professor at Moscow in 1903–11 and again in 1917–18 (having resigned in 1911, together with

REFORMIST TRENDS · *189*

many other liberal and radical members of the teaching staff, in protest against a measure of the Minister of Education that infringed upon the autonomy of the university). He was also director of the newly founded Moscow Commercial Institute and later (1922–24) founder and dean of the Russian Juridical Faculty (a kind of *émigré* university) in Prague. He was active in the Union of Liberation and in the Constitutional Democratic Party and in 1906 was elected by his native Ekaterinoslav province (in the Ukraine) to the First State Duma.

Already in his early writings (*The Historical School of Jurists*, 1897; *Kant's and Hegel's Teachings on Law and State*, 1902; *State and Law*, 1904), Novgorodtsev advocated the revival of the doctrine of natural law. He was most emphatic in his insistence on the autonomy of the individual: the state must recognize the free human personality as the limit of its dominion; it must recognize the existence of a sacred sphere—not available for state interference—of thoughts and sentiments, of personal self-determination. Being thus limited in its relations with its subjects, the state must also abandon its exclusiveness vis-à-vis the outside world, must open itself up toward this outside world and recognize the rights of other nations and other peoples. Novgorodtsev believed that modern states were in fact developing in both these directions; it was becoming increasingly clear that there were certain firm principles and unquestionable elements of law over which the state had no power. In 1903, Novgorodtsev edited a collection of essays by like-minded people, entitled *Questions of Idealism* and chiefly directed against Positivism in philosophy and jurisprudence. A notable feature of the volume was the participation in it of the former leading Russian Marxists P. B. Struve, S. N. Bulgakov, N. A. Berdyaev and others (usually called Legal Marxists by historians—see Chapter 11), who now argued not only against Positivism but also against Marxism. Their appearance together with Novgorodtsev and other Idealists in *Questions of Idealism* signified the fusion of both groups into one movement, which on the whole retained its cohesion until 1918 and re-established itself in emigration during the 1920's and 30's.

In his later works (*The Crisis of Contemporary Legal Consciousness*, 1909; *On the Social Ideal*, 1917), Novgorodtsev traced the breakdown among the intellectual elite of belief both in the individualist state and in a paradise on earth. The idea of an earthly paradise—i.e., of perfect harmony—common to Rousseau, Kant, Hegel, Comte, Spencer, and Marx, could not withstand modern criticism, which had been anticipated in Russia by Karamzin and Herzen and which was supported by the findings of moral philosophy and of the evolutionary theory. To the ideal of complete and finite perfection Novgorodtsev opposed his own positive ideal of infinite striving and development which he called "free universalism." In 1918, Novgorodtsev contributed to the last collection of articles produced by the Landmarks Movement in Russia—*De Profundis*—an essay entitled "The Ways and Tasks of the Russian Intelligentsia" in which he rejected not only Socialism but also Liberalism (or rather, what was chiefly understood in Russia under this name—the views of the radical Milyukovist majority of the Constitutional Democratic Party), which, he said, lacking the experience of governing, was emotionally attracted to socialism without realizing that Russian Socialism, stemming from Bakunin, was devoid of any liberal elements. Under the impact of the 1917 revolution and of the first months of the Bolshevik regime, Novgorodtsev's "free universalism" finally took the shape of Burkean Conservatism.

The former leading Marxists who ostentatiously joined the Idealist camp in 1903 were a group of brilliant scholars and journalists who in their early youth—in the late 1880's and early 90's—had embraced Marxism, partly under the influence of Plekhanov's writings, but chiefly under the influence of the original works of Marx and his German disciples. In the mid-1890's, they had broken through the censorship and begun to publish their openly Marxist writings legally in Russia, thus earning the nickname of Legal Marxists. Being genuinely interested in theory, and intellectually honest, they soon discovered inconsistencies and other weaknesses in the Marxist doctrines and, like some of their contemporaries among West European Marxists, proceeded to revise them, so that around the turn of the century the term Legal Marxism became almost synonymous with Revisionism. In the process of revision they often took their clues (again, like the German Revisionists) from Neo-Kantianism, and soon completed the transition "from Marxism to Idealism" (as one of them, S. N. Bulgakov, entitled the essay he contributed to *Questions of Idealism*). Continuing the process, they soon combined Neo-Kantianism with the religious thought of Dostoevsky and Solov'ëv.

The leading spirit among the Legal Marxists, and later in the Landmarks Movement, was P. B. Struve (1870–1944). An economist of German descent educated at St. Petersburg University, he was the first to publish a book written from an avowedly Marxist standpoint (*Critical Notes on the Development of Our Economy,* 1894). But even in this book he qualified his Marxism, and two years later, in an article in a German theoretical Social Democratic journal, he began openly to revise it. Yet he edited the short-lived Marxist journals that were published in St. Petersburg in the late 1890's, retained close connections with the underground Social Democratic organizations, was on good personal terms with Lenin, and in 1898 wrote the Manifesto that announced the foundation of the Russian Social Democratic Labor Party. He left Social Democracy in 1900, and, joining forces with the Zemstvo constitutionalists, became one of the leaders of the liberal movement and edited abroad in 1902–5 its journal *Liberation*. He returned to Russia in 1905, joined the Constitutional-Democratic Party, and in 1907 was a member of the Second State Duma. Still a radical until the revolution of 1905, he now opposed Milyukov's radicalism and was the leader of the liberal right wing of the party, believing that under the new semiconstitutional regime liberals should cooperate with the government; his secret negotiations with the Prime Minister, Stolypin, about the participation of Constitutional Democrats in the government led to nothing because of opposition both from the radical majority of the party and the reactionaries surrounding the throne. Active as an academic economist (he occupied the chair of political economy at the new Polytechnic Institute in St. Petersburg, published a theoretical work in two volumes— *Economy and Price,* 1913–16—and was soon elected to the Academy of Sciences) and as a politician and journalist (editing the liberal monthly *Russian Thought*), Struve contributed the key essay, entitled "The Intelligentsia and Revolution," to the collection that gave the movement its name—*Landmarks* (published in 1909 and subtitled *A Collection of Articles on the Russian Intelligentsia*).

What had been intolerable under the pre-1905 autocratic regime in Russia, Struve argued in his essay, was that the autocracy had in advance set absolute limits to the life of the people and the development of the state. Anything that widened these limits, whether juridically or factually, or which merely threatened to widen them in the future, was not tolerated and was subject to repression. The breakdown of this policy had been unavoidable; speeded up by the growing complexity of social life and by the Russo–Japanese war, it came about very quickly. The granting of the constitution in October, 1905, should have ended the revolution, both in form and in substance. The fact that it had not done so was due to the peculiar role played in Russia by the intelligentsia. The intelligentsia was not identical or coextensive with the educated classes: It was that section of the educated classes which was alienated both from the traditional reality of the Russian state and from the state idea in general, the difference between the absolute rejection of the state by the Anarchists and the theoretically lesser hostility of other radicals being in practice insignificant. Bakunin had been the first representative of the intelligentsia and Chernyshevsky had continued his tradition. Neither Novikov, Radishchev, nor Chaadaev before them, nor Herzen and Solov'ëv among their contemporaries and later thinkers, nor any of the great nineteenth-century writers—Pushkin, Lermontov, Gogol', Turgenev, Dostoevsky, Tolstoy, Chekhov—had had the mentality of the intelligentsia. By its alienation from the state and hostility toward it, the intelligentsia of the second half of the nineteenth and the beginning of the twentieth centuries resembled the Cossacks of the seventeenth and eighteenth centuries, and it played the same political role of providing leadership for the elementally rebellious oppressed and exploited popular masses. The retreat of the monarchy in October, 1905, opening up a prospect of constitutional development, was greeted by the intelligentsia with a call "to stamp out the reptile with a last kick." This anarchic and nihilist frame of mind had its deeper roots in another kind of alienation of the intelligentsia—its irreligiousness. Irreligion precluded the intelligentsia from having a real sense of moral responsibility, for which the cult of "the people" was a bad substitute, resulting not in up-lifting the oppressed popular masses but in pandering to their instinctive appetites and hatreds. The tragedy of Russia lay in the coincidence of the reception of West European atheistic socialism with the social and political realities of the country at the time of this reception.

Struve had formulated his positive liberal program in 1905, immediately after the granting of the constitution, and he held to it until the revolution of 1917. In his view, what the country needed was equal freedom and equal political rights for all citizens, a "normal flow of economic life," and solid social re-forms. The threat of dictatorship was hanging over Russia—a dictatorship either of "those who are called the Black Hundred" or of "those who call themselves the revolutionary proletariat." But any dictatorship was unnecessary and repellent to the coun-try. Out of the elemental popular mass must be born a nation consisting of free citizens compromising with each other. The task was to create a nation and to carry Russian culture safely through the crisis without diminishing and weakening, but on the contrary enriching and strengthening it.

The dominant thread of Struve's political writings between the two revolutions was (as he pointed out in the preface to the collec-tion of his articles published under the title *Patriotica* in 1911) anxiety about the future of Russia. Criticizing both the intelli-gentsia and the government, he maintained that nothing short of a real regeneration of both would suffice. His criticism of the intelligentsia proceeded from the "severe but healthy religious individualism which appeals to the ideas of personal responsibility and personal value," while his criticism of the Russian govern-ment originated from an idea of law "the acceptance of which excludes any absolutism of the authorities, whatever its camou-flage and justifications."

Other contributors to the *Landmarks* collection (all save one of them former Marxists) mainly elaborated some of the chief points of Struve's essay. The effect produced by the appearance of the volume was rather similar to that of the publication of

Chaadaev's "Philosophical Letter"—it was felt to be a bomb explosion and provoked violent antagonism and hostility on the part of those who were the principal target of its criticism: the radical majority of the Constitutional Democratic Party, the Socialist Revolutionaries and the Social Democrats of all shades. The action of the *Landmarks* group was seen as a betrayal of all that the Russian intelligentsia had traditionally stood for. Especially singled out for protests was a sentence (later considered by Struve and by the author himself to have been unfortunate) in the preface to the volume, written by the one contributor who was not an ex-Marxist—M. O. Gershenzon—which revealed the intensity of the group's antirevolutionary sentiments: "Such as we are," Gershenzon wrote, "so far from dreaming of union with the people, we ought to fear the people more than any executions by the government and bless this government which alone, with its prisons and bayonets, still protects us from the people's fury."*

Undeterred by the reaction to the symposium, its participants proceeded with what they considered to be their duty—liberating progressive Russian thought from the mystique of revolution. United in "the recognition of the primacy both in theory and in practice of spiritual life over the outward forms of society, in the sense that the inner life of the individual . . . and not the self-sufficing elements of some political order is the only solid basis for every social structure"† (in the words of the preface), they were not unanimous as to what political consequences flowed from this recognition. While Struve and the majority of other participants of the movement adhered to conservative liberalism, or liberal conservatism as Struve later called this trend (in *Russian Thought,* which he revived abroad and was publishing in Sofia, Prague, Berlin, and Paris in 1921–27), Berdyaev and Bulgakov continued Fëdorov's tradition of Christian Socialism. Berdyaev's thought will be dealt with in greater detail in Chapter 13. Bulgakov (1871–1944), who was, like Struve, an academic economist (he taught at Kiev and Moscow universities and pub-

* Quoted by Leonard Schapiro in "The *Vekhi* Group and the Mystique of Revolution," *The Slavonic and East European Review,* XXXIV, December, 1955.
† *Ibid.*

lished two major works on economics—*Capitalism and Agriculture*, 1900; and *Philosophy of the Economy*, 1912), developed in his political writings (*Two Cities. Studies on the Nature of Social Ideals*, 1911; *Quiet Thoughts*, 1918) the theory according to which modern radicalism (from Feuerbach onward) was a kind of secular religion of man-godhood opposed to the Christian religion of God-manhood. He later became an Orthodox priest, an outstanding theologian and professor at the Russian Orthodox Institute in Paris.

The Landmarks movement failed to carry with it the bulk of the intelligentsia, which continued to hold to its radical beliefs until disillusioned by the realities of the Communist regime in the 1920's and 1930's. But the political philosophy of the movement, combining in effect spiritual Slavophilism with political Westernism, strongly influenced subsequent Russian thought and has now been revived in Solidarism.

A philosophical position similar to that of the Landmarks movement, and also under the influence of Dostoevsky and Solov'ëv, was occupied by A. F. Kerensky (born 1881). The son of a headmaster from the Volga area, he studied law at St. Petersburg University and distinguished himself as defense counsel in political cases. A romantic revolutionary in 1904–5, Kerensky became a reformist afterwards, retaining his Populist sympathies and democratic convictions. He was leader of the Labor Group (a group of semisocialist deputies) in the Fourth Duma and one of the leading members of the political Masonic organization which took the initiative in organizing the democratic forces on the eve of the February, 1917, revolution and in preparing a *coup de palais* in order to prevent a spontaneous revolution during the war. As Minister of Justice and later Prime Minister, he took a leading part in the democratic transformation of Russia embarked upon by the Provisional Government and enjoyed great popularity, but he failed to prevent the seizure of power by the Bolsheviks.

11. Social Democratism

THE YEAR 1881 had an impact upon Russian radical thought that may be compared to that of 1825. The collapse of the Decembrist uprising had signified and symbolized the apparent failure of Russia to go the "European" way, to follow France and other Continental states of Western Europe in transition from absolutism and serfdom to constitutional government and equality of civil status. And this apparent failure had provoked Chaadaev to raise the whole problem of Russia's relation to Western Europe and had precipitated the rift between the Westernists and the Slavophiles. Now there was a similar failure. The assassination of Alexander II by the People's Will Party did not lead to a disintegration of the Imperial government and its replacement by a revolutionary socialist dictatorship, and this, coming as it did only a couple of years after the breakdown of the second Land and Freedom organization's Bakuninist strategy, was interpreted by many radicals as the final failure of attempts to find a specific "Russian" way to socialism, bypassing capitalism. This led to a new schism in political thought—between Populists who still clung to the ideal of "Russian Socialism" and those who came to the conclusion that there was no separate path for Russia and that the Marxist view of capitalism as the stage in social development preceding socialism should be extended to include Russia. This conclusion was first reached by the leaders of the Black Repartition, headed by Plekhanov, who became the father of Russian Marxist Social Democracy.

Marxism

Marxism was not, of course, unknown in Russia. The Russian Left-Hegelians of the 1840's, Bakunin and Belinsky, were acquainted with it from its very inception. Bakunin later translated the *Communist Manifesto* and began to translate *Das Kapital*. The first volume of the latter (translated by a Populist) appeared in Russia in 1872—before it was translated into any other language. Already in the 1860's, Tkachëv had declared himself to be in agreement with the Marxist theory, and both Bakunin and Lavrov accepted Marx's analysis of the capitalist system. Lavrov called Marx his teacher; Lavrov's followers in Russia in the 1870's were loosely referred to as Marxists. Finally, academic economists in Russia had begun to accept Marx's economic theory. What was new in the views of Plekhanov and his friends was not their acceptance of Marxian views, but their insistence on Marxism to the exclusion of all other economic and political theories.

G. V. Plekhanov (1857–1918) came of a noble landowning family and was a student at the Mining Institute in St. Petersburg when he joined the revolutionary movement in 1875. He took part in forming the second Land and Freedom organization in the following year and was one of its leading theorists. When the organization split in 1879 into the Tkachëvist People's Will and the Bakuninist Black Repartition, it was Plekhanov who, by his opposition to the Tkachëvist turn, effected the split. Together with the other leading figures of Black Repartition, he went abroad in 1880, with no intention at first of abandoning the Bakuninist path. He remained in emigration (in Switzerland and France) until after the fall of the monarchy in 1917. Within two years of going abroad, Plekhanov became a convinced Marxist, and in 1883, he and his fellow *émigré* leaders of Black Repartition openly broke with Populism and formed a small organization of their own, the Liberation of Labor group, with the aim of interpreting Russian conditions and developments in Marxist terms, propagating Marxism in Russia, and paving the way for the formation of a Marxist Social Democratic Party. Plekhanov's pamphlets published abroad—*Socialism and the Political Struggle* (1883), *Our Disagreements* (1885)—and two books published legally in St. Petersburg—*On the Question of the Development of the Monistic View of History* (1895) and *The Justification of Populism in the Works of Mr. V. Vorontsov* (1896)—were written for this purpose and were devoted to criticizing both revolutionary and liberal Populism. Further writings of a theoretical character (*Essays in the History of Materialism,* 1896; *The Materialist Conception of History,* 1897; *The Role of the Individual in History,* 1898; *Fundamental Problems of Marxism,* 1910) established for Plekhanov the reputation of one of the leading Marxist theorists in Europe, ranking immediately after Kautsky and Bernstein. Plekhanov was the most rigid and doctrinaire of all the leading Marxists of his time, and he fiercely defended orthodox Marxism against the "revisionists"—Bernstein, Struve, Bogdanov, and others. He did much to reduce Marxism to a series of immutable dogmatic propositions, which it still largely is in Russia today.

"If we wish," Plekhanov wrote, "to summarize the views of Marx and Engels on the relation between the famous 'basis' and the no less famous 'superstructure,' we shall get something like this:

1. the *state of the productive forces;*
2. *economic relations* conditioned by these forces;
3. the *socio-political system* erected upon a given economic foundation;
4. the *psychology of man in society,* determined in part directly by economic conditions and in part by the whole sociopolitical system erected upon the economic foundation;
5. *various ideologies* reflecting this psychology."

The development of the productive forces themselves was determined by the peculiarities of the geographical environment—here Plekhanov introduced into Marxist theory an element of "geographical materialism" that was not contained (at least not explicitly) in the writings of Marx and Engels. But Plekhanov's main deviation from the views expressed by Marx was his insistence that Russia had to pass through the capitalist stage before it could reach socialism: Marx (who had admired the People's Will terrorists and was rather scornful of Plekhanov and his small band of *émigrés*), when this question was directly put to him shortly before his death by a colleague of Plekhanov's, came down after some hesitation on the side of Populists, who thought that Russia—thanks to the existence of the peasant village commune—might manage to avoid the horrors of capitalism. Although Russia had entered the capitalist path (which was especially evident from the fact that the village commune was disintegrating), there were two peculiar features in the Russian social and political situation which set it off from Western Europe and which demanded different tactics from Social Democracy. The Russian bourgeoisie was weak and too dependent in its business activity on the support of the government (which was promoting industrialization) to be able to fight resolutely for the overthrow of the absolutism and the establishment of a constitutional government. It therefore fell to the working class to exercise "hegemony" in this "bourgeois" revolution, and the Social Democratic Party must play the leading role in the struggle against autocracy. The Russian autocracy itself appeared to Plekhanov as an "Oriental" despoty, the characteristic feature of this type of government being that all land and the people who tilled it were deemed to be owned by the despot. And Plekhanov opposed the inclusion into the party program of a demand that privately owned land be nationalized, for in his view it would strengthen the element of "Oriental despotism" in the social life and mentality of Russia.

Secret Social Democratic organizations began to spring up in Russia simultaneously with the setting-up of Plekhanov's Liberation of Labor group abroad. The Party of Russian Social-Democrats (1883–87) was organized by former adherents of Black Repartition and former Lavrovists, and its program reflected Marxist, Lassallean, and Lavrovist influences. Social Democratic groups and circles multiplied, until the Russian Social Democratic Labor Party was founded at a secret gathering in 1898. Plekhanov enjoyed high esteem in the party, whose ideological outlook he had largely shaped, and he represented it for many years in the executive bureau of the Socialist International, but he never became the political leader of the party. The spread within the Social Democratic Party of "revisionism" and of the tendency that Plekhanov labeled "Economism" (in fact, a preoccupation in the practical work of the party with improving the workers' conditions) prompted Plekhanov to cooperate in 1900–3 with Lenin, whose battle cries were Marxist orthodoxy and primacy of political struggle against the autocracy. After the formal split of the party, in 1903, into a Leninist ("Bolshevik") and an anti-Leninist ("Menshevik")* faction, Plekhanov for the most part vacillated between the two, hoping for a reunification. Both in 1905 and in 1917, he stuck to his view that a more or less prolonged period of "bourgeois" constitutional regime was necessary before a socialist revolution could take place, and he consequently condemned the uprising in Moscow in December, 1905, and the Bolshevik seizure of power in 1917. But between the two revolutions, in 1910–13, he supported Lenin against the ideological heterodoxy of Bogdanov and the political line of Potresov and his friends, who favored abandoning the old underground party organization. The final break with Lenin came during World War I, when Plekhanov took the anti-German side, fearing that a German victory would jeopardize the prospects of socialism throughout Europe. Plekhanov's small Social Democratic group, "Unity," consisting chiefly of his old admirers, did not join in the formation of the Menshevik party in the autumn of 1917, and they put up candidates of their own in the election to the Constituent Assembly. After his death, the group continued to exist until 1930, in the guise of a committee to commemorate Plekhanov.

Apart from Plekhanov, two Social Democratic politicians deserve attention as intellectual leaders of distinctive trends within orthodox Marxist Social Democracy—Martov and Potresov. Yu. O. Martov (1873–1923), whose real name was Tsederbaum, came from a prosperous Jewish family with a tradition of public-mindedness: Martov's grandfather had founded the first modern newspaper in Hebrew. As a student at St. Petersburg University, Martov played the leading role in a Social Democratic circle, which was named the St. Petersburg Group of Liberation, to stress its solidarity with Plekhanov's group abroad. Expelled from the university and banished from the capital, Martov became what Lenin later termed a professional revolutionary. He lived for a time in Vil'na, taking part in the Jewish Social Democratic circles there. These circles, following the example of Polish Socialists, were shifting the main stress in their work among the

* The meaning of these two terms is explained on p. 219.

factory workers and artisans from the propagation of Marxist theory to practical agitation for better working conditions. One of the Vil'na Social Democrats wrote a pamphlet (*On Agitation*) in 1894 in which the new tactics were formulated; Martov gave the pamphlet its final shape and it was secretly distributed to all the centers of Social Democratic activity. Martov persuaded Lenin, who was the leader of another, more influential, circle in St. Petersburg, to combine forces, and in 1895 they formed the St. Petersburg Union of Struggle for the Liberation of the Working Class. Both circles—Lenin's and Martov's—had originally belonged to the periphery of a semi-Social Democratic secret organization (which will be considered in the section on Leninism); this organization had a special group for propaganda among the workers that coordinated and directed such propaganda throughout the capital. The setting-up of the Union of Struggle was in a way a reintegration of this earlier propaganda group, though the work it was to coordinate and direct was now to consist chiefly of agitation on the basis of specific grievances.

The tactics of agitation, though seemingly new, were in fact already known in the Russian revolutionary movement. They had been used to some extent by the Decembrists, were included in Ogarëv's plan, and later survived in the Bakuninist tradition, even as the tactics of propaganda survived in the Lavrovist tradition. Agitation was widely practiced by the second Land and Freedom organization, but after the 1879 split it was neglected by both the People's Will and the Black Repartition, though never formally dropped. The tactics of agitation were adopted in the mid–1890's in most of the main centers of the Social Democratic movement in Russia, and produced an effect that had not been intended by its originators. They had been introduced as a means of attracting the workers to the Social Democratic organizations; but in the process of applying the new tactics, many Social Democrats came to the conclusion (rather like Kablits among the Populists fifteen years earlier) that organizations speaking in the name of the workers should reflect the genuine views and interests of the workers and not try to impose views held by radical intellectuals, and that the workers themselves should be given a voice in directing Social Democratic activities. Martov resented this tendency, and in 1900, when he was released from banishment to Siberia, he joined Lenin and Plekhanov in combating it. Three years later, however, Martov put himself at the head of the opposition to Lenin's dictatorship within the party, and from 1903 until the end of his life, he remained the best-known leader of the Menshevik faction (from 1917 the Menshevik Party). The Mensheviks advocated and practiced a much looser organization than the Bolsheviks, and were much more genuinely democratically minded. Opposing Lenin's dictatorial methods in the party (*The Struggle Against the State of Siege in the Russian Social Democratic Labor Party*, Geneva, 1904, and *Saviors or Annihilators?*, 1911), Martov came round to the view—which he had combated as "Economism" before 1903—that the workers could to a considerable extent be relied upon to progress by themselves, in the course of their struggle with the employers, to Marxist views on the nature of the capitalist state. Martov was usually anxious to reestablish the unity of the party, or at least to cooperate with Lenin wherever possible, though he strongly disapproved of Lenin's lack of scruples in politics. During the 1905–7 revolution, the Mensheviks were active as members of the numerous local coalitions of the revolutionary socialist forces: in the strike committees, Soviets of Workers' Deputies, headquarters of local uprisings, etc. This performance was repeated after the fall of the monarchy in 1917, most Soviets having a Menshevik majority. Most Mensheviks gave qualified support to the Provisional Government and later in the year several of them entered it. But Martov himself in 1917 was heading a minority subfaction that opposed the Provisional Government's policy of "revolutionary defensism"—that is, of defending Russia, now that it had got rid of the monarchy, in the war against Germany. Martov had taken up a "Centrist" position after the outbreak of the war in 1914: pacifist and internationalist, in accordance with the prewar decisions of the Socialist International, but without breaking party ties with those Social Democrats who supported their country's war effort. Most Mensheviks shared Martov's position until the February revolution of 1917, when the majority became "revolutionary defensists" while he remained an internationalist. After the Bolshevik coup, Martov supported negotiations with the Bolsheviks in an effort to establish an all-socialist coalition government. Martov and the Menshevik Party, formed under his leadership in the autumn of 1917, thought that the social basis of Lenin's rule was the working-class and that the Bolsheviks were laying the foundations of a socialist order, although in a wrong and often very unpleasant way (*Questions of Social Democratic Politics*, Berlin, 1920). They therefore generally supported the Red side in the Civil War, and many, perhaps the majority, joined the Bolshevik Party. Martov himself and several other leading Mensheviks had to emigrate (for the third time) in 1920–22; they founded a monthly journal, *Socialist Courier*, which still exists (originally published in Berlin, it was transferred to Paris in 1933 and to New York in 1940). The period of semilegal existence of the Menshevik Party in Russia ended in 1922, and only small secret Menshevik groups continued to exist until most of their members were exterminated in the Great Purge of the 1930's.

But Martovism as a trend of Russian political thought was not confined to members of the various Menshevik organizations. Many Bolsheviks of the 1920's who had never had any connections with official Menshevism—those who took the Marxian teaching seriously and wholly accepted it, believed in the historic mission of the proletariat and considered it their duty to make the proletariat fulfill its mission—should perhaps more properly be regarded as Martovists, even if they had always been in Lenin's party. They usually had little understanding of problems of power, and equally little interest in them. They were usually dissatisfied with Lenin's and his successors' terroristic methods as applied to themselves, but justified them in relation to others. Those of them who were in the more or less organized oppositions within the Bolshevik Party (such as the Democratic Centralism Group or the Workers' Opposition) tried, as the Mensheviks did, to impress upon the Leninists the necessity of concessions to themselves in order that they should be able to cooperate more effectively. Stalin's terror put an end to this trend. But Martovism continued to exist among the *émigrés* abroad, and at the end of World War II, Martov's successor, F. I. Dan (1871–1947), who had for many years shared in the Menshevik leadership and was

the official leader of the majority of the faction in 1917, precipitated a new split in the Menshevik group by openly adopting a
pro-Communist attitude, though the majority of the group was by
then decidedly anti-Communist. In his book *The Origin of
Bolshevism* (New York, 1946), Dan justified the setting-up of the
Communist regime as a way of resolving the old nineteenth-
century dilemma of Russian revolutionaries—the impossibility of
establishing simultaneously socialism and democracy—through
creating, by means of a dictatorship, a socialist economy that
would be able to serve as a basis for political democracy. He now
believed that with the victorious end of the war, the time for
such a democratic evolution had come.

While the Centrist trend in Russian Social Democracy was
symbolized by Martov, its right wing was symbolized by A. N.
Potresov (1869–1934). Like Martov, Potresov did not take up his
final position from the beginning of his political career. Of a
noble family, he had been greatly influenced by the revolutionary
literature of the 1860's and 1870's, which was well represented in
the family library. Studying law and economics at St. Petersburg
University, he became attracted to Marxism, joined the circle of
young Marxist theorists headed by Struve, and at the same time
became acquainted with Martov's secret Social Democratic circle.
He visited Plekhanov abroad in 1893, and for the next few years
was the main contact man between the Liberation of Labor group
and the St. Petersburg Marxists. Potresov conceived the idea of
publishing Marxist political writings legally and succeeded in
bringing out a book by Struve, one by Plekhanov, and a collection of articles by various people (though this last was immediately confiscated). After the arrest of Lenin and Martov, Potresov
was one of the leaders of the St. Petersburg Union of Struggle,
until he himself was arrested and banished. Following his release
in 1900,he joined Lenin and Martov in a triumvirate to fight the
"revisionism" of Struve and his other former young Marxist
friends and the Economism prevalent in the local committees of
the Social Democratic Party. However, close cooperation with
Lenin in this period disillusioned Potresov once and for ever.
Rejection on moral grounds of the principle of amoralism in
politics shared by Lenin and Plekhanov, and of Martov's accom-

modating attitude—for reasons of expediency—toward practices of which he in principle disapproved, was the cornerstone of Potresov's political stand. Having lived in emigration in 1900–5, he remained in Russia after the 1905 revolution and became the leader of the right wing of the party, which laid the main emphasis on work in the newly established State Duma, in trade unions, cooperatives, workers' educational associations, and other legal institutions, and was averse to reviving the old conspiratorial party apparatus that had largely disappeared in 1908–9. This last attitude earned Potresov and his followers the pejorative nickname of "Liquidators" from Lenin and Plekhanov. Potresov was the editor of the main theoretical journals of this trend, *Renaissance* and *Our Dawn,* which were published legally in Russia. During the war, Potresov and his adherents took up a defensist position (the collection of essays *Self-Defense,* 1916) and supported the War Industries Committees, forming workers' groups in some of them despite the hostile attitude of the government toward these groups. In 1917 and after the Bolshevik coup, quite logically, the problems of preserving and regaining democratic freedoms came to the forefront of Potresov's and his friends' political thinking. They had no illusions about the Leninist policy and sharply attacked the Martovists for having such illusions. They also recognized the reasons for the latter's illusions— the Martovists' clinging to the obsolete concepts of Marxist propaganda (Potresov's impression of the Menshevik conference in December, 1917, was summarized in two words—"Dead souls!"). Reformist in their approach to practical problems before 1917, they were tempted to try the same approach under Lenin, particularly after the introduction of the New Economic Policy in 1921. They were mostly concentrated in cooperatives, then also in the trade unions and economic organs. Even among the Bolsheviks there were people in the early 1920's who openly propagated views akin to Potresov's, e.g., G. I. Myasnikov and his group. But not all Potresovists considered the reformist approach suitable in conditions of Lenin's rule, and many placed their hopes in a more or less distant new anti-Bolshevik revolution.

Potresov was allowed to emigrate in 1925, and from abroad he continued active opposition to the Communist regime, attacking the half-heartedness of the Martovist Menshevik leadership (*In the Captivity of Illusions,* Paris, 1927). After the split in the Menshevik *émigré* group at the end of World War II, the majority of the group, most of them former Martovites, in effect adopted Potresov's view of the Communist regime as a dictatorship of party bureaucracy over the rest of the population.

Bernsteinism

"Revisionism" in West European Marxist thought at the turn of the century was chiefly connected with the name of Eduard Bernstein, a German Social Democrat who had been influenced by the English evolutionary socialists of the Fabian Society. In a series of articles in 1896–98, Bernstein showed that Marx's predictions of progressive impoverishment of the proletariat in the advanced capitalist countries and of social polarization resulting from the disappearance of small enterprise had been wrong. He also advocated the abandonment by Social Democrats of the notion of socialist revolution as a seizure of power by violent means and the establishment of a dictatorship, identifying this notion as a "Jacobin" element in Marx's thinking. Bernstein's articles found a wide response in Russia (he even claimed that the majority of Russian Social Democrats were on his side), but there was only a small group of people who fully accepted his views and called themselves Russian Bernsteinians. The theorists of this small group were E. D. Kuskova (1869–1959) and her husband S. N. Prokopovich (1871–1955), a couple who in some ways resembled Sidney and Beatrice Webb in England. They had been among the first Marxist Social Democrats in Moscow in the early 1890's and were later associated with editing *Workers' Thought,* an illegal newspaper published by the St. Petersburg Union of Struggle in the late 1890's with the aim of reflecting the workers' own views. In 1897, Kuskova drafted a document that became known as *Credo;* not intended for publication, it was printed by Plekhanov abroad. In it, Kuskova maintained that a separate Social Democratic party was premature in Russia and that Russian Marxists should participate in the constitutional movement of the liberal bourgeoisie while assisting the workers in their efforts to improve their economic position. This view, which can be described as genuine Economism, had little in common with the ideas of those who, as we have seen, were also labeled Economists by Lenin and Plekhanov and who never doubted the desirability of a Social Democratic party but thought that it should be partly guided by workers and should have their immediate interests at heart.

The Prokopovich couple left the Social Democratic Party, in 1900–1904 took an active part in the formation of the political Masonic organization referred to earlier and of the Union of Liberation, and in 1905 took up a position to the left of the Constitutional Democrats. Continuing the tradition of undogmatic social reformism, they were among the founders of the trade unions after the 1905 revolution, were active in the cooperative movement, and exercised a strong influence on the semi-socialist deputies of the State Duma who were known as the Labor Group. The political Masonic organization, which was composed of members of various liberal and socialist parties and of nonparty intellectuals, was active during World War I in furthering the war effort, largely prepared the overthrow of the monarchy in 1917, supplied most of the leading members of the Provisional Government, and inspired many of the Provisional Government's administrative and social reforms. Prokopovich himself entered the Provisional Government as Minister of Food. Opposing the Bolshevik seizure of power, the Prokopoviches disapproved of violent methods and took no part in the Civil War, but were active in the committee that in 1921 secured foreign help for the victims of famine in Russia. In 1922, they were expelled from Russia, together with many other leading intellectuals, and, living in Prague and later in Geneva, devoted themselves to the academic study of economic and social conditions in Russia and to the advocacy of a peaceful and gradual evolution of the Soviet regime toward democracy.

Bogdanovism

Apart from the genuine Economists, there were two main groups of "revisionists" in Russian Social Democracy around the turn of the century. One comprised almost all the leading young

Marxists of the mid-1890's, with Struve at their head. These thinkers, commonly known as Legal Marxists, soon abandoned Marxism and Social Democracy altogether, and they will be considered in the chapter dealing with twentieth-century reformism. The other was a group of equally young and very enthusiastic men headed by Bogdanov. While Struve and his friends abandoned Marxism for neo-Kantian idealism, Bogdanov was drawn in the opposite direction—toward Positivism.

A. A. Bogdanov (his real name was Malinovsky, 1873–1928) was a physician by profession, and his scientific training had a strong influence upon his whole thinking. Having joined a Social Democratic circle in Kharkov in the mid-1890's, he soon distinguished himself as a theorist and propagandist and was banished to the north of European Russia. The several years he spent in banishment were devoted to intensive philosophical discussions with his fellow exiles (among whom were Lunacharsky and Berdyaev) and to writing. Bogdanov favored Lenin's "political" trend within the Social Democratic Party, and in 1904, when Lenin had lost control of the party apparatus (the Bolshevik Central Committee turning against him), Bogdanov joined forces with him and set up in Russia a network of unstatutory Leninist organizations of "stone-hard Bolsheviks" that recaptured the Bolshevik faction of the party. During the revolution of 1905-7, Bogdanov was a recognized leader of the Bolshevik faction, second only to Lenin. The break beween them came in 1909 (when they were both living in emigration), and the reasons for it—still not completely clear to historians—involved a dispute over the control of party funds as well as a disagreement on tactics. Bogdanov disapproved of Lenin's view that the revolution had ended and that the party now had to concentrate on the use of "front" organizations. Bogdanov headed the break-away left-wing subfaction "Forward," which disintegrated after a few years, returned to Russia after an amnesty in 1913, and during World War I served as a military surgeon. He was very active as a publicist in 1917 and was the inspirer and intellectual leader of an educational mass organization called "Proletarian Culture," formed in 1917 before the Bolshevik coup, which preserved its autonomy until 1919. Treasuring his intellectual independence,

Bogdanov did not rejoin the Bolshevik party after 1917, and consistently declined offers of high political office. In 1923, he left politics and thereafter devoted himself to problems of blood transfusion, founding the first institute of blood transfusion in Russia; he died as a result of performing an experiment upon himself.

Bogdanov's theoretical views were developed in a number of books published between 1896 and 1929: *A Short Course of Economic Science; From the Psychology of Society; Empiriomonism; A Course of Political Economy; Tectology, A Universal Organizational Science; The Science of Social Consciousness; Problems of Socialism; On Proletarian Culture, 1904–1924;* etc. At the center of Bogdanov's thought and activities was a striving for harmony: He was always preoccupied with problems of achieving harmony in thought, between thought and actions, and in social life. He considered himself to be a Marxist and a Social Democrat, but he went his own way in his treatment of Marxian teaching. Bogdanov found the doctrine of dialectical materialism unsatisfactory in the light of modern thought. It had been the first attempt to work out a proletarian world outlook and it had been based on the materialistic philosophy of the contemporary bourgeoisie. But meanwhile a new class had arisen, the technical intelligentsia, which had produced its own philosophy of empirio-criticism—a modern version of Positivism—developed by Mach, Avenarius, and Petzoldt. The proletariat, Bogdanov thought, now had to build on the basis of this modern philosophy, which was intellectually far superior to the old materialism. He denied the universal nature of dialectical processes, and where he did see them taking place he laid the stress on the equilibrium before and after the struggle between opposite tendencies. The Marxist doctrine of historical materialism seemed on the whole acceptable to Bogdanov, though it also was deficient. It failed to explain satisfactorily the phenomenon of ideology, and some of its basic concepts were imprecise and ambiguous—in particular the concept of the "economic structure" of society (because it includes "property relations," although law in general is regarded as a part of superstructure or ideology) and that of the productive forces (because it includes both the material means of production and the mental faculties of the producers). There was in fact little left of traditional historical materialism in Bogdanov's social philosophy. He defined society as "a system of cooperation in the widest sense of the word"; ideology as "an organizing method in the work and the struggle of society for existence"; custom, law, and morality as "a special series of organizing methods directed toward achieving the most harmonious mutual relations between people in the social process of labor"; progress as "an increase in the fullness and harmony of conscious human life"; and maintained that social existence and social consciousness were, "in the exact meaning of these words," identical.

With these general notions on society, Bogdanov viewed history as a process primarily motivated by the need to struggle against nature and the resulting technical advance (including scientific research), with various organizing methods (or adjustments—the Russian word used is *prisposoblenie*) being as a rule developed accordingly to facilitate and ensure further progress. Bogdanov did not ignore instances of retrogression, attributing them to the failure of one or another ideological form. He distinguished three main stages in historical development, each with an integrated system of economy, ideological forms, and types of thought. The first is the stage of authoritarian society, with a natural self-sufficient economy, authoritarian institutions, and religion as an authoritarian form of thought. The second stage is that of exchange economy, with individualist norms of behavior and speculative thought, a variety of philosophic schools, and a multiplication of the branches of science and learning. It is at this stage that the individual human personality, whose emergence had marked the transition from the authoritarian society, acquires considerable autonomy. This autonomy, however, which at first contributes to progress, later becomes an obstacle to further progress, since the strife of individual interests contradicts the unifying tendencies of the machine age. The victory of these tendencies will inaugurate the third main stage in history— that of the collective self-sufficient economy and "the fusion of personal lives into one colossal whole, harmonious in the relations of its parts, systematically grouping all elements for one common struggle—the struggle against the endless spontaneity of nature.

. . . An enormous mass of creative activity, spontaneous and conscious, is necessary in order to solve this task. It demands the forces not of man but of mankind—and only working upon this task does mankind as such emerge." All ideological forms, including philosophy and the sciences, merge at this stage into one "universal organizational science" necessary for the great task of harmonizing the efforts of mankind. Bogdanov undertook to lay the theoretical foundations of this future all-embracing science, which he called tectology. This argument reveals, as does his later concern with saving and prolonging human lives through blood transfusion, a strong Fëdorovist streak in Bogdanov's thought, although it could be argued that Bogdanov further developed here some ideas that can be found in a rudimentary form in the writings of Marx and Engels.

Bogdanov's theory of revolution also differs from the traditional Marxist approach. According to him "even fairly considerable differences between the elements of a whole do not yet mean that contradictions are necessary; contradictions arise . . . only when these elements are not merely different but also *develop in different directions.* However, in this case too, the possibility of eliminating contradictions through organizing adjustments does not completely disappear. . . . There is only one case when differences between elements of a social whole must turn into an insoluble contradiction, and that is when the groups of society develop in *opposite directions:* one in a progressive direction toward expanding the struggle against external nature and perfecting the means of productive work, the other in a regressive direction toward parasitism and the consumption of products of the labor of others." In such a situation a revolution occurs and the progressive class takes over the direction of society, provided that it has developed the necessary organizational abilities (e.g., the bourgeoisie in the French Revolution)—otherwise the elimination of the parasitic class in the revolution will lead to retrogression and a general decline of society similar to that which marked the transition from antiquity to the Middle Ages.

This is the root of Bogdanov's idea of proletarian culture, which in his view should be essentially identical with the future socialist culture. A practical program for the development of this

new culture was devised by him in *Cultural Tasks of Our Time,*
published in 1910. The two central tasks were the creation of a
"proletarian encyclopedia," which should play a role analogous
to that played by the great French *Encyclopédie,* and the establishment of a workers' university as a comprehensive educational
and scientific institution outside the existing educational system
and academic bodies and in the end to supersede them. The chief
task of these undertakings, and thus the main content of proletarian culture, would be the elaboration and implementation of
Bogdanov's "tectological" views.

Seen against this theoretical background, the Russian revolution of 1905 had the task of removing the survivals of the authoritarian period, and it failed because neither the bourgeoisie nor
the proletariat had the necessary organizational abilities to take
over. The revolution of 1917 had to complete the task by securing a democratic order of society, eliminating in the process those
retrogressive authoritarian features in social life whose emergence had been caused by the war. Bogdanov constantly warned
against utopianism and "maximalism," against expecting the
realization of socialism "tomorrow," against the view that socialism "first conquers and then is implemented." "As long as the
working class does not control its organizational tools, and, on the
contrary, is controlled by them . . . it obviously cannot and
must not attempt to solve directly the organizational task of the
world, to implement socialism." Under a democratic republic it
was possible to use parliamentary methods for settling the contradictions of interests, for counting the forces, for finding out
what concessions are necessary, for peaceful subordination of the
side that turned out to be the weaker but expects to become
stronger in the future. Under Lenin's "republic of Soviets" this
way out was closed, and there was a great risk of a civil war involving "a colossal squandering of the best forces of the nation."
Lenin's plan, a product of the authoritarian way of thinking, was
completely incompatible with a scientific conception of the state
and of class relations. The task of the proletariat in Russia, as in
other countries, was, while continuing the former struggle and
the organization, "consciously and consistently to gather, develop
and systematize the emerging germs of the new culture—the ele-

ments of socialism in the present." The gradual "creative realization of the socialist class order" would in the end lead the proletariat "to that victory which will transform this order into one embracing all humanity. Socialist development will find its consummation in the socialist revolution."

The essence of Bogdanov's approach to Marxism—finding obsolete elements and gaps in the Marxian doctrine and trying to replace them and fill the gaps by modern ideas or by products of one's own thought—was shared by a number of other Social Democratic theorists, most of them Bolsheviks. They first appeared as a distinct trend in the symposium *Essays in Realistic Philosophy* (1904); two more collections followed in 1908 and 1909—*Essays in the Philosophy of Marxism* and *Essays in the Philosophy of Collectivism*—and in the latter year the Bogdanovists formed the separate faction Forward within the Social Democratic Party. But before this split, the majority of prominent Bolshevik intellectuals were Bogdanovists, and Plekhanov deplored the fact that Bogdanovism appeared to be the official Bolshevik philosophy. A whole bunch of Bogdanovist theories was developed by these people, of which the following had a more direct bearing on political thought: S. Vol'sky's ethics (*Philosophy of Struggle*, 1909); M. N. Pokrovsky's conception of history; M. A. Reisner's legal theory (*The Theory of Petrazhitsky, Marxism and Social Ideology*, 1908); and the religious theory of "god-building" advanced by A. V. Lunacharsky in his *Religion and Socialism* (2 vols., 1908–1911) and by Maxim Gorky in his *Confession* (1908). To these were added, after 1917, P. P. Blonsky's theory of education (*The Unified Labor School*, 1919), A. M. Kollontay's "winged Eros" theory of sex relations, and P. M. Kerzhentsev's theory of the "scientific organization of labor" as the real essence of socialism. In 1917, most Bogdanovists joined the Proletarian Culture organization and rejoined the Bolshevik party, and until Stalin consolidated his power in the late 1920's and early 1930's, the Bogdanovists were in charge of the educational and cultural policy of the Soviet Government (Lunacharsky being the Commissar—Minister—of Education until 1929, and Pokrovsky Deputy Commissar until his death in 1932).

12. Communism

COMMUNISM first began to be distinguished from socialism in the 1860's, when Chernyshevsky accepted the view, then widely held in Western Europe, that communism represented a higher degree of socialization; he thought that it was therefore a higher social ideal and would be reached later than socialism. Tkachëv was the next prominent adherent of the communist ideal; unlike Chernyshevsky, however, he did not relegate its realization to a distant future but stated that the introduction of communist features would be the immediate task of the revolutionary dictatorship that was to be established after the overthrow of the existing regime. After the 1870's, the term "communism" was chiefly used by anarchists (among whom, as we have seen, there was a communist trend) until Lenin adopted the title *Kommunist* for a journal he and Bukharin edited in 1915.

However, the Chernyshevsky-Tkachëv tradition in the revolutionary movement had continued uninterrupted, though its adherents had for a time lost sight of the distinction between socialism and communism. What distinguished them from all other revolutionaries and socialists was their acceptance of the Ogarëvist views on revolutionary organization and, to a lesser extent, on strategy and tactics. After the disintegration of the People's Will Party in the early 1880's, some of its peripheral adherents and admirers abandoned the practice of terrorism as useless and concentrated on building strong underground organizations, training revolutionary leaders from among young radical intellectuals, and propagating socialist ideas among the intelligentsia and the industrial workers; like the People's Will, they neglected agitation. Organizations of this type existed in the 1880's in most university cities of European Russia, with branches in other towns.

They had no common name, but since they all stressed the preparatory nature of their activities, it may be appropriate to call the whole trend "preparatory." Existing side by side with Social Democratic organizations, the organizations of the preparatory trend at first distinguished themselves from the former, but gradually they themselves fell under a strong Marxist influence, and by the early 1890's, most of their members regarded themselves as Social Democrats. They differed from the early Social Democrats principally in their strong elitist feeling, which expressed itself in the existence of different degrees of initiation and a rejection of electoral practices within the organizations and in their extensive use of "front" organizations. The typical features of the more Marxist wing of the preparatory trend later crystallized in Leninism.

The subsequent development of the Communist doctrine and practice can be divided into three stages: Leninist, Stalinist, and the post-Stalin Neo-Leninist.

Leninism

V. I. Lenin (1870–1924), whose real name was Ulyanov, was the son of an official in the provincial school administration in the Volga area who shortly before his death had become a hereditary nobleman by virtue of the rank he had attained in government service. On his mother's side Lenin was of German origin. His elder brother joined the People's Will Party and was executed in 1887 for an attempt on the life of Alexander III, but he also belonged to the St. Petersburg organization of the preparatory trend and held Marxist views on economics and the philosophy of history. Lenin entered Kazan University in 1887, but was expelled almost immediately for participating in student disorders; however, he took the final examination in law as an external student at St. Petersburg University in 1891, receiving the highest marks in all subjects. He was a practicing lawyer for a year or two, but soon abandoned his practice to devote himself entirely to revolutionary activities and became what he later called a professional revolutionary. In 1887–93, he belonged to several circles of the preparatory trend in the Volga area, gradually becoming a leading figure among the more specifically Marxist wing of that trend. In 1893, he moved to St. Petersburg and joined the so-called Elders' Circle, whose leading members had likewise belonged to the preparatory trend and which was chiefly concerned with propagating Marxism among factory workers. He also joined Struve's circle of young Marxist theorists. Lenin took an active part in the Marxists' campaign against Populism, writing three pamphlets which were produced illegally under the common title *What Are the 'Friends of the People' and How They Wage War Against the Social Democrats.* At the same time, he turned against Struve's qualified acceptance of Marxism (in the article "The Economic Content of Populism and Its Critique in Mr. Struve's Book"), defining Struve's position as a "reflection of Marxism in bourgeois literature"; later he justified his cooperation with the "legal Marxists" as a tactical alliance. In 1895, Lenin accepted the tactics of agitation among the workers on the basis of their economic grievances, and together with Martov effected a fusion of their two circles (both of which had their roots in the preparatory trend) into the St. Petersburg Union of Struggle for the Liberation of the Working Class. Arrested in December, 1895, he spent more than a year in prison and was then banished to southern Siberia for three years. While in prison and banishment, he continued the theoretical argument against the Populists (*Development of Capitalism in Russia*, 1899), wrote a draft program for the Social Democratic Party which was about to be formed, and resolutely opposed all forms of "Economism."

The Russian Social Democratic Labor Party, which was formed in Lenin's absence in 1898, and which was essentially a fusion of the early Social Democrats with the Marxist wing of the preparatory trend, consisted of diverse elements—orthodox Marxist and revisionist, "Economist" and more politically minded. For Lenin, who had consistently upheld Marxist orthodoxy and opposed Economism, such a situation was intolerable, and he devised a plan of capturing the party with the help of an unstatutory organization within the party consisting of adherents of orthodoxy and "politics." Together with Martov and Potresov, who joined him in a triumvirate for this purpose, he formed such an organization—The Spark—after his return from banishment in 1900. He emigrated in the same year and lived abroad (chiefly in Munich, London, and Geneva) until 1905. In the pamphlet *What Is To Be Done?* (1902), which is the most important single work of Leninist theory, and in the *Letter to a Comrade on Our Organizational Tasks* (a kind of supplement to *What Is To Be Done?*), he laid down views on party organization and on political strategy and tactics to which he consistently adhered throughout his life and which have since formed the backbone of Communist political thought. The pamphlets were essentially a restatement of Ogarëvist views, culled from the writings of Chernyshevsky and Tkachëv (besides the published writings of Ogarëv himself), as well as from the publications and the practice of the People's Will Party and the organizations of the preparatory trend, reinforced and supplemented by similar views of Marx, Engels, and Kautsky; the principal ideas of the two pamphlets can be summarized as follows:

The role of the vanguard fighter in the political struggle can be fulfilled only by a party that is guided by an advanced theory. Personal conviction and success in the political struggle are the two criteria by which the "advanced" theory can be recognized (though Lenin does not say so in so many words). Because of the function of theory in the political struggle, any departure from it means to weaken one's own side and to strengthen the enemy. Theories develop in the heads of intellectuals and are not born spontaneously among the masses, and socialist theory is no exception to this rule. Left to themselves, the workers merely produce demands aimed at improving their position in relation to the employers. A policy based solely on these demands is essentially a bourgeois policy, since it leaves the employee-employer relationship intact. The task of revolutionary Social Democracy is to struggle against the "spontaneity" of the labor movement in order to divert it from this "bourgeois" path. The opposite concept to spontaneity is "consciousness," by which Lenin means acceptance by the workers of the correct revolutionary and socialist theory. The labor movement is the main, but not the only movement, and the industrial workers the main, but not the only class, that must be utilized by the party. All classes and groups of the population which are opposed, for whatever reason, to the enemy

one is fighting must be utilized. From these strategic principles follow the tactical precepts. To win the cooperation of an individual
or a group, one must appear as the champion of the cause that this
person or group holds to be of paramount importance. Every
such particular cause should, if possible, be reduced to a general
one, or at least made to appear as an aspect of a wider cause—this
is clear from Lenin's insistence on substituting a general antagonism to the autocracy for the different grievances of the various
social, religious, and ethnic groups in Russia. In any given situation, one should try to find a key task ("the decisive link," as
Lenin called it later), the solution of which would lead to the
solution of all the main tasks of the movement. The idea of the
"decisive link" was new both to the Ogarëvist tradition and to
Marxist doctrine. Lenin's views on the structure and internal
functioning of the party and of organizations controlled or influenced by the party are purely Ogarëvist. The sole source of
authority is the party center. It delegates as much authority as is
expedient to a multiplicity of "executive agents," all of whom are
absolutely responsible to it. No other focus of loyalty is permissible, no minor leaders with authority of their own. Fixed rules of
procedure are of little importance and may be replaced by regular
reports to the higher party authority on all aspects of each group's
life and work.

What Is To Be Done? and the *Letter to a Comrade* were intended to guide Lenin's followers in the Spark organization in
their efforts to conquer the Social Democratic Party from within.
Additional instructions were given in numerous letters from
Lenin to his adherents, and these letters constitute an important
source of our knowledge of Lenin's political thought. The main
conclusion to which a study of these letters leads is that Lenin
was free from moral scruples in matters of politics; he frequently
urged his supporters and agents to disregard rules, agreements,
and promises, while at the same time insisting that they should,
whenever opportune, make use of legitimate means and legalistic
arguments. The efforts of the Spark were crowned with success:
the Sparkists captured several local committees of the party, secured the collaboration of several other organizations and groupings, and packed the second congress of the party in 1903 with

their supporters. The success was ensured mainly by the activities
of the network of mobile agents of the center, the importance of
which Lenin had rightly stressed in *What Is To Be Done?*. Similar
unstatutory organizations were resorted to by Lenin in 1904, 1906,
and again in 1910–12, each time after he had lost control of the
party apparatus and each time with considerable success. On each
occasion, Lenin's closest collaborators of the moment, who had
recognized him as their leader because of particular policies
championed by him at the time, were unable to adjust themselves
to his refusal to treat them as equal partners and to his tendency
to impose changes of policy as he thought fit. The first such division occurred at the second congress of the party in 1903, when
the Sparkists themselves split into the "hard" and the "soft"; this
led to the split of the whole party into a Leninist ("Bolshevik,"
i.e., "Majority") and an anti-Leninist ("Menshevik," i.e., "Minority") faction, roughly along the lines of the former division
between the Social Democrats and the preparatory trend. In 1904,
when the majority of the Bolshevik faction took up a conciliatory
attitude toward the Mensheviks, Lenin, together with Bogdanov,
organized a radical subfaction of "stone-hard" Bolsheviks with an
unstatutory central body (the Bureau of the Majority Committees) and a network of agents to recapture the party apparatus.
When the whole party was officially reunited in 1906, Lenin
formed a secret Bolshevik center, which coordinated the activities
of his adherents even after 1907, when the Bolsheviks secured a
majority in the Central Committee. Having broken with Bogdanov and other radicals in 1909, partly over the issue of the utilization of legal opportunities under the new constitutional regime
(a policy rejected by the radicals), Lenin in the following year lost
the support of the "conciliatory," or "party-minded," Bolsheviks;
the latter opposed the practice of "expropriations," i.e., armed
robberies with the purpose of replenishing the Bolshevik chest,
and were against a new split with the Mensheviks, who also opposed such robberies. A conference called by an unstatutory organizing commission and consisting of a dozen hand-picked Leninists, declared that it had the authority of a party congress, elected
from among its members a "central committee," and "expelled"
from the party in advance all those who would not recognize this

central committee. Lenin's activities before 1917 thus consisted to
a large extent of conspiring within and against the Russian Social
Democratic Labor Party of which he was ostensibly a member;
and all along he taught his followers the art of such intraparty
conspiracy.

The use made by Lenin of whatever party organization he had
at his disposal was always consistent with the principles that he
had laid down in *What Is To Be Done?*. His aim was to weaken
and ultimately to overthrow the existing government, whether
autocratic as before 1906, semiconstitutional as between 1906 and
1917, or democratically-minded as after the February revolution
of 1917. Almost any other parties and groups that would cooperate were welcomed by him as temporary allies, open or secret,
according to circumstances. Nonparty organizations such as trade
unions, cooperatives, educational associations, and, in 1905 and
1917, Soviets of Workers' (and in 1917 also Soldiers') Deputies
were extensively used as front organizations.

The party could operate effectively only if it carefully studied
the changing circumstances in which it had to act. This, in Lenin's
view, meant appreciation of long-term trends of social development as well as of shifts in the balance of political power. Having
in the 1880's and 1890's accepted and actively propagated Plekhanov's view that Russia had entered the capitalist stage of economic and social development, Lenin returned to this problem
during World War I. Adopting Rosa Luxemburg's view of monopolistic capitalism, Hilferding's theory of the role of banks in
the monopolistic stage of capitalism, and Hobson's economic
theory of imperialism, Lenin (following in the footsteps of Bukharin, who had done a similar job a year earlier) in 1916 wrote
his *Imperialism as the Highest Stage of Capitalism*. According to
the criteria used by Lenin in this treatise, Russia, although it had
entered the capitalist path later than the principal countries of
Western Europe and the United States, had already reached the
last stage of capitalist development, that immediately preceding
a socialist revolution. Lenin did not suggest that there was anything peculiarly Russian in this; indeed, Japan—where capitalism
was even younger than in Russia—was also included in his list of
the most advanced capitalist countries. The explanation lay in

the unequal rate of development of different countries under capitalism, especially toward the end of the capitalist epoch, when all the contradictions inherent in it became particularly sharp. The unevenness of capitalist development at the imperialist stage made it possible to find the weakest spot in the imperialist "front." For a number of reasons, Russia was this weakest spot, and a socialist break-through was therefore easier in Russia than elsewhere. Yet despite this apparent theoretical certainty, Lenin twice in 1917 displayed a curious lack of conviction of victory. Shortly before the outbreak of the February revolution, he delivered a speech in Switzerland (he had again lived in emigration after 1907, chiefly in Paris, Austria, and Switzerland) in which he expressed doubts about the chances of people of his generation seeing the revolution in Russia. And later in the year, when urging the Bolshevik Central Committee to hurry up with the intended coup aimed at filling the power vacuum—in his own words, picking up the power that was lying in the street—he repeatedly said: "Now or never!" Like Tkachëv before him, Lenin feared that the bourgeoisie might establish a stable government (in this case a democratic one).

What should happen after a successful revolution? Like all Marxists, Lenin distinguished between a bourgeois revolution, which would establish a democratic government and thus remove all obstacles to the further development of capitalism but also greatly facilitate socialist propaganda and organization, and a subsequent proletarian revolution, which would inaugurate a transition to socialism. Accordingly, the program of the Russian Social Democratic Labor Party adopted in 1903, which had been drafted by Plekhanov and Lenin, was divided into a minimum and a maximum program. The former included the overthrow of the autocracy and the establishment of a democratic republic, an eight-hour working day, the return to the peasants of those agricultural lands which they had cultivated before the abolition of serfdom but which had been retained by the landlords, as well as the equality of all peoples inhabiting Russia and their right to self-determination. The maximum program spoke of a socialist revolution and of a dictatorship of the proletariat during the period of transition to socialism. "Dictatorship of the proletariat" was a Marxian concept that had not been adopted by the Social Democratic parties of Western Europe, and its revival by the Russian party marked an important stage in the process of theoretical differentiation between Social Democratism and Communism. Considering the special conditions of Russia, Lenin accepted Plekhanov's idea of a "hegemony of the proletariat" in the coming bourgeois revolution. But, unlike Plekhanov, he appreciated the potentially revolutionary nature of the peasantry, and in his *Two Tactics of Social Democracy in a Democratic Revolution* (1905) he defined the regime to be established after such a revolution as a "revolutionary democratic dictatorship of the proletariat and the peasantry." In a series of articles and pamphlets written in 1917 (of which the "April Theses" and *State and Revolution* are the most important), he argued that the strong position of the Soviets of Workers' and Soldiers' Deputies within the system of "dyarchy" that followed the overthrow of the monarchy meant in effect that the "revolutionary democratic dictatorship of the proletariat and the peasantry" had been realized and that the party should immediately proceed to the socialist revolution.

Three different levels are discernible in Lenin's argument in 1917: abstract theoretical, practical organizational, and demagogic. On the abstract theoretical level, which also had a demagogic tinge (especially in *State and Revolution*), he argued that the bourgeois state machine should be completely broken and an entirely new mechanism of the dictatorship of the proletariat put in its place; that the replacement of the democratic republic by a "republic of Soviets" (which was a suitable form for the new state machine) would mean the replacement of "formal" democracy by "genuine democracy of the toiling masses"; that the business of government would be so simplified under the dictatorship of the proletariat that every cook would be able to govern the state. He also revived the old differentiation between socialism and communism as being mainly concerned with distribution: socialism provided for distribution according to work done, communism according to need. On the practical organizational level, Lenin argued that "state capitalism"—that is, the measures adopted during the war to control and mobilize the country's economy for the war effort—had created many forms of economic control and administration which could simply be taken over and used for running the large-scale industry, banks, etc., that were to be nationalized; that the Socialist Revolutionaries' program of confiscation of all privately owned land and its distribution among the peasants should be adopted; that the party should make all the necessary practical preparations for the seizure of power, such as forming and training armed detachments of sympathizers from among factory workers, securing Bolshevik majorities in the soviets of Workers' and Soldiers' Deputies in the main cities and in the committees of army units garrisoned in these cities, etc. On the demagogic level, Lenin manipulated with extreme skill a multiplicity of slogans designed to appeal to diverse social and political groups among the population, winning over some of them and neutralizing others. The most important of these slogans (some of which were taken over from the Socialist Revolutionaries, syndicalists, pacifists, etc.) were: "All power to the soviets"; "Peace to all peoples"; "Factories for the workers"; "Workers' control in factories"; "Land for the peasants"; "Bread for the hungry"; and "Loot what has been looted." The seizure of power itself was carried out under the pretext that the Provisional Government of Kerensky was deliberately delaying the elections to the Constituent Assembly and was preparing to suppress the Soviets.

Lenin became the head of the government that was formed after the coup of November, 1917, and remained in this post until his death. It is often held that with the change of task—from the destruction of the monarchy and of the capitalist order to the construction of a new order—Lenin's approach to many political problems changed from that of an underground revolutionary to that of a statesman. This view ignores the fact that Lenin's approach had basically always been positive—achieving power is no less positive a task than maintaining, extending, and intensifying it; all these tasks can be looked at as different stages or aspects of the one general task of maximizing one's power. And a close analysis of Lenin's activities leaves little doubt that this was how he himself perceived the problem. The main instrument remained the same—the Party, now renamed the Russian Communist Party (Bolsheviks). Its many subsidiary organizations, which had previously been used as "fronts," now became "transmission belts" from the Party to the masses. The state apparatus took its place as the most important subsidiary organization of the Party. The process of takeover largely consisted in grafting onto various branches of the state apparatus embryonic organizations with somewhat similar functions that had already existed (in accordance with the provisions of *What Is To Be Done?*) in the Party or as its subsidiaries. Lenin's tactics also remained the same: attracting people to particular policies and generalizing the resulting attachment into attachment to the "Soviet power"; suppressing dissidents and opponents by administrative means, both within the Bolshevik Party (the process culminating in the general prohibition by the Tenth Party Congress in 1921 for Party members to form organized factions) and outside it (the gradual outlawing of all other parties by 1922); making concessions and retreats when opportune from the point of view of maximizing the power of the Party and of himself as its leader (the most notable examples being the toleration of non-Communist views held by "bourgeois specialists," whose cooperation in running the economy was essential, and the abandonment in 1921 of the policy of "War Communism" in the face of peasant resistance). The freedom from moral scruples characteristic of Lenin as a politician before 1917 was clearly discernible when he was the head of the government; it expressed itself, for example, in dispersing the Constituent Assembly, signing a separate peace treaty with Germany (events which precipitated the Civil War), receiving financial assistance from the German Government in 1917–18, the conquering by the Red Army of several of the independent states that had been established in 1917–18 by various non-Russian peoples in the border areas of the former Russian Empire, and resorting to terror on a large scale even after the end of the Civil War.

The political regime established after the seizure of power by the Bolsheviks was described as Soviet power. The ideas of the division of powers, as well as of universal and equal franchise, direct elections and secret ballot, were expressly rejected as bourgeois. The supreme authority in the state was, according to the Constitution of 1918, the All-Russian Congress of Soviets of Workers', Peasants', and Red Armists' Deputies elected by provincial

congresses, which in turn were elected by town and district Soviets. People who before 1917 had belonged to privileged estates
(nobility, clergy, and merchants), as well as those who were or had
been employing hired labor, were disfranchised; the vote of an
urban resident weighed five times as much as the vote of a peasant. This was only one aspect of a comprehensive system of legal
inequality introduced by the Bolsheviks, who thus undid the
achievement of the Provisional Government, which had decreed
the full equality of all citizens before the law. The privileged position of the urban workers was meant to substantiate, if only
for appearances' sake, the theory that the Soviet system was a dictatorship of the proletariat. In fact, the Bolshevik Party, which
was not assigned any governmental functions by the Constitution,
managed all elections as it wished with the help of such devices as
voting by show of hands and terror against members of other
parties. The 1918 Constitution described Russia as a Socialist
Federal Soviet Republic. The term "federal" in this official name
of the state lacked a precise meaning, since the government structure described in the Constitution was not federal. However,
when the Union of Soviet Socialist Republics was formed in 1922,
Lenin (who had previously favored unitary government but now
thought that a concession to federalists was opportune) insisted
on giving it a quasi-federal structure, with the four constituent
republics of the Union (R.S.F.S.R., the Ukraine, Belorussia, and
the Transcaucasian Socialist Federal Soviet Republic) being ostensibly equal. Yet the federal structure had little substance, for
the real holder of power everywhere, the Communist Party, was
strictly centralized.

There were three major phases of the administrative, economic,
and social policies pursued by Lenin's government. The first
lasted for a few months, from the October coup until the middle
of 1918. It was the period of the takeover of the central and local
administrative apparatus; of the elimination of local government
combined with the practice described as "local power" (when the
local organs of the new regime exercised considerable discretion
in implementing the policies decreed by the central government);
of the "agrarian revolution," i.e., nationalization (without compensation) of all land and its distribution for use by the peasants

on an egalitarian basis; and "workers' control" in industry, exercised by factory committees. The second phase is known as the period of War Communism (1918–21). This policy was aimed at supporting the Bolshevik effort in the Civil War and at accomplishing rapidly the transition to conditions of communism, despite Lenin's earlier view that there should be a prolonged intermediate period of socialism. In practice, the period was marked by the nationalization (without compensation) of industry and trade and their management by centralized state agencies; wages in kind for workers and employees; compulsory food deliveries by the peasants; and obligatory labor service by the bourgeoisie. The Bolsheviks won the Civil War, but by the end of it, the country's economy was ruined and the peasants antagonized. The New Economic Policy, inaugurated in 1921 on Lenin's initiative, was designed to restore the economy by making concessions to private enterprise in agriculture, industry, and trade, and to neutralize the peasants politically. The policy was successful, but Lenin did not live to see its full effect.

Little needs to be said about Lenin's views on foreign affairs, for they were essentially an extension of his views on internal political matters. He seems to have been equally hostile to all "bourgeois" governments (that is, governments not controlled by his party or its close associates)—whether in Russia, in independent states that formed themselves after 1917 in various parts of former Imperial Russian territory, or in foreign countries. According to circumstances, he fought them, made peace with them, tried to keep them neutral or to attract them to his side, rather in the same way as he treated different political groupings within Russia. After 1917, in relations with foreign states, he simultaneously used both the conventional instruments of foreign policy and the Communist International, founded in 1919 as a special apparatus for undermining foreign governments from within their own countries. Thus in this field as in others, he remained true to the main political ideas which he had formulated at the turn of the century.

The second most prominent Communist politician of the Leninist period was L. D. Trotsky (real name Bronstein, 1879–1940). The son of a Jewish farmer from the southern Ukraine, he became involved in underground Social Democratic activities while a first-year student at Odessa University and was arrested and banished to Siberia. Escaping from banishment, he became a professional revolutionary, joined Lenin's Spark organization, and distinguished himself as a brilliant journalist. When the Social Democratic Party split in 1903, he became one of the leaders of the Mensheviks, predicting that adherence to Lenin's organizational principles would result in a one-man dictatorship. From then on, until he joined the Bolsheviks after the February revolution in 1917, he tried to reunite all the factions and subfactions into which the Russian Social Democratic Labor Party was perpetually splitting. Unlike Lenin, who kept in the background, Trotsky was one of the most familiar public figures during the 1905 and the 1917 revolutions, becoming on both occasions chairman of the Soviet of Workers' Deputies in St. Petersburg. He was Lenin's foremost collaborator in preparing the seizure of power and was the chief architect of the coup in Petrograd. He became Commissar (Minister) for Foreign Affairs in Lenin's government formed after the coup, but changed to Military and Naval Affairs when he disagreed with Lenin on the issue of the Brest-Litovsk peace treaty with Germany in 1918 and lost his erstwhile majority on this issue in the Party's Central Committee. He was the chief organizer and leader of the Red Army during the Civil War and was generally regarded as the second man in the Party leadership, though he again opposed Lenin in the Party-wide debate in 1920–21 on the role of trade unions. Trotsky lost the struggle for power after Lenin's death, was dismissed from all his leading positions, expelled from the Party, banished to Central Asia, and finally expelled from the U.S.S.R. (in 1929). Having had many adherents not only in the Russian Communist Party but also in the other parties of the Communist International (of which he had been a leader), he organized them into a Fourth International and continued bitterly to attack Stalin and his rule until he was murdered in Mexico by Stalin's agents.

Trotsky considered himself a Leninist from 1917 until his death, and his political thought during this period was an important variety of Leninism. Less flexible than Lenin, and more strongly influenced by the Social Democratic view that a socialist

revolution in the most advanced capitalist countries was necessary
for a transition to socialism anywhere, he thought that the Russian revolution could only succeed if it sparked off proletarian
revolutions in Western Europe. Hence his opposition to the peace
treaty with Germany in 1918, and later to Stalin's policy of first
"building socialism in one country." The same lack of flexi-
bility showed itself when Trotsky advocated turning the trade
unions into a part of the state apparatus to a greater extent than
they already were. But his disagreements with Lenin after 1917
were of minor importance compared to his acceptance of Lenin's
views on the role of the Party and on the methods of Party rule,
including terror (*The Defense of Terrorism,* 1921). Trotsky's interpretation of Leninism after Lenin's death is of greater importance. It began in 1924, with the publication of his pamphlet
Lessons of October. According to Trotsky's understanding of the
events of 1917, Lenin, after the overthrow of the monarchy, had
been converted to the idea of "permanent revolution" to which
Trotsky himself had adhered since 1905. The term "permanent
revolution" had been used by Marx, but had not been adopted
by anyone else except the Russo-German Social Democrat Parvus
and by Trotsky. It meant that a bourgeois revolution might in
certain circumstances grow into a proletarian revolution without
an intervening period of bourgeois rule, and Trotsky was convinced that this was the right solution for Russia. It seems that
Trotsky was substantially right in thinking that Lenin also had
come to this conclusion in 1917. However, Trotsky almost certainly deviated from Lenin's way of thinking on matters of the
internal functioning of the Party. Having opposed Lenin's views
on this subject before 1917, he was then able to cooperate with
Lenin at a time when the latter, under the pressure of extreme
necessity, tolerated a considerable diversity of opinions among
Party members, including the advocacy of views opposed to his
own and, until 1921, even the existence of organized factions.
When Stalin reverted to Lenin's pre-1917 intolerance, Trotsky
perceived it as the abandonment of Lenin's practice, and he was
strengthened in this belief by Lenin's condemnation of Stalin's
excesses. Trotsky attributed Stalin's practices to a bureaucratic
(that is, to his Marxist way of thinking, bourgeois) degeneration

of the Party apparatus. This bureaucratic degeneration was facilitated by the New Economic Policy and by the idea of building socialism in one country, which dampened the revolutionary ardor of the Party and attracted bourgeois elements into its ranks. Salvation, according to Trotsky, lay in continuing the "permanent revolution"—a more strongly antipeasant policy at home and the fanning of Communist revolutions abroad. Although Trotsky and his followers were branded as deviationists and later as "enemies of the people" (most of them were executed or died in concentration camps), their thought in fact had a great practical significance. Stalin adopted the Trotskyists' idea of financing the industrialization of the country mainly at the expense of the peasants, and in our own days the Chinese Communist Party is advocating a Trotskyist revolutionary course for the Communist parties on the world scene. Trotsky's notion of a bourgeois degeneration of the Russian Communist Party after Lenin's death has greatly influenced many foreign observers and interpreters of the Soviet scene. It was also the starting point of the process of theorizing that culminated in James Burnham's theory of managerial revolution and managerial society.

The third outstanding theorist of Communism in its Leninist stage was N. I. Bukharin (1888–1938). The son of a school teacher from Moscow, he studied economics at Moscow and Vienna universities, though he did not bother to finish the courses at either. As early as 1905, he had joined a revolutionary organization of schoolboys, and from 1906, he was a member of the Bolshevik faction of the Social Democratic Party. Banished from Moscow to northern Russia in 1910, he escaped abroad and within a few years distinguished himself in polemics against the opponents of the Marxist economic doctrine (*Political Economy of the Leisure Class*, written in 1912–13, although it did not appear in print until 1919). During World War I, he took up the Leninist position of advocating defeat for one's own country and was active in the antiwar propaganda among Russian *émigrés* and among Social-Democrats of the countries in which he lived (Sweden, Norway, U.S.A.). In his second major work, *World Economy and Imperialism,* written in 1915, he largely anticipated Lenin's theory of imperialism. An attempt to edit a theoretical journal

(*The Communist*) jointly with Lenin had to be given up after the first issue because of Lenin's intolerance. Bukharin disagreed with Lenin on the questions of national self-determination (he thought, following Rosa Luxemburg, that this idea was harmful to the international solidarity of the proletariat) and of the fate of the state after the socialist revolution—unlike Lenin, he envisaged a speedy disappearance of the state. In 1917, Bukharin played a leading part in the preparation of the seizure of power in Moscow, and after the coup he became the editor of *Pravda* (*Truth*), the Party's chief daily paper. In 1918, he led the faction of "left-wing Communists" who bitterly opposed the conclusion of the Brest-Litovsk treaty and advocated a revolutionary war against Germany. And he again opposed Lenin in 1920–21, joining Trotsky in the debate on the trade unions. But despite these disagreements, Lenin retained respect and even affection for Bukharin and called him "the darling of the Party." Bukharin was the youngest and the most theoretically minded of the Party leaders. He was Lenin's chief collaborator in drafting the new Party program adopted in 1919, and took a leading part in drafting two programs of the Communist International.

Bukharin's somewhat mechanical and apolitical mind (Lenin said that he had never properly understood dialectics) always inclined to a most consistent and radical interpretation of whatever political position he occupied. In accordance with his general leftist standpoint at the time, he did not foresee in his *Economy of the Transition Period* (which was a theoretical justification of the policy of War Communism) the change-over to the New Economic Policy. But he accepted it when it came and became its most prominent advocate. He therefore sided with Stalin against Trotsky, Zinoviev, and other left-wing oppositionists in the mid-twenties, but opposed Stalin's adoption of Trotskyist policies against the peasants in 1928. As the theoretical leader of the Right Opposition, he lost his seat in the Party's Political Bureau, the editorship of *Pravda,* and the leadership of the Communist International (which he had taken over from Zinoviev in 1926). He repented, and even took part in drafting the Stalin Constitution of 1936, but was arrested in the following year, and in 1938 figured as the chief defendant at one of the big show trials of the Great Purge. He was accused of heading, together with Zinoviev, an underground "Bloc of Rightists and Trotskyites," alleged to be inspired by Trotsky from abroad and aimed at assassinating Stalin and other Stalinist Party leaders, the overthrow of the Soviet regime, and the restoration of capitalism. He confessed to all the charges, except those of having been in the pay of several foreign intelligence services and of having plotted the assassination of Lenin in 1918. For this stubbornness, the public prosecutor, Vyshinsky, called him a "damned bastard of a pig and a fox." Bukharin was condemned to death and shot.

As a political thinker, Bukharin was chiefly influenced by Marx, Plekhanov, Lenin, and Bogdanov, the Bogdanovist influence being especially noticeable in his *Theory of Historical Materialism* (1921). In this work, which is largely a systematic exposition and interpretation of the views of Bukharin's teachers, the problems of equilibrium—between society and nature, between different elements of society, the loss and restoration of social equilibrium—are treated very prominently. Bukharin was not content with exegesis and tried to develop the theory of historical materialism beyond the stage reached by his predecessors, maintaining that he was doing it "along the line of the most orthodox, materialistic, and revolutionary understanding of Marx." His main innovations, which he pointed out himself, are the following: Contrasting mechanical and organic processes has become meaningless in the light of modern science; apparently "mechanistic" explanations of social processes are therefore perfectly legitimate. Thus the theory of equilibrium is a legitimate theoretical foundation for the dialectical method (not a substitute for dialectics, as with Bogdanov). The theory of equilibrium is particularly useful in explaining why the productive forces ultimately determine social development: It is because the productive forces express the relation between society and nature, and the relation between a system and its environment is always the quantity that ultimately determines the movement of the system; the relation between society and nature is understood by Bukharin as the quantity of material energy (definite at any given moment) on which society lives and which is transformed in all sorts of ways in the process of social life. (This notion of Bu-

kharin's is reminiscent of Speransky's analysis of social forces.)
Bukharin suggested a materialistic definition of the Marxist concept of production relations—a coordination of people (regarded
as "living machines") in space and time in the labor process. He
outlined a more differentiated picture of the "superstructure"
than that given by Plekhanov; every superstructure, including the
state, consisted of three main spheres—the material tools (e.g., the
government buildings, artillery, office equipment, etc., in the
state), relations between people (e.g., the bureaucratic organization), and ideology, i.e., a system of ideas, images, norms, sentiments, etc., operative in or associated with a given superstructure.
He claimed that such a view of superstructures greatly facilitated
the solution of a number of theoretical and practical problems,
such as the desirable size of the intelligentsia as a social group.
Bukharin picked up Marx's term *Vorstellungsweise,* neglected by
other Marxists, and interpreted it as the "style" of superstructures
corresponding to a given style of the economic basis. Also new in
Marxist thought was Bukharin's theory of the "materialization
of social phenomena"—i.e., the accumulation of culture in the
shape of things (books, libraries, museums, etc.), which are social
psychology and ideology in a "solidified" form and which make
up a part of the material basis for the further development of the
superstructures. Struggling against teleology in the study of society, Bukharin rejected the usual formula of the "growth of
productive forces" as the starting point of the theory of historical
materialism. This formula, according to him, did not encompass
either the periods of retrogression or the revolutionary transition
periods, including the one through which Russia was going.
Bukharin defined such periods as periods of a retreat of the productive forces under the influence of superstructures, the extent
of the retreat being limited by the previous state of productive
forces. It is clear that most of Bukharin's innovations were in fact
suggested by Bogdanov's ideas, and the accusations of Bogdanovism leveled against Bukharin in 1928–30 were substantially correct. His concern for economic equilibrium, which lay at the root
of his opposition to the destruction of well-to-do peasant farms,
also stemmed from the same source. Bukharin's views on matters
of social theory and economic and social policy, unmentionable

under Stalin, have to some extent been revived during the 1950's, especially in Yugoslavia and Poland, though his authorship is rarely acknowledged.

There was a clearly perceptible difference between the attitudes to political theory of the three foremost Communist thinkers of the Leninist stage. Lenin's attitude was the most manipulative of the three. Being mainly concerned with practical problems of attaining and maintaining power, he seems to have regarded theory in all its forms and aspects—rational appraisals of reality, truthful statements about aims, myths calculated to arouse passions and a determination to act, or fictions designed to induce ostensibly conformist behavior—almost exclusively as a weapon in the political struggle. Trotsky was far more genuinely captivated by the Social Democratic elements in Marxism, being akin in this respect to Martov, and was often ready to sacrifice political advantage to theoretical conviction. Bukharin was primarily a theorist; a political situation, problem, or action seem to have interested him mainly as material for reflection or as a challenge for his intellectual ingenuity and skill. Of the three, it was Lenin's approach that became and has remained predominant among Communists. It was best understood and further elaborated by Stalin.

Stalinism

I. V. Stalin (real name, Dzhugashvili, 1879–1953) was a Georgian. The son of an artisan, he was educated at the Orthodox Theological seminary in Tiflis, but was expelled in his last year, apparently for his connections with underground revolutionary circles. He joined the Social Democratic Party in 1898, and consistently adhered to all the successive Leninist factions, from the Spark organization onward. He was an active but not particularly important underground professional revolutionary, fomenting strikes, publishing articles in the local Bolshevik papers, arguing and scheming against the Mensheviks, and organizing armed robberies. He was banished six times to northern Russia and to Siberia, but escaped each time except the last, when he decided to remain in southern Siberia for the duration of the war. He first rose to prominence in the Party after the overthrow of the monarchy in 1917, when he turned out to be the second in seniority (after Kamenev) among the Bolshevik leaders who were present in Petrograd before the arrival of Lenin from abroad. As editor of *Pravda*, Stalin fell in with Kamenev's policy of giving a conditional support to the Provisional Government, but unlike Kamenev, he quickly changed his mind after Lenin's "April Theses" had given the signal for preparing a Bolshevik seizure of power. He was in favor of Lenin's appearance in court when Lenin, who was wanted in connection with a charge of receiving money from the Germans, went into hiding to escape arrest. But after the summer of 1917, he undeviatingly stuck to Lenin until 1922. Like Lenin and Trotsky, he was a member of the Party's Political Bureau and was particularly close to Lenin during the 1918 crisis, when both Trotsky and Bukharin opposed Lenin, and Lenin on the other hand had not yet forgiven Zinoviev and Kamenev for their more than lukewarm attitude toward the coup in 1917. Stalin was made Secretary General of the Party's Central Committee in 1922, and this appointment gave him a chance to manipulate the Party apparatus to his own advantage. Lenin was aware of the fact that Stalin had accumulated great power, and in his notes (known as his "political testament"), which he dictated shortly before his final collapse, Lenin recommended the replacement of Stalin by some other person: Stalin was the most gifted man among the Party leaders excepting Trotsky, Lenin said in this document, but he was too crude and disloyal to his comrades, he was "a cook who could prepare only hot dishes." Lenin's suggestion was not followed, and during the 1920's Stalin was able, through a series of skillful maneuvers as well as police measures, to eliminate all the other contenders for succession to Lenin and to emerge, by 1929, as the undisputed leader of the Communist Party and the Communist International. He ruled the country together with a dozen or so of his supporters, who made up the Party's Political Bureau, until 1934. An attempt in that year, in which some members of the Political Bureau were involved, to dislodge Stalin from his position of power had the opposite result: Stalin established a regime of unlimited personal dictatorship, which soon developed into a reign of terror that lasted until his death. The terror involved mass arrests of absolutely innocent people (from Party and military leaders to simple workers and peasants) followed by an immediate branding of the arrested as "enemies of the people," physical and mental torture during interrogations to extort false confessions (of espionage, sabotage, separatism, attempting to assassinate Stalin and to overthrow the Soviet regime, etc.), mock trials by special boards (established in 1934 and consisting of security officials), executions or sentences of up to twenty-five years in corrective-labor camps, large-scale deportations (including deportations of entire ethnic groups), and two severe famines (1932–33 and 1946–47), which were at least partly artificial. The victims of Stalin's terror must be counted in millions, though no exact figures are available. There were two periods—1937–38 and 1949–52—when the terror reached levels surpassed in modern history only by Hitler's policy of extermination of the Jews. The demoralizing effect of Stalin's terror was probably greater than that of Hitler's, for it was not directed against a specified and identifiable minority but—especially in 1937–38 (a period usually referred to outside Russia as the period of the Great Purge)—was deliberately made universal. The years of World War II were, in comparison with the preceding and following years, a period of relaxation and greater freedom. The terror and the consequent universal dissembling on the part of the population were the most characteristic features of Stalin's rule.

But the quarter of a century during which Stalin wielded absolute power was also full of other developments, many of them with far-reaching consequences. Forcible collectivization of agriculture was carried out in 1929–34. This measure, called by Stalin a "revolution from above," reversed the "agrarian revolution" of 1917, destroying practically all peasant farms, and setting up instead "collective farms" managed by Party appointees. Collectivization encountered stiff opposition from the bulk of the peasantry, ranging from sporadic uprisings and the slaughter of nearly a half of the country's livestock in 1930, to passive resistance taking the forms of persistent truancy and slackness at work. Although advantageous for the Party authorities, since it facilitated political control and economic exploitation of the countryside, collectivization dealt a severe blow to the efficiency of agriculture and, despite a great deal of mechanization, continues to impede its progress. Stalin's other main policy in the economic field was the resumption, after an interruption that had lasted for a full decade, of rapid industrialization of the country. Whereas the pre-1917 industrial expansion (also very rapid) had to a considerable extent been financed by foreign capital (either in the form of state loans or of direct investment by private firms), Stalin's policy was to finance industrialization almost exclusively by forced savings, largely through the sale at high prices of agricultural products obtained through compulsory deliveries. This resulted in a prolonged depression of the living standards of both the peasants and the urban population. But, unlike Stalin's agricultural policy, his industrial policy was largely successful and through a series of five-year development plans it propelled the Soviet Union from the fifth to the second place in the world in terms of industrial output.

Stalin's social policy was unique in the modern world. On the one hand, it included such progressive features as universal education up to the age of fourteen (the denial of educational facilities to children of "socially alien elements," practiced during the 1920's and early 1930's, was stopped in 1935) and almost free medical services (these had been started on a modest scale by local government bodies before 1917, but was also denied during the 1920's and early 1930's to "socially alien elements," which in some areas made up as much as one-fifth of the population). On the other hand, Stalin revived such archaic social institutions as slavery and serfdom. Inmates of corrective-labor camps—who counted in millions—were treated as slaves with no civil rights; their lives depended on the whims of the camp administration and the guards, and they were employed in enterprises (in lumbering, mining, construction of railways, canals, hydroelectric stations, etc.) run by the security service (thus largely paying for its upkeep), or hired out to other government departments or to collective farms (the security service appropriating as a kind of feudal rent, the difference between their earnings outside and the cost of keeping them alive). The peasants pressed into collective farms became a kind of state serfs, suffering many of the humiliations of serfdom besides compulsory labor, such as in cases when collective-farm chairmen forbade women members to marry outside their own collective farm; collective farm members were (and still are) generally forbidden to travel outside their own rural district. Conditions akin to serfdom were extended in 1940 to industrial workers and other state employees (private business in industry and trade having being suppressed ten years earlier): They were forbidden to change their places of employment, and the additional labor necessary for the expansion of industry was thereafter mainly obtained through compulsory recruitment among the peasants and a system of partial "call-up" of school-leavers for trade apprenticeship. A complicated system of wage and salary differentials, official ranks and decorations, and a proliferation of uniforms made Soviet society strikingly hierarchical and bureaucratic, both in appearance and spirit. The Leninist social stratification (in terms of prestige) was considerably modified. The intelligentsia was placed above industrial workers, while the privileged elite, which in Lenin's time had been practically coextensive with the membership of the Communist Party, became more complicated—it included the whole of the security service, the officers of the armed forces, occupants of the higher ranks in all the other institutions (Party, state administration, economic management), and the leading intellectuals, as well as selected war heroes and "heroes of socialist labor" from among industrial workers and peasants, who served as a kind of decorative elite. The reintroduction of military and civilian ranks was only one aspect of the policy of restoring traditional social forms; its other important aspects were full recognition of the family and restoration of the secondary school as a means of controlling social mobility—both these institutions having been undermined and the latter practically ruined by Bogdanovists in the 1920's.

On the political plane, the policy of restoration of pre-Communist forms expressed itself in the reintroduction by the Constitution of 1936 of universal and equal franchise, direct elections, and secret ballot. Any possibility of this having an adverse effect on the Communist dictatorship was removed by the practice of putting up one candidate, selected by the Party authorities, in each constituency. But participation in general and local elections, although devoid of practical significance, familiarized the population with some of the external forms of democracy.

Stalin's cultural policy was as self-contradictory as his social policy. The so-called "cultural revolution" carried out under his direction had two aims: raising the educational level—and therefore the efficiency—of the population at large, and replacing the old intellectual elite—largely hostile to the Communist regime—by a new one, brought up under this regime and if not genuinely loyal to it at least not openly disapproving. Modernistic tendencies in education and art (which had been disapproved of but tolerated by Lenin and actively promoted by the Bogdanovists) were mercilessly suppressed. The arts and social sciences were reduced at first to supplying illustrations to Party slogans, and toward the end of Stalin's life to the glorification of Stalin, with the content and form being prescribed in detail by himself. Even the natural sciences and medicine were subject to Stalin's whims, and cybernetics, for example, was proscribed as a "bourgeois pseudo science."

Limited freedom of organization and worship was conceded in 1943 to most Christian denominations, as well as to Islam and to Buddhism, and antireligious propaganda was almost absent for a whole decade, in return for the churches' support for the war effort and for the Communists' "peace" campaign after the war. However, the relative freedom granted to other denominations was denied to the Roman Catholic Church and to Judaism. The last years of Stalin's life were a period of mounting chauvinism and anti-Semitism.

The highlights of Stalin's foreign policy were the advocacy in the League of Nations of collective security and the signing of nonaggression treaties with most of the Soviet Union's neighbors; intervention in the Spanish Civil War on the anti-Fascist side; a friendship pact with Hitler in 1939, which made it easier for Hitler to start World War II; annexation of parts of or the whole territory of several of the states with which nonaggression pacts had been concluded; dissolution of the Communist International in 1943; imposition of Communist regimes on all the countries of Europe that were occupied by the Soviet Army at the end of the war and their economic exploitation; break with the Yugoslav Communist leader Tito, who rebelled against attempts to subject Yugoslavia to similar treatment; acceptance of help from the U.S.A. and Britain during World War II and subsequent initiative in dividing the world into two hostile camps and in waging a Cold War against the "imperialist" states by means of diplomacy and internal subversion.

The political theory of Stalinism must be considered against this background of Stalin's practical policies. The theory was largely developed by Stalin himself, in his lectures at a Party school entitled *Problems of Leninism* (1924), in speeches at Party congresses and conferences (especially one delivered in 1937, "On Deficiencies in Party Work and on Measures for the Liquidation of Trotskyist and other Double-Dealers"), in his report on the new Constitution in 1936, in various notes and letters (some of which were published) and in *ad hoc* oral statements on the most varied occasions; the 1936 Constitution itself (invariably referred to as the "Stalin Constitution" in his lifetime, but not now) and the book published in 1938 under the title *History of the Communist Party of the Soviet Union (Bolsheviks)*, both edited and partly written by Stalin, are also among the most important texts of Stalinist political theory. Finally, some parts of the theory were enunciated by Stalin's chief aides, notably Molotov, Zhdanov (who was for many years in charge of cultural policy), and Vyshinsky (on legal matters). The term "Stalinism" was never used to describe either Stalin's theory or his practice, though the adjective "Stalinist" was freely applied to them. Stalin maintained that his theory was merely an elaboration of orthodox "Marxism-Leninism" and its further development in new historical circumstances. He pictured himself as a faithful pupil and loyal comrade-in-arms of Lenin, describing Leninists as those Marxists who "switch the center of gravity of the problem from the outward recognition of Marxism to its implementation," paying most attention to designing ways and means of realizing Marxism that correspond to circumstances and changing these ways and means when circumstances change. At first, Stalin's policies were represented as the realization of Lenin's intentions, and Stalin himself as the executor of Lenin's will, but from the mid-thirties on, he was represented as the Great Leader and Teacher in his own right, deriving his authority simply from his superior wisdom.

Stalin claimed that the construction of socialism had been in the main completed in the Soviet Union by 1936, and that the country had entered the stage of the final completion of socialism and transition to communism. There were no more exploiting classes, Soviet society consisting of two friendly classes—workers and peasants—and an "intermediate stratum"—the "toiling intelligentsia"—which originated from the two classes and served their interests but was not a class in itself. All Soviet citizens were happy and prosperous and were growing ever happier and more prosperous. The Soviet Union was the only truly free and democratic state, and its 1936 Constitution was the most democratic constitution in the world, guaranteeing full protection for the rights of all citizens. The U.S.S.R. was a genuinely federal state, and its constituent republics were free to leave the federation if they so desired; but naturally no one in his senses would wish to leave such a happy Fatherland. There was complete moral and political unity among Soviet citizens, and therefore there was no need for any other party but the Communist Party, which was a voluntary association of the most active and politically conscious citizens. The Party, being the leading and guiding force in Soviet society, constituted the core of all state institutions and social organizations. Soviet citizens were full of love for the Soviet regime, the Communist Party, and above all for Stalin, but nevertheless the class struggle did not recede but on the contrary was intensified with the approach to full socialism, especially as the remnants of native "class enemies" were supported by the capitalist states that surrounded the U.S.S.R. The class enemies and their agents, who were at the same time agents of foreign imperialists, were trying by the most criminal means to sabotage socialist construction and to overthrow the Soviet regime. They would not succeed, but it was necessary to exercise extreme vigilance and to have an efficient and powerful security service. In dealing with the enemies of the people, it was unnecessary to make use of proper judicial procedures: Confession on the part of the accused was sufficient evidence of his guilt. The Soviet security service was effectively thwarting all the nefarious plans of the imperialists and their agents and was therefore entitled to —and was in fact enjoying—the support, gratitude, and love of the whole population. If capitalist encirclement continued to exist even after the completion of communism in the Soviet Union (which was quite possible), the state would remain even under full communism, despite the traditional view that the disappearance of the state was one of the necessary features of communism.

Although Leninism was the main source of intellectual inspiration for Stalin, other sources are also clearly discernible. Thus, the Fëdorovist theme of conquering and changing nature was much in prominence, both in the 1930's and again after World War II. Even more important was the contribution of National Bolshevism (which will be considered in the next chapter): It accounted for the revival in the 1930's of patriotism as one of the main aspects of the official outlook. Pan-Slavism was incorporated into the official theoretical armory for a period during and immediately after the war. Finally, the bureaucratism, obscurantism, and anti-Semitism of the last years of Stalin's rule were strongly reminiscent of the theory and practice of Official Nationality.

Many theories have been advanced to explain Stalinism as a system of political thought and practice. The explanations range from defects of Stalin's character to peculiarities of the Russian political tradition (Stalinism being seen as a new version of Muscovite autocracy) and to the Soviet Union's geopolitical situation. Most of these theories are valuable, since they illuminate certain aspects of Stalinism, but the theory put forward by Dr. R. Redlich seems to be the most helpful, for it draws attention not so much to what Stalinism has in common with other political systems as to what most clearly and significantly distinguishes it. According to this theory, at the basis of Stalinism lies a hierarchy of values in which power occupies the highest place. We have seen that Lenin had already to a very great extent concentrated his thoughts on the problems of achieving and maintaining power. Stalin was in this respect his most faithful pupil, but he went much further than Lenin. Having achieved a high degree of control over most aspects of the people's behavior, he then set out to dominate their

242 • RUSSIAN POLITICAL THOUGHT

minds. But this domination was of an unusual kind. Sensing that genuine intellectual conviction and emotional devotion could only be won on a limited scale, he resorted to a large-scale application of fictions. Fictions are an old device, which had frequently been used in the past by authorities of all kinds, especially in the field of law. Jeremy Bentham analyzed their logical structure and functions: In his definition, "a fictitious entity is an entity to which, though by the grammatical form of the discourse employed in speaking of it existence is ascribed, yet in truth and reality existence is not meant to be ascribed. . . . The fiction . . . is the mode of representation by which the fictitious entities thus created . . . are dressed up in the garb, and placed upon the level, of real ones." Stalin's political theory was for the most part fictitious. To profess full and enthusiastic acceptance of it at its face value was humiliating to people's intelligence and integrity, and by making such professions incessant and universal—indeed, by restricting public utterances of Soviet citizens almost solely to reciting parts of the theory and glorifying its creator as the source of limitless wisdom and benevolence—Stalin demonstrated to what extent they were in his power. There is little doubt that Stalin intended people to be aware of the fictitious nature of the theory, for an attempt on the part of the population to treat it as truthful (e.g., to believe that they enjoyed freedom of speech) would undermine the whole of his system of rule. Therefore any action based on belief (genuine or pretended) in the truthfulness of the official theory was treated as a most serious political offense. A profession of belief was obligatory; an action implying belief was severely punished. It seems that Stalin came to be indifferent to people's genuine views that might lie behind the mask of dissembling, and the fictions were used merely as a means of ensuring the appearance of conformist thought, i.e., as a means of controlling an aspect of external behavior. The divorce between private conviction and public utterance, which had often been noticeable in Russia in the past, assumed greater proportions than ever before. But whereas in the past dissembling was primarily resorted to in order to appear better than one in fact was —nobler, more just, more enlightened, etc.—in Stalin's time people more often than not felt compelled to appear worse than they were—more cruel, more obscurantist. The degradation of public morals is likely to remain the aspect of Stalin's heritage most difficult to eradicate.

The significance of Stalinism for general political theory is twofold. It demonstrated that, given willingness and skill in operating the twin instruments of terror and fictions, a political authority can achieve a very high degree of control of most socially relevant aspects of human life. But it also demonstrated that even the determination and ruthlessness of a Stalin are not sufficient to effect a genuine transformation of the human spirit, and that therefore the totalitarian ideal is probably unattainable.

Neo-Leninism

Politically, the decade that has passed since Stalin's death can be divided into two periods: the period of struggle for the succession among the party leaders, which went on until 1957, when Khrushchev defeated his rivals, and the subsequent period of his ascendancy. Until 1957, the ruling group of Stalin's former chief aides presented a fairly united face to the public, except for the fall of Beria, head of the security service, in the summer of 1953, and his execution—on a typically Stalinist charge of having been an agent of foreign imperialist governments since 1918. In 1957, the defeated leaders (among whom were Molotov and Malenkov, Stalin's closest collaborators from the 1920's until his death, and Marshal Zhukov, the most outstanding military leader of World War II) were not permitted to state their views (which were branded as "anti-Party" and anti-Leninist) in public—in contrast to the situation after Lenin's death, when Trotsky and other rivals of Stalin were able to enjoy considerable publicity. Since 1957, the composition of the ruling group has undergone several more changes, but political accusations have not been brought against those who were removed from their positions.

The general political course throughout the post-Stalin decade has been one of de-Stalinization, in the sense of removing some of the worst aspects of Stalinism. The security organs lost their preponderance in the state and much of their political power; most corrective-labor camps were abolished and a greater measure of legality has been observed; some of the Stalinist fictions have been dropped. The situation in agriculture and the position of peasants have improved a bit, as have the manufacture and supply of consumer goods; workers and employees were again allowed to change their place of work at will, working hours were reduced, pensions and the wages of lower-paid categories were raised, and a serious effort made to tackle the housing situation. The reorganization of the economic administration gave somewhat greater scope to the managers, and a more liberal policy has been pursued toward the intellectuals. The extreme chauvinism and xenophobia of Stalin's last years, as well as isolationism in foreign policy and pronounced hostility to all states governed by non-Communists or by dissident Communists, also abated. The policy of de-Stalinization has in most fields been very slow and intermittent, with halts and reversals, but Russia is now a far freer country and the people are better off materially than at any time under Stalin. The post-Stalin leadership, Khrushchev in particular, have firmly adhered to the Leninist principles of the political monopoly of the Communist Party, of Party organization, and of "partyness" (i.e., Party spirit) as the criterion of correct behavior in all spheres of life. Such distinctive Stalinist policies as fictitious elections, compulsory collective-farm membership and a higher rate of expansion for producer- than for consumer-goods industries have been retained, and an attempt is being made to repeat Stalin's "cultural revolution," to change once again the social composition of the intelligentsia.

There has been a good deal of official theorizing during the past decade. The early contributions to political theory after Stalin's death were as if under the spell of the old doctrine—the first post-Stalin issue of the Party's theoretical organ, *Communist*, consisted almost entirely of articles designed to prove that Stalin was the only creator and initiator of all the more important aspects of Soviet policy. But the spell was soon to break. This time there was no "execution of the will," as there had been after Lenin's death. Although the new rulers were at first presented to the public, and acclaimed in the Party press, as old, trusted, and close collaborators of Stalin, this was not emphasized as their only, or even their main, qualification for leadership. They were at the same time described as "talented pupils of Lenin" and the most prominent representatives of a larger body—the Central Committee of the Party. Great stress was laid on the fact that Stalin had been succeeded not by a single person but by a group of people exercising "collective leadership," and Lenin was credited with the authorship of the principle of "collective leadership."

The next step was the abandonment of the Stalin cult, or "cult of personality" as it was usually referred to until 1956. The expression "cult of personality" seems to have been used first (in relation to Lenin and Trotsky) immediately after the Bolshevik seizure of power in 1917 by a dissident Bolshevik, Lozovsky. It was later taken up by Trotsky in his struggle against Stalin and was occasionally used in the *émigré* press during the last decade of Stalin's rule. In June, 1953, *Pravda* published an unsigned article which sharply criticized the belief that important historical developments could be ascribed to any single person; this was stated to be an "idealist cult of personality," entirely alien to Marxism and characteristic of the nineteenth-century Populists and their epigones, the Socialist Revolutionaries. A further step in the same direction was taken in the following month, on the fiftieth anniversary of the formal birth of Bolshevism (the Second Party Congress of 1903), when the Agitation and Propaganda Department of the Central Committee and the Marx-Engels-Lenin-Stalin Institute, in a joint exposition of the Party's history and the current situation, limited Stalin's contribution to political theory merely to "a correct interpretation of Marxism-Leninism in new circumstances" and "an enrichment of it on some points." They went so far, indeed, as to urge that the "cult of personality" should be completely eliminated from Party propaganda. This directive was clearly intended to convey that the cult of *Stalin* should be eliminated, for in the same exposition Lenin alone was credited with developing the theory of the proletarian revolution, the theory of the Communist Party destined to bring about this revolution, and with the building up of the Party and the conduct of the revolution itself, while toward the end of Stalin's rule he had invariably been presented as Lenin's near equal in precisely these achievements. Even the chief milestones of the Stalin era—the industrialization of the country (with heavy industry predominating), the collectivization of agriculture, and the "cultural revolution"—appeared in this exposition as no more than the realization of a program already designed by Lenin. Thus for the post-Stalin rulers, the theoretical importance of being "Lenin's pupils" increased; by implication, they were even promoted (although this was manifestly untrue) to the status of Lenin's "collaborators," since the phrase was used "Lenin, Stalin, and their collaborators."

Even more interesting was the development of the third element in the new rulers' theoretical basis of authority—that of being the leading representatives of the Central Committee. This tendency first appeared in various pronouncements after Stalin's death in the vague and rudimentary form of references to "the policy worked out by the Party." Later attempts to define what was meant in this connection by "the Party," and to clarify why it should have worked out this particular policy, resulted in a further splitting of the source of authority, so that there are now five distinct sources, all stemming from this one root. The most frequently mentioned is the Party's alleged knowledge of the "objective laws of historical development"; these laws are still supposed to be revealed by the doctrine of Marxism-Leninism, though there was a period when they were often referred to simply as the "scientific basis" of Party policy. Another source of authority now occupying a prominent place is the Party's supposed knowledge of the needs of the people. Each of the measures taken by the government to improve the standard of living has been followed in the press not merely by a flood of thanksgiving —as was the case in Stalin's day—but by statements such as "the Party knows the needs of the people." Quite often the emphasis on the Party's supposed connection with the people at large goes further and takes the shape not merely of knowledge of the people's needs, but of the Party as a tool of the people. In the campaign against the "cult of personality," the doctrine that was most commonly brought into play was that of the decisive role of "the people": "Collective experience of the toiling masses" was the ultimate basis of Party policy. The policy, therefore, and the aims of the Party, were "clear and comprehensible for the people, and the people consider the implementation of this policy as their immediate task." The other doctrine advanced against the "cult of personality" has been that of the "collective wisdom of the Central Committee." This notion appeared in official propaganda immediately after Stalin's death, in the form of an editorial in *Communist*, March, 1953, when the origin of this wisdom was said to derive from Stalin's training and influence. Very soon, however, all mention of Stalin was dropped, and the doctrine was even turned against him through being opposed to the "cult of personality." It was now no longer Stalin who had designed the "great and clear program of the construction of Communism," but the Central Committee. The sources of the Central Committee's wisdom in turn were its "collective political experience" and the "collectivity" of its decisions, which cannot therefore be "one-sided" but are weighed from all sides and therefore are right. The fifth doctrine of the Party's source of authority is that it is contained in the Party tradition as embodied in the resolutions of the various Party congresses, conferences, Central Committee meetings, etc.

Since the new rulers did not at once declare a complete break with the Stalinist regime, the people had no reason to expect any new doctrine to be anything but a new fiction. The series of minor reforms that ensued, however, must have caused some to wonder whether official doctrine too would develop more realistically, and in fact some of the new notions on the source of authority—for example, the collective sense of the Central Committee, or their knowledge of the needs of the people—might in due course, given good intentions on the part of the rulers, develop into more realistic conceptions.

What were the reasons for the very swift development after Stalin's death of official doctrine regarding the source of authority in the Soviet Union? It would appear that the new policy-makers were first of all anxious to dash any possible assumption that the death of Stalin would weaken the topmost layer of the power apparatus; hence the insistence that the policies to be pursued were those worked out by Stalin and that they would be implemented by those same people who would have been implementing them had he not died. Their second thought was, perhaps, to try and heighten the appearance of their own suitability for the job by projecting their experience of authority right back to the time of Lenin. Yet they must have been aware of the fact that Stalin's policy was thoroughly unpopular, not only with the mass of the people but also with the bulk of the Party and presumably with the majority of its higher ranks. From the earliest days, therefore, they embarked upon measures designed to create the impression that they were gradually breaking away from Stalin's heritage and that they might ultimately even abandon it entirely. Such a course required a new ideological basis to replace the "Great Leader and Teacher" and his testament. A hastily constructed preliminary formula was found in "the policy worked out by the Party," but since this was too indefinite to be of much use in future practice, a search began for a doctrine that could be used to justify and explain future decisions. This search resulted in various formulas (already familiar in Stalin's time, but used then merely as attributes of the all-powerful Leader) being invested with the function of the theoretical source of authority. During the period of this search, one can sense that there was a certain indecision among the policy-makers as to which of the various slogans advanced should be given precedence. Nor, indeed, is it surprising that they should have hesitated, for the possible implications of their various choices were very different and might be profound and far-reaching.

This survey of Communist political theory in the first years after Stalin's death shows that most important statements on the subject were impersonal, but the gradual strengthening of Khrushchev's position within the Party leadership was paralleled by his emergence as the Party's chief political theorist. N. S. Khrushchev (born 1894) comes from a peasant family from the border area between Great Russia and the Ukraine. He received little education and was a locksmith in the Donets coal-mining basin when he joined the Bolshevik Party in 1918. He took part in the Civil War as a minor political commissar in the Red Army and after the war became a professional party official. In the course of his Party career, he often had as his superiors people whom he defeated in the struggle for power after Stalin's death and branded as an "anti-Party" group. In the 1920's, Khrushchev had consistently followed these men in supporting Stalin, and in the 1930's, he was an obedient tool in their hands in carrying out Stalin's policies, until he himself was made a member of the Political Bureau in 1939, thus joining the circle of Stalin's principal aides. Khrushchev's main chance came in 1953, when, shortly after the death of Stalin, he replaced Malenkov as First Secretary of the Party's Central Committee. In his rise to power, he closely followed the technique that had been employed by Stalin before 1934, and his position now is similar to that of Stalin's between 1930 and 1934.

Khrushchev first appeared in the role of the chief theorist of the post-Stalin regime at the Twentieth Congress of the Party in 1956, when he delivered the official report and a speech (still not published in Russia, but read out at the time at many meetings) on Stalin and de-Stalinization. His subsequent numerous theoretical pronouncements (reports and speeches at Party congresses, Central Committee plenary sessions, and other official or semi-official gatherings) deal chiefly with three groups of problems: de-Stalinization, international affairs, and the advance to Communism. The term "de-Stalinization" is never used by Khrushchev or other Party theorists: They speak of "overcoming the consequences of the cult of Stalin's personality" and of "re-establishing Leninist norms in Party and state life." Stalinism, according to Khrushchev, was due to Stalin's bad character, the mental illness from which he suffered in the last years of his life, and the evil intentions of Beria. Khrushchev is not consistent in depicting his own attitude to Stalin in the past, stressing sometimes his devotion to Stalin and claiming on other occasions that he had realized the true situation and even secretly opposed Stalin. The Party had now, on its own initiative, told the people the truth about Stalin and his rule, and was successfully eradicating the last vestiges of arbitrariness and dogmatism. The Party had done everything that was necessary to ensure that there would be no return to arbitrariness and terror. (On closer examination, however, such measures seem to be limited to subordinating the security organs to the supervision of the Party apparatus, i.e., restoring the situation that had existed before the mid-1930's.) Khrushchev emphasizes that the policy of the Party must be understood correctly and that criticism of "the cult of personality and its consequences" must not be allowed to turn into criticism of the Soviet regime itself, of the Communist Party, or of its aims. In particular, any attempt to interpret de-Stalinization as permitting the removal of any intellectual or artistic activity from the control of the Party is a surrender to the hostile bourgeois ideology. L. S. Il'ichëv, who is now in charge of intellectual and cultural matters (as Zhdanov was in the 1930's and 1940's), clearly formulated Khrushchev's position when, attacking oppositional intellectuals in 1962, he stated that there was freedom in the Soviet Union to fight for Communism but not to fight against it. This is a truthful statement, provided it is understood that the final decision as to what is favorable to Communism and what is not lies with the Party authorities.

Two doctrines of fundamental importance have been advanced by Khrushchev on international affairs, both in his report to the Twentieth Party Congress in 1956. One is that wars between the socialist and the capitalist countries are not inevitable now that the socialist camp is so mighty and the anti-imperialist forces in the capitalist world so strong. The correct foreign policy for the Soviet Union and other socialist states is therefore one of "peaceful coexistence," i.e., competing with the "capitalist" countries in military, political, technological, and economic strength while avoiding the danger of a major war. However, there must be no peaceful coexistence in ideology, the Communist and the "bourgeois" ideologies being directly opposed to each other. Khrushchev and his government have in fact consistently adhered to this policy. The other main theoretical innovation in the field of foreign affairs was Khrushchev's statement (resurrecting an old idea of Engels') that different roads to socialism are feasible in different countries. In some countries, the road might even be peaceful, that is, without a civil war. But in all cases, a period of "dictatorship of the proletariat," led by a Communist Party, would be necessary. As a result, the Soviet leadership recognized the complete independence of Yugoslavia and considerably loosened its control over the other Communist-ruled European countries; however, the establishment in Hungary in the course of the revolution of 1956 of a coalition government of various socialist parties, headed by the dissident Communist Imre Nagy, led to the suppression of the revolution by Soviet armed force.

Problems connected with the idea of transition from socialism to communism became topical when Khrushchev declared at the Twenty-first Party Congress in 1959 that the Soviet Union had finally completed the construction of socialism and was entering the period of a rapid transition to communism. These problems had not been permitted to be discussed in public from the late 1930's until the publication of Stalin's last theoretical work, *Economic Problems of Socialism in the U.S.S.R.*, in 1952. After the denunciation of Stalin in 1956, the taboo was definitely removed and the need for theoretical elucidation of these problems recognized. They are treated at length in the new program of the Party, prepared by a committee under the chairmanship of Khrushchev, and in Khrushchev's report on the draft of the program at the Twenty-second Party Congress in 1961. The program is intended for a period of two decades. Its economic part sets production targets for 1980 the achievement of which would create the "material basis" of Communism. Both in absolute figures and calculated per head of population, the envisaged output is higher than the current output figures in the United States. Most independent students of the Soviet economy think that the industrial targets are attainable, but that those for agriculture are extremely unlikely to be reached if the collective-farm system is retained without major changes. Social policy envisaged in the program, if consistently pursued, will bring Russia in this respect roughly to the level of the advanced welfare states of today. The economic and social sections of the program are thus in the main realistic. However, the other two principal aims of the program —the gradual "withering away" of the state and the creation of a "new man"—are clearly utopian if they are understood literally. But a closer analysis shows that the "withering away of the state" merely means a transfer of administrative functions from government organs to a variety of so-called "social organizations," i.e., ostensibly voluntary associations; these bodies would function, as the government organs have functioned hitherto, under the direction of the Communist Party, whose role is even to be strengthened. So reinterpreted, the concept of a stateless Communist society loses its utopian character—but also any attraction it may have possessed. The program includes a "moral code for a builder of Communism," consisting of the traditional Communist mixture of Christian and humanist norms with intolerance and hatred of opponents.

The program gives the following definition of Communism: "Communism is a classless social system with an undivided ownership by the whole people of the means of production, full social equality of all members of society, where an all-sided development of the people will be accompanied by the growth of the productive forces on the basis of constantly developing science and technology, all sources of social wealth will flow in full stream, and the great principle 'From each according to his abilities, to each according to his needs' will be realized. Communism is a highly organized society of free and conscious working people in which social self-government will be established, work for the good of society will become the first vital need for all and a recognized necessity, and the abilities of each will be applied to the greatest benefit of the people." As a result of the implementation of the program, "a Communist society will in the main be built in the U.S.S.R." by 1980; "the construction of Communist society will be fully completed in the subsequent period."

13. Post-1917 Reformist Trends

THE ESTABLISHMENT of the Communist dictatorship confronted thinking Russians once again with an almost total failure—this time the failure of all the other trends of political thought to assert themselves in the face of a force that only a few months earlier had seemed quite insignificant. As on similar occasions in the past, failure gave impetus to new thinking, and a number of new political trends which attempted to cope with the new situation—some in a reformist and others in a revolutionary way—appeared on the scene.

National Bolshevism

Chronologically, the first new reformist trend was the "Change of Landmarks" movement, which appeared in 1920, both in Russia and among the *émigrés* abroad, among people who had been on the anti-Communist side during the Civil War. The political philosophy of the movement was appropriately called National Bolshevism. In 1920, its adherents published a symposium, *Change of Landmarks,* abroad, later a journal under the same title, and still later a number of journals in Russia as soon as the New Economic Policy made private publishing ventures possible. The chief theorist of the movement was N. V. Ustryalov (born 1890), a historian by profession and a former prominent member of the Constitutional Democratic Party who had taken part in the anti-Communist struggle in Siberia. In his contribution to the symposium and in his other writings (*In the Struggle for Russia,* 1920; *Under the Sign of Revolution,* 1925), he traced the philosophy of the Change of Landmarks to the original Landmarks. Arguing against Struve, who was irreconcilably anti-Communist, he claimed that it was Struve himself who had taught Ustryalov and his generation to disregard the various "people-loving" ideologies of the intelligentsia and to hold the state in high esteem as a value in itself, irrespective of who was governing it at a given moment.

According to Ustryalov, the trend of thought he advocated had manifested itself for the first time in General Brusilov's appeal in October, 1917, to all national-minded people to save the country from disintegration, to preserve its independence and territorial integrity, if necessary without and against the government. The logical concomitant to this was that if the government itself demonstrated willingness and ability to act in this sense it should be supported, whatever its complexion. And in fact, when the Soviet Government early in 1918 proclaimed the slogan of "The Socialist Fatherland in Danger" (of being crushed by the German army), even Purishkevich, who was held in prison, expressed his willingness to serve the Bolsheviks in whatever capacity they might find suitable. Foreign intervention in the Civil War enhanced these sentiments, and the majority of former officers of the Imperial Army who were commanding the Red forces (Brusilov among them) were inspired by them. The former opponents of the Bolsheviks who joined the Change of Landmarks movement now aimed at a reconciliation with the Soviet Government, believing that the Bolsheviks were the only party in existence that was capable of governing Russia effectively and of defending her national interests. With the beginning of the New Economic Policy period, a new element entered the ideology of National Bolshevism—the idea that Russia was following the course of the French revolution and entering a period of "normalization." The economic policy of War Communism had always been considered by National Bolsheviks to be harmful, and now they rejoiced at the picture of Soviet Russia being "like a radish—red outside and white inside." Their hope was that Krasin and other businessmen would eventually replace the "utopians" in the leadership of the Party.

Several leading adherents of the Change of Landmarks movement among the *émigrés* (notably Ustryalov himself and the writers Count A. N. Tolstoy and Ilya Ehrenburg) soon returned to Russia. The Communists at first felt that National Bolshevism was an alien and to some extent even a hostile trend and often branded it as bourgeois and chauvinistic. But in 1934, much of it was incorporated by Stalin and Zhdanov into the official doctrine and in the following years, leading National Bolsheviks (usually referred to as "non-Party Bolsheviks," officially presumed and largely pretending in public to share the Stalinist views completely) became prominent members of the privileged intellectual elite. Prompted by the growing danger of Nazi Germany, they drew very close to the Party leaders and took an active part in the glorification of the Soviet regime and in the adulation of Stalin, hoping in return to strengthen and consolidate the patriotic turn that was being taken by official policy.

An important role in this process was played by B. D. Grekov, the head of the National Bolshevik school of historiography. Having previously suffered frequent attacks from Pokrovsky and other Bogdanovist and Leninist historians for their "bourgeois" views and methods of research, Grekov and his school were raised in the mid-thirties to the position of the officially recognized and supported trend. The price of this recognition (which in effect saved serious research in Russian history from extinction) was ostensible acceptance of the Marxist philosophy of history and of Stalin's (and Lenin's, where these did not contradict those of Stalin) views on particular historical problems. Together with Tolstoy and Ehrenburg, Grekov was prominent during the war as a spokesman of the National Bolshevik-minded intellectuals; they were also the leading exponents of Pan-Slavist sentiments. The National Bolshevik school of historiography was apparently about to be crushed (for paying little attention to problems of Socialist and Communist construction) when Stalin died in 1953. Saved from annihilation, it has nevertheless been obliged during the past decade to yield some ground to a more genuinely Marxist approach. National Bolshevik sentiments in general, however, remain an important source of strength for the Communist regime.

There were a number of movements after 1917 among the non-Russian peoples of the country that resembled the Great Russian National Bolshevism. Local nationalisms were blended with the official Bolshevik theory, which offered self-determination to all peoples. Often these minority National Bolsheviks were given re-

sponsible positions in the administration of their respective territories, and in the 1920's and 1930's, they were largely in control
of educational and cultural matters there. But most of them were
sooner or later accused of "bourgeois nationalism" and removed
from positions of influence. Nearly all of them disappeared during the Great Purge; those who survived had to profess at least
outward allegiance to Stalin's ideal of culture—"national in form
and socialist [i.e., Stalinist] in content."

Eurasianism

The second post-1917 evolutionary trend, Eurasianism, was born
almost simultaneously with the Change of Landmarks movement
in 1920; but unlike the latter, which had a considerable following
inside Russia, Eurasianism was an almost purely *émigré* intellectual trend. During the 1920's and early 1930's, the Eurasians developed a lively publishing activity, issuing a series of symposia
(starting with *Exodus to the East* in 1921; most volumes bore the
title *Eurasian Journal*) and a number of separate monographs
dealing with the philosophy of history, aspects of Russian culture,
and political problems.

The founder of Eurasianism was Prince N. S. Trubetskoy
(1890–1938), philologist and philosopher who from 1923 occupied
the chair of Slavonic philology at Vienna University. In his pamphlet *Europe and Mankind* (Sofia, 1920) and in the collection of
his articles published under the title *On the Problem of Russian
Self-Knowledge* (Paris, 1927), he revived Danilevsky's doctrine of
cultural types and accepted the traditional Slavophile view on the
deficiencies of "European" (Romano-Germanic) civilization. Unlike the Pan-Slavists, however, he rejected the idea of a Slavic cultural type, and postulated instead the existence of a Eurasian
civilization, based on two ethnic elements—eastern Slavs and
Turks. The Russian national character had many affinities with
that of the Turks. The spiritual life of the Turks was dominated
by one basic feature—the clear schematization of a comparatively
poor and simple material. This feature of Turkic mentality—
which Trubetskoy regarded as positive—had played a beneficial
role in Russian history: the Russian mental make-up before Peter

the Great had belonged to this type. The Russian Muscovite state had been rooted in the Tatar state of the Golden Horde, and the transformation of Tatar statehood into Russian had been due to the influence of Orthodox Christianity. Turanian statehood was founded on the idea of unconditional submission, but this idea extended to the supreme ruler himself, who was always thought of as being equally unconditionally subordinated to some higher principle, which at the same time was the guiding light in the life of each of his subjects. The Orthodox faith had been such a principle in Muscovite Russia. A foreign yoke was not only catastrophe for a nation but also a lesson. The foreign yoke under which Russia had been smarting was its subjection since Peter the Great to Romano-Germanic values. These values were not organically assimilated but imposed from above. Some of them— e.g., the idea of the rule of law—had been badly assimilated by the upper strata of Russian society and not at all by the common people. Unlike the classical Slavophiles, who had valued many aspects of the West European impact upon Russia, or Danilevsky, who had expected the future Slavic civilization to be a synthesis that would include some West European traits, Trubetskoy called for a shaking off of the "European" concepts and a return to the "Eurasian" principles.

Trubetskoy left the Eurasian movement in 1928, and the role of the most influential theorist passed to the geographer and economist P. N. Savitsky (born 1895), who argued (e.g., in *Russia as a Peculiar Geographical World*, Prague, 1927) that Eurasia was not only a historical and cultural but also a geographical unit, roughly coextensive with the territory of the Soviet Union and different both from Western Europe and from Asia "proper," i.e., Southeast Asia.

The leading political scientist in the Eurasian movement was N. N. Alekseev (born 1879), a former professor of Moscow University whose first books had been published in Russia before the emigration (*General Theory of Law*, Simferopol', 1919; *Outlines of a General Theory of State*, Moscow, 1920) and who became influential with the *émigré* youth around 1930. His main works of the Eurasian period were *On the Ways to Future Russia* (with the subtitle *The Soviet System and Its Political Potentialities,*

1927), *Property and Socialism* (subtitle *An Attempt at Laying a Foundation for a Social and Economic Program of Eurasianism,* 1928) and *Theory of the State* (1931). An analysis of contemporary political theory (mainly French and German) and practice (mainly of Soviet Russia and Fascist Italy) had led Alekseev to the conclusion that liberal-democratic parliamentary government was unlikely to withstand the rise of Socialism, Communism, and Fascism. He did not regret this prospect, for the defects of the liberal-democratic form of government were more obvious to him than its advantages. Rejecting the notion of a perfect state form, he outlines a picture of a "relatively perfect" state. Many of the factors that determine conditions in a state are either natural data or result from spontaneous developments. The territory of the state, with all its geographical peculiarities and natural resources, belongs to this category. Most advantageous in respect of territory are the "world states" that embrace whole continents or similarly large areas (like Russia). The population of a state is another natural or elemental datum. An ethnically diverse population with a single supranational culture has the best chance of fruitful development; here again, Russia is in a fairly good position. The "relations of authority" are also, according to Alekseev, a spontaneously developing aspect of the life of a state. The exercise of authority in a perfect state could be completely automatic and smooth, based on persuasion alone, without any need for violent means; the degree of approximation to this ideal is indicated by the necessary minimum of violence in the practice of a given state. Finally, the formation of a leading stratum from among the population of the country is an unavoidable, spontaneous process. Different types of leading strata may develop, and the one which is purely functional and not based on a particular social class is the best. Alekseev devoted much attention to the problem of the best organization of the leading stratum. It should not be incorporated into the government apparatus, lest it become merely an agency of the government; on the contrary, the leading stratum should be a voluntary autonomous association, similar in some respects to a monastic order. It should not be split into parties representing sectional interests, but rather be organized in a single association dedicated to service to the common interests of the state as a

whole. Selection of new members should be based on what Alekseev calls the "eidocratic" principle, to avoid the use of the term
"ideocratic," which is associated with domination by particular
ideas rather than by a vision of the common interests. Alekseev
used the Ciceronian idea of justice (to each what is his due) to
advocate an "equilibrium" between the duties and rights of citizens and a mixed economy. He rejected the idea of pure "merito-
cracy" (as we might now call such a system)—a government run by
the competent members of the leading stratum without popular
participation—in favor of a system combining a pyramid of elected
bodies, based on indirect vote and representing varied real, sectional interests, with an executive consisting of a head (whether
he is called president or monarch does not really matter) and his
appointees. The "eidocratic" and the "demotic" principles are
reconciled when public opinion is deliberately "stabilized," becomes a conviction shared by the whole people and transforms itself into popular will. Following the Slavophile tradition, Alekseev thought that in the last resort there could be only moral
guarantees against arbitrariness; but in his opinion, the Slavophiles had gone too far in considering the law to be a purely external limitation. The law and the idea of legality were valuable
forms of expression of moral norms.

Applying his general criteria to Soviet Russia, Alekseev thought
that the revolution (always a social illness), although eliminating
many of the old evils, had also created new ones. It was futile to
imagine that the revolutionary ills could be cured by a return to
the pre-Soviet concepts of absolute or constitutional monarchy or
of parliamentary democracy. One should start with an appraisal
of the existing situation and then try to suggest how it could be
improved. Alekseev thought that most of the new ills stemmed
from the Marxist theory and from attempts to act in accordance
with it. This West European theory should be abandoned and
Russia should revert to the pre-Petrine ideal (Alekseev in fact
quoted Nil of the Sorka) of personal perfection as the true aim after
which people should strive. A just state was one that realized the
principle of spiritual freedom. But while the policies of the Communist Party were indefensible, one should not identify the Soviet system itself with them. The Soviet system had not been set

up in accordance with a preconceived plan; it had been born largely spontaneously in the process of the revolution. Alekseev held that there were several positive features in the Soviet system. It had produced a strong government, because it embodied the principle of substitution, according to which lower-level Soviets had the same competence as higher-level ones and could "substitute" themselves for the latter if there was need for issuing a decision; this feature should be retained as a general principle, though some powers should be reserved to the central legislature. The existence of a clearly identifiable ruling group—the Communist Party—was another reason why the Soviet system had produced a strong government. But the Communist Party, because of its adherence to Marxism and its party character, was ill suited for the role of a leading stratum, which, in Alekseev's view, should have no sectional interests at heart. The other positive feature of the Soviet system was that it was the first attempt at a democratic organization of the Russian people, in the sense of drawing large numbers into some sort of participation in governing the country. But as an idea, the Soviet system was not entirely new in Russia: It had been foreshadowed by Speransky's constitutional project. In this way, Alekseev came to the formula: "Russia with Soviets, but without Communists"—a formula very similar to that believed to have been advanced by the Kronstadt sailors during their uprising in 1921.

Alekseev emphasized the difference between his standpoint and that of the Change of Landmarks people, describing the latter as purely opportunist. Soviet Russia should abandon Marxism, reject the Communist Party, and embrace Eurasianism, not the other way around. But there were Eurasians who went further than Alekseev in seeing Soviet Russia as a reincarnation of the Muscovite Russia that was dear to their hearts, and some of these followed the Change of Landmarks example in returning to Russia. Others resented the growth of pro-Soviet feeling within Eurasianism, and it was this growth that prompted many prominent members to withdraw from the movement.

Eurasianism as a coherent trend did not survive World War II. After the war, some of its former leaders (including Savitsky) found themselves in Soviet concentration camps, where they con-

tinued to preach their doctrine. While the direct political effect of
Eurasianism was confined to some softening of the attitude of a
section of *émigré* intellectuals towards the Soviet regime, its intellectual significance has been considerable. Drawing attention to
the hitherto much neglected Asiatic connections in Russian history and culture, the Eurasians made an impact upon Russian
historiography that is likely to be lasting; one might say that a
version of Eurasianism has found its way into the official Soviet
historiography, where the concept of the "history of the peoples
of the U.S.S.R." has since the mid-1930's replaced the old concept
of Russian history. On the other hand, the Eurasians (especially
Alekseev's writings) helped to develop a "postrevolutionary," anti-
restoration approach to the problems of Russia's political future,
an approach that was gradually adopted by the *émigré* intelligentsia, especially of the younger generation. Many of Alekseev's
specific suggestions concerning the features of a "relatively perfect" state were incorporated into the early programs of the Popular Labor Union, which will be dealt with in the next chapter.

Personalist Socialism

Unlike National Bolshevism and Eurasianism, both of them
trends of thought that animated more or less coherent movements
and were formulated theoretically by leading members of these
movements, Personalist Socialism was the name given to the social
and political aspects of his philosophy by one thinker, N. A.
Berdyaev (1874–1948). A Marxist and member of the early Social
Democratic circles in his youth, Berdyaev, together with a number of other young Marxist intellectuals, turned to Idealism
(*Subjectivism and Individualism in Social Philosophy*, 1901) and
later to Orthodox Christianity. He continued to be sympathetic
toward the revolutionary movement until the revolution of 1905,
but he became disillusioned and took part in the Landmarks
symposium in 1909. Although he considered the outcome of the
1917 revolution to be inevitable, and in the social sense just (he
had, indeed, forecast a victory for the Bolsheviks ten years before), he became an opponent of the new regime because of its suppression of human freedom. Berdyaev was elected to the chair of

philosophy at Moscow University, where he became extremely popular with the students, and in 1921 he founded, together with S. L. Frank, the Free Philosophical Academy, in which lectures were open to the public. The Academy had a sensational success, but Berdyaev was expelled from Russia in 1922, together with other leading intellectuals. He settled first in Berlin, where he founded the Russian Academy of Philosophy and Religion; but later, he had to leave Germany and spent the last years of his life in France. The philosophic genius of Berdyaev, which had already manifested itself in his *Meaning of Creativeness* (1916), now developed to its full extent, and he became a leading Christian philosopher, exercising considerable influence on contemporary thought. Of his many writings, *Slavery and Freedom* (1939) and *The Realm of Spirit and the Realm of Caesar* (published posthumously) are especially important for an understanding of his political philosophy in its mature stage.

Man, according to Berdyaev, is at once a natural, a social, and a spiritual being. By virtue of being natural and social he belongs to the realm of necessity, by virtue of being spiritual to the realm of freedom. Freedom is the inner, creative energy of man that constitutes his godlike nature. Although every man has some freedom, it is not easy, for freedom is not a right—as liberals tend to regard it—but an obligation: freedom presupposes a readiness to struggle for it and is realized to the extent to which the realm of necessity is narrowed by conscious effort. The realm of freedom in man is his personality. Human personality cannot be considered as a part of some larger whole. The realm of freedom is not divisible, not capable of fragmentation, and therefore the human personality encompasses the whole realm of freedom. Personality cannot be a means to something else—it is a primary value, an end in itself. The concept of personality should not be confused with the concept of the individual, either as a part of society or in contradistinction to it; and personalism, the assertion of personality as a primary value, has little in common with individualism. The destiny of man is to exercise his creative energy and to enlarge the realm of freedom. But this destiny can itself only be fulfilled freely, man cannot be compelled to fulfill it, freedom cannot be enlarged through compulsion. The greatest obstacle in

the path of fulfilling man's destiny is the danger of falling prey
to the temptation of a multiplicity of partial and relative values.
Absolutization of relative values leads to their idolization and
thus to the enslavement of man. Monism is the philosophical
basis of slavery; the absolutization of relative values and self-
enslavement to them lead also to the enslavement of others.

In *Slavery and Freedom,* Berdyaev gives a systematic exposition
of the whole range of forms of self-enslavement, according to the
values that are absolutized and idolized: the slavery of man to
himself, to nature, society, civilization, the philosophic slavery to
being, and even slavery to God—for man can treat God as an idol
and thus enslave himself. Absolutization and idolization of particular social values and phenomena—sovereignty, war, nation,
aristocracy, property, revolution, collectivism—lead to particular
forms of social slavery.

Berdyaev regarded earthly sovereignty as an illusion, and the
acceptance of the idea of sovereignty by Christians as the result of
a misunderstanding of St. Paul's words that there is no authority
but from God: Berdyaev maintained that St. Paul had merely
advised Christians on how to behave in a pagan state and that his
words had no religious significance. Their misinterpretation has
led to the attribution to Christian monarchs of sacred rights (in
imitation of pagan practices), and later these sacred rights had
come to be attributed by democrats to the people as a whole and
by Communists to the proletariat. The Christian truth about
society had not yet been revealed, thought Berdyaev, but only
freedom proceeded from God, not authority, and the only principle compatible with Christianity was the recognition of man's
inalienable rights. The rejection of the idea of sovereignty did
not mean the rejection of any public authority and the acceptance of the anarchist utopia of happy statelessness. In conditions
of this world, the functions of the state will always remain. But
the state is of only functional and subordinate significance, and it
must be denied sovereignty, otherwise it tends toward totalitarianism—all states have this tendency, not only Communist and
Fascist ones. At the basis of totalitarianism lies a reaction against
fragmentation of human life and autonomization of its various
spheres, but attempts to restore unity through absolutization of

one or another of these spheres can lead only to slavery or tyranny. True liberation will come only with the elimination of the idea of sovereignty, regardless of the subject to which sovereignty is attributed.

Berdyaev similarly proceeded against all the other forms of slavery. He believed that socialism was right on the practical level —at least in its rejection of individualism, of the bourgeois spirit, and of capitalist exploitation (describing capitalism in very Marxist terms)—but he opposed its egalitarianism and collectivism. People are equal before God, and they should be equal before society, in the sense that society has no right to discriminate among them on the basis of privilege. But personalities are qualitatively distinct and unequal, and the contrary view leads to tyranny. Collectivism aims at compulsory justice, but good ends cannot be achieved by evil means, justice is impossible without freedom, and Berdyaev supported the Slavophile concept of conciliarism against collectivism.

Although Berdyaev's view of the contemporary world was rather pessimistic, he conceived a brighter future in which men, through a spiritual effort, would emancipate themselves from slavery and enlarge the realm of freedom. Not taking part in any organized political movement among the *émigrés,* Berdyaev came nevertheless to be considered as representative of a tendency fairly widespread among the left-wing *émigrés* in the 1920's and 1930's of trying to find a new basis—in the Christian view of man—for their belief in human freedom.

Post-Stalin Reformism

The abandonment by the Neo-Leninist leadership of preventive terror and the relaxation of the political atmosphere that followed—public or semipublic discussion of political matters—made possible a revival of political thought in the country. Much of the discussion has been oral and has not yet found its way into print, so that the student of present-day Russian thought is often reduced to attempts at interpreting vague hints or elucidating the implications of a person's or a group's practical activities. A large part of the new thought is reformist in its approach, falling into two main sections, one of which strives to effect more or less significant changes in the official theory and practice without abandoning Communism as the main symbol and the final aim, while the other rejects Communism.

Neo-Leninism itself is in a sense a moderately reformist trend of the first kind. It is flanked on the Left by a cluster of attitudes that are fittingly designated by the Neo-Leninists as "modern revisionism," for what they have in common is a revision of the spirit of Leninism. This takes different forms, but all point toward further liberalization of the regime, so that the whole trend might perhaps be called Liberal Communism. It seems that at the basis of this trend lies the view that the infallibility of the Party leadership is a harmful myth that should be discarded and that individual Communists should be accorded the right to independent opinion and judgment. Some proceed from this to the demand that Party policies should be determined through genuinely democratic processes, with genuine elections within the Party and genuine majority decisions (which could then be accepted as binding for Party members). Others concentrate on the need to allow individual Communists to exercise discretion in deciding what is in the interests of the Party and conducive to the attainment of the Communist ideal. A prominent representative of this trend is the poet A. T. Tvardovsky (born 1910), who, as editor of the literary journal *Novy Mir,* initiated the "thaw" in literature immediately after Stalin's death by exposing the mechanism of ensuring the conformity of authors under Stalinism and thus unmasking a number of the Stalinist fictions.

A more radical reformist trend is that which advocates abandonment of the notion that "partyness" is a universally applicable and obligatory criterion, or simply abandons it in practice. Adherents of this trend advance as substitutes for partyness such criteria as rational calculation in economic policy, sincerity or "self-expression" in literature, etc. Such arguments lead logically to recognizing the autonomy of various fields of human effort and to a pluralistic view of the problems of society as a whole. The danger of such a position from the point of view of the Party leadership is that people who take it up can easily lose sight altogether of the Party interests and of the Communist aim.

A peculiarly radical position, somewhat reminiscent of Bog-danovism, has been evolved by a group of young intellectuals headed by the poet E. A. Evtushenko (born 1933). Their starting point is a strong emotional revulsion against Stalinism, which they reject mainly on moral and aesthetic grounds. The present-day Party leadership consists of the "heirs of Stalin" who had faithfully served the despot while he was alive and have only half-heartedly abandoned his ways. It is the duty of the young people to cleanse public life of all the filth that has accumulated there. One must in a sense work one's way back to Lenin's days, to re-capture the revolutionary spirit that animated Communists in the past. At the same time, Evtushenko and his group accept and practice modernism both in art and in their style of life, which is a Bogdanovist, not a Leninist, trait. Another Bogdanovist fea-ture is the revival of the "god-building" idea by Evtushenko's friend A. A. Voznesensky, for whom Lenin is an eternal spirit of goodness and perfection of which the living man Ulyanov was only one, albeit the most perfect, embodiment. Speaking of his attitude to the present-day state of Russia and the world, Evtu-shenko said in answer to a question: "Maturity means both the ability to see the good in people and to fight for it. That is why I have remained an optimist. But my optimism is not light-blue or pink in color. All the colors that exist, including black, enter into it." And of the Communist future, he says: "I envisage Com-munism symbolically, as a state in which truth is president and tenderness and strictness are ministers. In my opinion these two ministers will be enough under Communism." Evtushenko be-lieves that "the poet must be a sort of prototype of this Commu-nist state"— and this is yet another Bogdanovist idea.

A more radical departure from hitherto accepted Communist traditions is suggested by a trend of which the most prominent representative is the novelist L. M. Leonov (born 1899), who has always been regarded as continuing the Dostoevskian tradition in literature. People belonging to this trend advocate a more spir-itualized and more humane approach to social and political prob-lems. Writers and literary critics among them discuss in print such Dostoevskian problems as the effect of suffering (e.g., in Stalin's concentration camps) on human behavior and the corrupting and dehumanizing effect of absolute power. Leonov himself, in his speech at the official celebration of the fiftieth anniversary of L. N. Tolstoy's death, suggested that the time had come when the Leninist approach, explicable in the past, should be to some extent replaced by the Tolstoian approach to human beings and to ways of treating them.

The Christian element clearly discernible in the thinking of Leonov permeated the whole thought of B. L. Pasternak (1890–1960). In his novel *Doctor Zhivago* (published abroad in 1957, its publication in Russia having been forbidden) the great poet depicted the Communist revolution of 1917 as a spiritual reaction, a counterrevolution directed against the true spiritual revolution of Christ. In the "Epilogue" to the novel, Pasternak gave this classic analysis of Stalinism and its role in the life of Russia:

> Collectivization was an erroneous and unsuccessful measure and it was impossible to admit the error. To conceal the failure people had to be cured, by every means of terrorism, of the habit of thinking and judging for themselves, and forced to see what didn't exist, to assert the very opposite of what their eyes told them. This accounts for the unexampled cruelty of the Yezhov period, the promulgation of a constitution that was never meant to be applied, and the introduction of elections that violated the very principle of free choice.
>
> And when the war broke out, its real horrors, its real dangers, its menace of real death, were a blessing compared with the inhuman reign of the lie, and they brought relief because they broke the spell of the dead letter.
>
> It was felt not only by men . . . in concentration camps, but by absolutely everyone, at home and at the front, and they all took a deep breath and flung themselves into the furnace of this deadly, liberating struggle with real joy, with rapture.
>
> The war has its special character as a link in the chain of revolutionary decades. The forces directly unleashed by the revolution no longer operated. The indirect effects of the revolution, the fruit of its fruit, the consequences of its consequences, began to manifest themselves. Misfortune and ordeals had tempered characters, prepared them for great, desperate, heroic exploits. These fabulous, astounding qualities characterize the moral elite of this generation.

And of the postwar years he said:

Although victory had not brought the relief and freedom that were expected at the end of the war, nevertheless the portents of freedom filled the air throughout the postwar period, and they alone defined its historical significance.*

Vilified by official spokesmen and time-servers, Pasternak not only became the recognized spiritual leader of that section of the post-Stalin intellectual opposition—whether reformist or revolutionary—which rejected Marxism, but the heroic figure of the old writer who openly challenged all the foundations of the official political philosophy itself served as a source of inspiration to the opposition as a whole.

* Boris Pasternak, *Doctor Zhivago*, trans. Max Hayward and Manya Harari (New York, 1958), pp. 507–8, 519. Reprinted by permission of Pantheon Books, a division of Random House, Inc.; © Copyright, 1958, by Pantheon Books Inc.; © 1958 Wm. Collins & Co., Ltd.; © 1957 Giangiacomo Feltrinelli Editore.

14. *Revolutionary Anti-Communism*

REVOLUTIONARY anti-Communism dates almost from the moment of the seizure of power by the Bolsheviks in 1917. After the coup, and especially after the dispersal by the Bolsheviks of the Constituent Assembly in 1918, a number of anti-Bolshevik committees and secret societies sprang up in Petrograd and Moscow, most of them consisting of liberal or moderate socialist politicians. A series of uprisings was organized by the Socialist Revolutionaries in provincial towns near Moscow, and later in the year the Civil War began in earnest in the east, north, and south of the country. The opponents of the Communists in the Civil War soon acquired the colloquial name of "Whites."

The White Movement

People of very diverse political views fought on the White side, ranging from the right wing of the Socialist Revolutionaries to the extreme reactionaries. The Volunteer Army in the south of European Russia, the most important both numerically and strategically, was also relatively the most coherent politically. Founded by Generals Kornilov and Alekseev, both of whom had served as commanders-in-chief of Russian armies under the Provisional Government in 1917 (Kornilov, indeed, was a republican and had, in his capacity as commanding officer of the Petrograd Military District, arrested Nicholas II after his abdication), it preserved on the whole a moderately right-wing outlook. The views of P. B. Struve, who was one of the leading intellectuals on the White side and became Minister of Foreign Affairs in General Wrangel's government in the Crimea in 1920, corresponded fairly closely to those of the young wartime officers who were the mainstay of the Volunteer Army. Struve formulated his views on the nature of

Bolshevism, the causes of its success in the 1917 revolution, and ways of combating it in two public lectures which he delivered in Rostov-on-Don in 1919.

The World War, according to Struve, had been started by Germany in pursuit of the utopian aim of dominating the world. It had been primarily directed against Russia, which had to be destroyed. The Germans therefore planned and organized a revolution in Russia, which made their object of destroying Russia more easily achieved. Russia's Western allies did not understand this, mainly because they had identified Russia as a great power with a particular form of government—the autocracy—and considered the fall of this autocracy a good thing. This attitude toward Russia had been facilitated by the wartime propaganda of the Western allies, according to which they fought the war not for state interests but for democratic principles. Since it turns against the Russian national interests, this democratic propaganda must be rejected by Russians. Russians must reject any suggestion that allied assistance to the Whites can be combined with political interference by the allies. It is in the allies' own interest to assist in the struggle against Bolshevism, for Bolshevism is an essential episode in the World War as a whole. Created by German propaganda and with German assistance, Bolshevism is a world danger; the restoration of Russia as a great power is necessary for the restoration of the balance of power in the world.

Apart from German assistance, there were two forces that created Bolshevism in Russia. One of them was elemental and economic in its nature—the desire of every member of the working masses to work as little as possible and to receive as much as possible, a desire which leads to attempts to achieve this result by mass action regardless of means while avoiding harmful consequences to themselves of such behavior. The other force was the political movement aimed at the realization of socialism through seizure of state power. The combination of both forces produced Bolshevism.

But how was it possible that a people who had created a great state and a rich culture should have destroyed this great state, committed national suicide, for the sake of transient and illusory benefits? The roots of the catastrophe lay deep in Russian history. Russia's misfortune, and the main cause of the catastrophic character of the revolution, was that the people had not been gradually attracted into active and responsible participation in government. Struve recalled the constitutional attempt of 1730, and said that Lenin had been able to destroy the Russian state in 1917 because the Duchess of Kurland (i.e., the Empress Ann) had defeated Prince Golitsyn in 1730. This defeat had delayed political reform in Russia for 175 years and caused a perverse attitude on the part of the Russian educated class toward the state. The consolidation of serfdom was a compensation to the gentry for the withholding of political rights. Both the abolition of serfdom and constitutional reform came too late. The post-1905 constitutional regime could have worked if the government had sincerely adhered to its principles and, on the other hand, the intelligentsia had realized that the enemy of political liberty and social peace was no longer the government but those elements of the intelligentsia itself that continued a revolutionary struggle against the government. Failure to understand this, and idealization of the popular masses whom they scarcely knew, precipitated the revolution. Revolution was a combination of the abstract radical ideas on which the intelligentsia had been brought up and the anarchic, destructive, and egoistic instincts of the popular masses. But of all the political trends at the time of the revolution, only Bolshevism was consistent in its loyalty to the essence of the revolution itself, and that is why it succeeded. Struve drew a parallel between the revolution of 1917 and the Time of Troubles in the seventeenth century: There was the same spiritual instability not only of the popular masses but of the upper classes also, the same utilization by foreigners of the internal struggle. In the seventeenth century, Russia had been saved by a national movement initiated by the middle classes—the middle gentry and the townspeople—and inspired by the clergy, i.e., the intelligentsia of the time. There was a close similarity between this picture of the national forces in the seventeenth century and the Volunteer Army.

The defeat of the Whites in the Civil War did not appreciably change their political views. Organized in the emigration in the Russian Military League, the former soldiers remained loyal to "the White cause" for two decades, continuing to think in terms of a new military campaign against the Communist regime, i.e., of reopening the Civil War at some undetermined future date. The idea of restarting the Civil War was revived and given a new shape during World War II by the Vlasov Movement, so named after General A. A. Vlasov (1900–1946), who, having been captured by the Germans, was persuaded that cooperation with Germany would enable Russian anti-Communists—who were assumed to be sure of the support of the vast majority of the population of the Soviet Union—to fight effectively against the Communist regime. The leadership of the movement consisted of former Communist officials and generals, and its political complexion was mainly influenced by "liberal communist" ideas, not unlike those which came to the surface in the Soviet Union after Stalin's death, and by Solidarism, which will be considered in the next section.

While the idea of reviving the Civil War in the future was dominant among the former participants of the White movement in the emigration, a more active and politically minded minority among them evolved a new anti-Communist revolutionary doctrine designed to promote revolutionary activities without waiting for a new civil war. The intellectual leader of this revolutionary minority was I. A. Il'in (1882–1956), a former professor of philosophy at Moscow University who, together with other leading intellectuals, was expelled from Russia in 1922. In his pamphlet *On Resistance to Evil by Force* (Belgrade, 1926) and in many articles, especially in the journal *The Russian Bell,* which he published in Berlin in 1927–29, Il'in developed what might be called a theory of White Activism.

The starting point of this theory was that, thanks to divine providence, Russia was already beginning to arise spiritually from her humiliation and suffering. This awakening Russia will need all her faithful sons wherever they are and whatever they have been doing until now. They will all be joined in a new brotherhood. The first thing that Russia needs in this hour of awakening is a national idea. One must visualize an ideal Russia in its possible and coming perfection. It is an idea of a great Russia—great spiritually and therefore great as a state—built on the foundation of a truly Christian, strong, and noble statehood, the idea of a "God-serving and therefore holy motherland." This idea, at once merciful and powerful, rejects slavery and asserts brotherhood and chivalry. It gives man freedom for the spirit, love, and creation, but gives him no freedom for the lie, hatred, or villainy. It teaches man to accept voluntarily law and discipline and demands that he should earn freedom by spiritual self-restraint. It calls for brotherhood, seeing brotherhood not in equality but in justice and just ranking. It calls man to creative work and defends property, but conceives property as a responsible obligation and a call to generosity. It teaches man to build the state not on advantage and arbitrariness, but on duty and loyalty; not on intrigue and suspicion, but on respect and trust; not on ambition and conspiracy, but on discipline and conscientious loyalty to the leader. A monarch is therefore preferable to a republic.

Secondly, Russia needed, according to Il'in, chivalrous cadres with will and character, dedicated to the service of the idea of the perfect Russia of the future. Thirdly and finally, it needed "free and calm patriotic realism" to enable her to find a peaceful and creative way out of the revolution. Il'in realized that his teaching was akin to Fascism. He considered Fascism as one of the forms of the White movement in the world, but saw a fundamental difference between Fascism and his own doctrine in the absence of the Christian element in the former. When Hitler came to power, Il'in, who had been teaching at Berlin University, was forced to leave Germany and moved to Switzerland.

Il'in's teaching found a strong response among the young Russian *émigrés*, and there was an organization called the Brotherhood of Russian Truth, built on the lines of an order of chivalry, whose members engaged in terroristic acts against prominent representatives of the Communist regime, both in Russia and abroad.

Solidarism

Among those who were strongly influenced by Il'in's teaching were *émigré* students at various West European universities, who in 1930 set up the National Union of Russian Youth, an organization that still exists and is now called the Popular Labor Union (Russian Solidarists), better known under its Russian abbreviation NTS. They accepted Struve's explanation of the causes of revolution and the Communist victory, N. N. Alekseev's views on a "relatively perfect" state, and Il'in's call for activism and chivalry. They were less romantic and more sober than the Brotherhood of Russian Truth, and they rejected terrorism. The difference between the Union of Russian Youth and the Brotherhood somewhat resembled that between the People's Will and the preparatory trend in the 1880's. Indeed, the practical activities of the Solidarists have been strongly reminiscent of those of the preparatory trend organizations during the 1880's and 1890's: propagating their views in order to create a favorable climate of opinion—in the first place among the intelligentsia—and building up an underground network of small cells. They have often made use of front organizations of various kinds—the most important of these probably being the Vlasov movement during World War II, which was thoroughly permeated and strongly influenced by the Solidarists.

The political orientation of the NTS underwent a considerable change during and after World War II, partly as a result of the influx into the organization of many people who had grown up in the Soviet Union. Their better understanding of Soviet reality enabled these persons to work out the "axiological" theory of Bolshevism, which we have touched upon in the section on Stalinism and which is very similar to the one proposed later by Pasternak. The theoretical horizon of the organization was considerably widened and the term "Solidarism" adopted for its social and political philosophy. This term had not been used in Russian political thought until the 1920's (when it was adopted by Professor G. C. Guins, who proposed a Solidarist system of law), though it had been used in the West since the late nineteenth century as a designation for the Roman Catholic social and political doctrine and for the cooperativist trend of moderate socialism in France. The basic concept of Russian Solidarism, whose chief theorist is Dr. S. A. Levitsky (educated at Prague University and now teaching in the United States), is Khomyakov's old principle of Conciliarism, and the present-day Solidarists consider themselves as the heirs of all those thinkers and politicians who—whether explicitly or not—adhered to this principle, i.e., the Slavophiles, Dostoevsky, V. S. Solov'ëv, the Landmarks group, Kropotkin, and the Popular Socialists. On the other hand, they also feel themselves to be the heirs to the Russian revolutionary tradition from the Decembrists to the People's Will Party. The political program of the Solidarists now envisages a popular revolution against the Communist dictatorship and the establishment of a democratic multiparty system of government combining adult suffrage with the representation (in a separate chamber) of professional, regional, etc., bodies.

The tactics of the NTS are largely based upon building up a "molecular" organization in Russia, according to a theory formulated by its present chairman, Dr. V. D. Poremsky, a scientist by training and a professional revolutionary. But during the post-Stalin decade it has included indirect cooperation with the reformists, mainly by way of suggesting improvements that can be attained without an overthrow of the Communist government. The campaign of ostentatious public "silence," i.e., passive non-cooperation with the Party authorities, successfully carried out by the oppositional writers in 1956–58, had also been suggested by the Solidarists.

The NTS has a publishing house of its own, situated abroad, which produces a number of newspapers (including, since 1945, the weekly *The Sowing*) and journals, as well as pamphlets and leaflets; it also operates a pirate radio station from abroad called "Free Russia." Having abandoned the Stalinist practice of preventive terror against innocent people, the neo-Leninist leadership of the Communist Party treats its organized enemies all the more harshly. NTS members, if caught, are usually sentenced to death or to long-term imprisonment with work in uranium mines. In the 1950's, the Soviet security organs also organized several terroristic attempts against NTS leaders abroad.

Post-Stalin Revolutionism

The first events of a revolutionary nature after Stalin's death were a series of strikes and revolts in the main concentration-camp areas (Vorkuta in the north of European Russia, Noril'sk in northern Siberia, Karaganda in central Kazakhstan) in 1953–55, which were led by coalitions of Marxists (organized in groups of "True Leninists" and Trotskyists), "Vlasovites" (including NTS members) and nationalist organizations of non-Russians. Although they were all suppressed, they undoubtedly contributed to the urgency of de-Stalinization, especially the abolition of the camps themselves. Strikes ending in clashes with security units, sometimes very serious, have been occurring sporadically since then in many industrial centers, but they do not seem to have had any particular political coloring, only the arrival of troops serving to turn a peaceful strike or procession into a violent clash. Some of the many reported cases of attempts on the lives of members of the "popular teams for the preservation of public order"—i.e., voluntary vigilantes, which have been formed since the late 1950's to assist the police and the security organs—seem to be of a more political nature.

On the other hand, the radicalism of the intellectuals, particularly of the very young, often crosses the dividing line between reformism and revolutionism. Some revolutionary intellectuals join the NTS underground, but many form small revolutionary groups of their own, independent of any outside influence and not recognizing any outside leadership. They hold debates, publish journals (handwritten or duplicated), and sometimes even address large street meetings, thus making use of the tactics that have been revived by Evtushenko and his group (the crowd usually gathers to hear poetry readings). The content of these journals and oral addresses varies. Thus, the first issue of the duplicated journal *Phoenix,* published by a Moscow revolutionary youth group in 1961, besides containing poems with a certain political undertone or openly revolutionary, contains an open letter to Evtushenko from a young man who had been his admirer but had abandoned him because of his compromises with the authorities: Evtushenko is accused of having himself become a part of the Communist establishment. The poem "A Human Manifesto" by Yu. Galanskov in the same issue of *Phoenix* has an anarchist ring—the author calls upon the people to rise and destroy "the rotten prison of the state."

Far more mature is the "Free Philosophical Treatise" by A. S.

Yesenin-Volpin (born 1925), the son of the famous poet and Left Socialist Revolutionary Yesenin. One of the most brilliant mathematicians and logicians in Russia, Yesenin-Volpin, who has inherited a poetic talent from his father, openly professes his anti-Marxist and anti-Communist views. He was arrested in 1949, declared to be insane (reminding us of the treatment meted out to Chaadaev in his day), and placed in a psychiatric hospital, but in the following year he was banished to Karaganda. Released by amnesty after Stalin's death in 1953, he was again arrested in 1959 and again declared to be "mentally unstable," but was once more released and has recently been working in the Academy of Sciences. Shortly before his second arrest, he hurriedly drafted his "Free Philosophical Treatise" and sent it abroad to be published in case of his arrest. In the "Treatise," he rejects any belief in the reality of being, materialism, determinism, and monism—all of them basic concepts of Marxist-Leninist philosophy—and ridicules the Marxist notion of freedom as being "recognized necessity." Speaking of freedom, he says that people value freedom, conceived as the possibility of choice, not because they like to choose but because they desire to choose without compulsion. It was necessary to free oneself from confusing the concept of freedom with the concept of the good, which latter concept often sneaks into the place of freedom. There is an insoluble conflict between man as a living being (in which capacity he puts life above thought, i.e., above seeking the truth) and man as a thinking being (in which capacity he puts thought above life, i.e., above seeking advantage). The "so-called historical materialism, which sees in relationships originating in the sphere of economy the basis for all others, in particular for moral and legal relationships" is obviously erroneous. Its concepts "are inapplicable, for instance, to Soviet society, where a powerful state authority can change the economic system from an agrarian to an industrial one." "A true classification of society should proceed according to a psychological principle, and in political problems the psychological attitudes of various groups towards authority are of primary significance." In the Soviet Union the purely political tendency toward power prevails. The author's political ideal is anarchy, but "an attempt to realize it in practice would, in our time, be a revolting crudity, brigandage and demagogy, and would probably end in usurpation." It is not the role of ideals to be realized: It is enough if fine but unattainable ideals influence our morals. To be honest is the most important thing, and this means not to lie and not to become a traitor (it is not entirely clear from the text what is meant by "traitor"). Neither state nor culture must have power over the convictions of individuals.

Yesenin-Volpin's "Free Philosophical Treatise" ends with the words that have been used as a motto for this book:

"There is no freedom of the press in Russia, but
who can say that there is no freedom of thought?"

Bibliography

General Works

There is no single work covering the whole history of Russian political thought, but the following deal with large parts of it:

Sources

BLINOFF, MARTHE (ed.). *Life and Thought in Old Russia.* University Park, Pa.: The Pennsylvania State University Press, 1961.

BUNYAN, JAMES, and FISHER, HAROLD H. (eds.). *The Bolshevik Revolution, 1917–1918. Documents and Materials.* Stanford, Calif: Stanford University Press, 1934.

GOLDER, F. A. (ed.). *Documents of Russian History, 1914–1917.* New York and London: The Century Co., 1927.

KOHN, HANS (ed.). *The Mind of Modern Russia: Historical and Political Thought of Russia's Great Age.* New Brunswick, N.J.: Rutgers University Press, 1955.

Studies

BERDYAEV, NICOLAS. *The Russian Idea.* New York: The Macmillan Company, 1947.

BILL, VALENTINE T. *The Forgotten Class: The Russian Bourgeoisie from the Earliest Beginnings to 1900.* New York: Frederick A. Praeger, 1959.

BLACK, CYRIL E. (ed.). *The Transformation of Russian Society: Aspects of Social Change Since 1961.* Cambridge, Mass.: Harvard University Press, 1960.

———, *et al.* "The Nature of Imperial Russian Society," *Slavic Review*, XX, 1961.

BLUM, J. *Lord and Peasant in Russia from the 9th to the 19th Century.* Princeton, N.J.: Princeton University Press, 1961.

CHESHIRE, H. T. "The Radicals of the Sixties and Their Leaders," *Slavonic and East European Review*, I, 1922.

CiŽEVSKY, D. *History of Russian Literature from the 11th Century to the End of the Baroque.* New York: Humanities Press, 1960.

FLORINSKY, MICHAEL T. *Russia: A History and Interpretation.* 2 vols. New York: The Macmillan Company, 1953.

GRONSKY, P. P., and ASTROV, N. I. *The War and the Russian Government.* New Haven, Conn., 1929.

HANS, NICHOLAS. *History of Russian Educational Policy, 1701–1917.* London: P. S. King, 1931.

———. *The Russian Tradition in Education.* London: Routledge & Kegan Paul, 1963.

HARCAVE, SIDNEY (ed.). *Readings in Russian History.* 2 vols. New York: Thomas Y. Crowell Company, 1962.

HARE, RICHARD. *Pioneers of Russian Social Thought.* London and New York: Oxford University Press, 1951.

————. *Portraits of Russian Personalities Between Reform and Revolution.* London and New York: Oxford University Press, 1959.

HECKER, J. F. *Russian Sociology.* New York: Columbia University Press, 1916; 2d ed., London, 1934. (The 1934 edition includes the post-1917 period.)

IGNATIEV, P. N., *et al. Russian Schools and Universities in the World War.* New Haven, Conn., 1929.

KARPOVICH, MICHAEL. *Imperial Russia, 1801–1917.* New York, 1932.

KLYUCHEVSKY, VASILI. *History of Russia.* 5 vols. Translated by C. J. HOGARTH. New York: E. P. Dutton & Company, 1911–1913; New York: Russell & Russell, 1960.

KOVALEVSKY, M. *Russian Political Institutions.* Chicago: The University of Chicago Press, 1902.

LAPPO-DANILEVSKY, A. S. "The Development of Science and Learning in Russia," in J. D. DUFF (ed.), *Russian Realities and Problems.* Cambridge: Cambridge University Press, 1917.

LEDERER, IVO J. (ed.). *Russian Foreign Policy: Essays in Historical Perspective.* New Haven, Conn.: Yale University Press, 1962.

LEVIN, ALFRED. *The Second Duma.* New Haven, Conn., 1940.

McLEAN, HUGH, *et al.* (eds.). *Russian Thought and Politics.* ("Harvard Slavic Studies," Vol. IV.) Cambridge, Mass.: Harvard University Press, 1957.

MASARYK, T. G. *The Spirit of Russia: Studies in History, Literature, and Philosophy.* 2 vols. London and New York, 1919; 2d ed., New York: The Macmillan Company, 1955. (Originally published in German in 1913.)

MAZOUR, ANATOLE G. *Modern Russian Historiography.* Princeton, N.J.: D. Van Nostrand Co., 1938; 2d ed., 1958.

MILYOUKOV, P. "Continental Literature: Russia," *Athenaeum,* July, 1889.

MIRSKY, D. S. *Contemporary Russian Literature, 1881–1925.* Rev. ed. New York: Alfred A. Knopf, 1949.

————. *A History of Russian Literature.* Rev. ed. New York: Alfred A. Knopf, 1949.

————. *Russia: A Social History.* London: Cresset Press, 1931.

NAHIRNY, V. C. *The Russian Intelligentsia: From Men of Ideas to Men of Convictions.* ("Comparative Studies in Society and History," Vol. IV.) The Hague, 1962.

PLATONOV, S. F. *History of Russia.* London: Macmillan & Co., 1925.

POLNER, T. J., *et. al. Russian Local Government During the War and the Union of Zemstvos.* New Haven, Conn.: Yale University Press, 1930.

RAEFF, MARC. "The Russian Autocracy and Its Officials," in SIDNEY HARCAVE (ed.), *Readings in Russian History.*

RIASANOVSKY, NICHOLAS V. *A History of Russia.* London and New York: Oxford University Press, 1963.

SIMMONS, ERNEST J. (ed.). *Continuity and Change in Russian and Soviet Thought.* Cambridge, Mass.: Harvard University Press, 1955.

TOMPKINS, S. R. *The Russian Intelligentsia: Makers of the Revolutionary State.* Norman, Okla.: University of Oklahoma Press, 1957.

———. *The Russian Mind: From Peter the Great Through the Enlightenment.* Norman, Okla.: University of Oklahoma Press, 1953.

UTECHIN, S. V. "Bolsheviks and Their Allies After 1917," in SIDNEY HARCAVE (ed.), *Readings in Russian History.*

VINOGRADOFF, P. *Self-Government in Russia.* London: Constable & Co., 1955.

WALKIN, JACOB. *The Rise of Democracy in Pre-Revolutionary Russia: Political and Social Institutions Under the Last Three Czars.* New York: Frederick A. Praeger, 1962; London: Thames and Hudson, 1963.

ZENKOVSKY, V. V. *A History of Russian Philosophy.* 2 vols. New York: Columbia University Press, 1953.

Reference Works

FLORINSKY, MICHAEL T. (ed.). *McGraw-Hill Encyclopedia of Russia and the Soviet Union.* New York: McGraw-Hill Book Company, 1961.

HARKINS, W. E. *Dictionary of Russian Literature.* Paterson, N.J.: Littlefield, Adams & Co., 1959.

UTECHIN, S. V. *Everyman's Concise Encyclopaedia of Russia.* New York: E. P. Dutton & Company; London: J. M. Dent & Sons, 1961.

Bibliographies

FISHER, HAROLD H. (ed.). *American Research on Russia.* Bloomington, Ind.: Indiana University Press, 1959.

HORECKY, PAUL L. (ed.). *Basic Russian Writings.* Chicago: The University of Chicago Press, 1962.

HUNT, ROBERT N. CAREW (ed.). *Books on Communism.* London and New York: Oxford University Press, 1959.

MAICHEL, KAROL. *Guide to Russian Reference Books.* ("Hoover Institution Bibliographical Series," No. 10.) Vol. I, *General Bibliographies and Reference Books.* Stanford, Calif.: Stanford University Press, 1962.

MORLEY, C. *Guide to Research in Russian History.* Syracuse, N.Y.: Syracuse University Press, 1951.

SHAPIRO, D. *A Select Bibliography of Works in English on Russian History, 1801–1917.* London and New York: Oxford University Press, 1962.

"Western Books on the USSR Published in 1961," *Soviet Studies,*
XIV, 1963.

Periodicals

Bulletin of the Institute for the Study of the USSR. Munich.
Problems of Communism. Washington, D.C.
Russian Review. New York.
Slavic Review (formerly *The American Slavic and East European
Review*). Urbana, Ill.
Slavonic and East European Review. London.
Soviet Studies. Oxford.

Introduction

OBOLENSKY, D. "Russia's Byzantine Heritage," *Oxford Slavonic Papers,*
I, 1950.
PHILIPP, W. "Historische Voraussetzungen des politischen Denkens in
Russland," *Forschungen zur osteuropäischen Geschichte* (Berlin),
I, 1954.
TOYNBEE, ARNOLD J. "Russia's Byzantine Heritage," in *Civilization on
Trial.* London and New York: Oxford University Press, 1948.
WEIDLÉ, WLADIMIR. *Russia Absent and Present.* New York: John Day
Company; 2d ed., New York: Vintage Books, 1961.

Chapter 1: Medieval Russia
Chapter 2: Muscovite Russia
Sources

CROSS, S. H. (trans.). *The Russian Primary Chronicle.* ("Harvard Studies
and Notes in Philosophy and Literature," Vol. XII.) Cambridge,
Mass.: Harvard University Press, 1930.
DEWEY, H. W. "The White Lake Charter: A Medieval Russian Admini-
strative Statute," *Speculum,* XXXII, 1957.
MICHELL, R., and FORBES, N. (trans.) *The Chronicle of Novgorod,
1016–1471.* ("Camden Third Series," Vol. XXV.) London, 1914.
VERNADSKY, G. (trans.). "Medieval Russian Laws," in A. P. EVANS (ed.),
Records of Civilization, No. 41. New York: Columbia University
Press, 1947.
ZENKOVSKY, S. A. *Medieval Russian Epics, Chronicles, and Tales.* New
York: E. P. Dutton & Company, 1963.

Studies

ANDREYEV, N. "Filofey and His Epistle to Ivan Vasil'yevich," *Slavonic
and East European Review,* XXXVIII, 1959.
————. "Kurbsky's Letters to Vasyan Muromtsev," *ibid.,* XXXIII, 1955.
CHERNIAVSKY, MICHAEL. *Tsar and People: Studies in Russian Myths.*
New Haven, Conn.: Yale University Press, 1961.

DEWEY, H. W. "The 1497 Sudebnik: Muscovite Russia's First National Law Code," *The American Slavic and East European Review,* XXIX, 1951.

DVORNIK, FRANCIS. "Byzantine Political Ideas in Kievan Russia." ("Dumbarton Oaks Papers," Nos. 9 and 10.) Cambridge, Mass., 1956.

ECK, A. *Le Moyen Age russe.* Paris, 1933.

FENNELL, J. L. I. "The Attitude of the Josephians and the Trans-Volga Elders to the Heresy of the Judaisers," *Slavonic and East European Review,* XXIX, 1951.

HAMMER, D. P. "Russia and the Roman Law," *The American Slavic and East European Review,* XVI, 1957.

KEEP, J. L. H. "The Decline of the Zemsky Sobor," *Slavonic and East European Review,* XXXVI, 1957.

————. "The Regime of Filaret," *ibid.,* XXXVIII, 1960.

KLYUCHEVSKY, V. O. "St. Sergius: The Importance of His Life and Work," *Russian Review* (London), 1913.

LAPPO-DANILEVSKY, A. S. "L'Idée de l'Etat et Son Evolution en Russie depuis les Troubles du XVII*e* Siècle jusq'aux Reformes du XVIII*e*," in P. VINOGRADOFF (ed.), *Essays in Legal History.* London: Oxford University Press, 1913.

MASARYK, T. G. *The Spirit of Russia: Studies in History, Literature, and Philosophy.* Vol. I.

MEDLIN, W. K. *Moscow and East Rome: A Political Study of the Relations of Church and State in Muscovite Russia.* New York: Gregory Lorenz, 1952.

PHILIPP, W. "Ansätze zum geschichtlichen und politischen Denken im Kiewer Russland," *Jahrbücher für Geschichte Osteuropas,* Beiheft 3. Breslau, 1940.

RAEFF, MARC. "An Early Theorist of Absolutism: Joseph of Volokolamsk," *The American Slavic and East European Review,* VIII, 1949.

ŠEVČENKO, I. "A Neglected Byzantine Source of Muscovite Ideology." ("Harvard Slavic Studies," Vol. II.) Cambridge, Mass.: Harvard University Press, 1954.

SOLOVIEV, A. V. *Holy Russia: The History of a Religious-Social Idea.* New York: Humanities Press, 1959.

SPINKA, M. "Patriarch Nikon and the Subjection of the Russian Church to the State," *Church History,* X, 1941.

STREMOUKHOFF, D. "Moscow, the Third Rome: Sources of the Doctrine," *Speculum,* 1953.

SZEFTEL, M. "Aspects of Feudalism in Russian History," in R. COULBORN (ed.), *Feudalism in History.* Princeton, N.J.: Princeton University Press, 1956.

TCHÉREPNINE, L. "Le Rôle des Zemski Sobory en Russie lors de la guerre des paysans au debut du XVII siècle." (Études présentées à la Commission Internationale pour l'histoire des Assemblées d'États, Vol. XXIII.) 1960.

VASILIEV, A. "Was Old Russia a Vassal State of Byzantium?" *Speculum,* VII, 1932.

WOLFF, R. L. "The Three Romes: The Migration of an Ideology and the Making of an Autocrat," *Daedalus,* Spring, 1959.

Chapter 3: Petrine Russia

Sources

KARAMZIN, A. M. *Letters of a Russian Traveler, 1789–90.* Edited by F. JONAS. New York: Columbia University Press, 1957.

PIPES, RICHARD (ed.). *Karamzin's Memoir on Ancient and Modern Russia: A Translation and Analysis.* Cambridge, Mass.: Harvard University Press, 1959.

RADISHCHEV, A. N. *A Journey from St. Petersburg to Moscow.* Edited, with an Introduction and Notes, by R. P. THALER. Cambridge, Mass.: Harvard University Press, 1958.

Studies

ALEKSEEV, M. P. "Adam Smith and His Russian Admirers in the Eighteenth Century," in W. R. Scott, *Adam Smith as Student and Professor.* Glasgow: Jackson, Son & Co., 1937.

ANDERSON, M. S. "Some British Influences on Russian Intellectual Life and Society in the Eighteenth Century," *Slavonic and East European Review,* XXXIX, 1960.

KLYUCHEVSKY, VASILI. *Peter the Great.* Translated by L. ARCHIBALD. St Martin's Press, 1959.

LANG, D. M. *The First Russian Radical.* London: Allen & Unwin, 1959.

———. "Some Western Sources of Radishchev's Political Thought," *Revue des études slaves* (Paris), XXV, 1949.

LEONTOVITSCH, V. *Geschichte des Liberalismus in Russland.* Frankfurt/Main, 1957.

MCCONNELL, A. "Radishchev's Political Thought," *The American Slavic and East European Review,* XVII, 1958.

MCGREW, R. E. "Notes on the Princely Role in Karamzin's *Istorija gosudarstva Rossij'skago,*" *The American Slavic and East European Review,* XVIII, 1959.

MASARYK, T. G. *The Spirit of Russia: Studies in History, Literature, and Philosophy.* Vol. I.

MAZOUR, ANATOLE G. *The First Russian Revolution, 1825: The Decembrist Movement, Its Origin, Development, and Significance.* 2d ed., Stanford, Calif.: Stanford University Press, 1961.

RAEFF, MARC. *Michael Speransky: Statesman of Imperial Russia, 1772–1839.* The Hague, 1957.

———. "State and Mobility in the Ideology of M. M. Shcherbatov," *The American Slavic and East European Review,* XXIX, 1960.

ROGGER, HANS. *National Consciousness in Eighteenth-Century Russia.* Cambridge, Mass.: Harvard University Press, 1960.

SCHWARZ-SOCHOR, J. "P. I. Pestel: The Beginning of Jacobin Thought in Russia," *International Review of Social History*, III, Part 1, 1958.

STRAKHOVSKY, L. I. "Constitutional Aspects of the Imperial Russian Government's Policy Toward National Minorities," *Journal of Modern History*, XIII, 1941.

STUPPERICH, R. *Staatsgedanke und Religionspolitik Peters d. Grossen.* Breslau, 1936.

YARMOLINSKY, AVRAHM. *Road to Revolution: A Century of Russian Radicalism.* London, 1957.

ZETLIN, MIKHAIL. *The Decembrists.* New York: International Universities Press, 1958.

Chapter 4: The Theory of Official Nationality and Its Antidote
Sources

GOLDER, F. A. (ed.). *Documents of Russian History, 1914–1917.*

KOHN, HANS (ed.). *The Mind of Modern Russia.* (Chap. ii, "Russia's Place in Universal History: Chaadayev.")

Studies

BALMUTH, B. D. "The Origins of the Tsarist Epoch of Censorship Terror," *American Slavic and East European Review*, XIX, 1960.

BENNET, F. "The Campaign Against the Duma," *Russian Review* (London), II, 1913.

CURTISS, J. S. *Church and State in Russia: The Last Years of the Empire, 1900–1917.* New York: Columbia University Press, 1940.

KOYRÉ, A. "Russia's Place in the World: P. Chaadayev and the Slavophils," *Slavonic and East European Review*, III, 1927.

LEDERER, IVO J. (ed.). *Russian Foreign Policy: Essays in Historical Perspective.* New Haven, Conn.: Yale University Press, 1962.

MONAS, SIDNEY. *The Third Section: Police and Society in Russia Under Nicholas I.* Cambridge, Mass.: Harvard University Press, 1961.

MOSKOFF, E. *The Russian Philosopher Chaadaev: His Ideas and His Epoch.* New York, 1937.

RIASANOVSKY, NICHOLAS V. *Nicholas I and Official Nationality in Russia, 1825–1855.* Berkeley and Los Angeles: University of California Press, 1959.

VASILIEV, A. T. *The Okhrana: The Russian Secret Police.* Philadelphia, 1930.

Chapter 5: Slavophilism
Sources

DOSTOEVSKY, F. M. *The Diary of a Writer.* Translated by R. BRASOL. New York: George Braziller, 1954.

KOHN, HANS (ed.). *The Mind of Modern Russia.* (Chap. iii, "The Slav and World Mission of Russia: Pofodin"; chap. v, "Russia and the

Revolution: Tysetchev"; chap. vi, "Slavophil and Orthodox Russia: Khomyakov and Aksakov"; chap. x, "Russia and the West: Danilevsky.")

Studies

BERDYAEV, NICHOLAS. *Dostoevsky.* Cleveland and New York: Meridian Books.

CHRISTOFF, P. K. "A. S. Xomjakov," in *An Introduction to Nineteenth-Century Russian Slavophilism.* Vol. I. The Hague, 1961.

FADNER, F. *Seventy Years of Pan-Slavism in Russia: Karamzin to Danilevsky, 1800–1870.* Washington, D.C., 1961.

FLOROVSKY, A. "Dostoyevsky and the Slavonic Question," *Slavonic and East European Review,* IX, 1930.

FLOROVSKY, G. "The Historical Premonitions of Tyutchen," *Slavonic and East European Review,* III, 1924.

GRATIEUX, ALBERT. *A. S. Khomiakoff et le mouvement slavophile.* 2 vols. Paris, 1939.

KOHN, HANS. "Dostoevsky and Danilevsky: Nationalist Messianism," in E. J. SIMMONS (ed.). *Continuity and Change in Russian and Soviet Thought.*

———. *Pan-Slavism: Its History and Ideology.* Notre Dame, Ind.: University of Notre Dame Press, 1953; rev. ed., New York, Vintage Books, 1960.

———. *Prophets and Peoples: Studies in Nineteenth-Century Nationalism.* New York: The Macmillan Company, 1947.

LAVRIN, J. "Populists and Slavophiles," *Russian Review,* XXI, 1962.

LUBAC, H. DE. *The Drama of Atheist Humanism.* London and New York: Sheed & Ward, 1949.

MASARYK, T. G. *The Spirit of Russia: Studies in History, Literature, and Philosophy.*

PETROVICH, M. B. *The Emergence of Russian Panslavism, 1856–1870.* New York: Columbia University Press, 1956.

RIASANOVSKY, NICHOLAS V. *Russia and the West in the Teaching of the Slavophiles.* Cambridge, Mass.: Harvard University Press, 1952.

SEDURO, VLADIMIR. *Dostoyevsky in Russian Literary Criticism, 1846–1956.* New York: Columbia University Press, 1957.

ZENKOVSKY, V. V. "The Slavophil Idea Re-Stated," *Slavonic and East European Review,* VI, 1927.

Chapter 6: Westernism

Sources

BROWDER, ROBERT P., and KERENSKY, ALEXANDER F. (eds.). *The Russian Provisional Government, 1917.* 3 vols. Stanford, Calif.: Stanford University Press, 1961.

CHERNYSHEVSKY, N. G. *Selected Philosophical Essays.* Moscow, 1953.

FISHER, HAROLD H. (ed.) *Out of My Past: The Memoirs of Count Kokovtsov.* Stanford, Calif.: Stanford University Press, 1935.

GOLDER, F. A. (ed.). *Documents of Russian History, 1914–1917.*

GUCHKOV, A. J. "The Third International and Colonial Propaganda," *Slavonic and East European Review,* X, 1932.

————. "Types of Russian Oratory: The General Political Situation and the Octobrist Party." (Speech delivered on November 21, 1913, at the Conference of the Octobrist Party in St. Petersburg.) *Russian Review* (London), III, 1914.

————. "Types of Russian Parliamentary Oratory." (Speeches on the naval and military estimates of 1908.) *Ibid.,* II, 1913.

GURKO, V. I. *Features and Figures of the Past: Government and Opinion in the Reign of Nicholas II.* Stanford, Calif., and London, 1939.

HERZEN, ALEXANDER J. *My Past and Thoughts.* Translated by CONSTANCE GARNETT. 6 vols. London: Chatto & Windus, 1924–27.

KOHN, HANS (ed.). *The Mind of Modern Russia.* (Chap. vii, "Progressive Russia: Belinsky"; chap. viii, "Radical Russia: Chernyshevsky"; chap. ix, "Education to Liberty: Herzen.")

KOVALEVSKY, M. M. *Russian Political Institutions.* Chicago, 1902.

————. "The Upper House in Russia," *Russian Review* (London), I, 1912.

LVOV, N. "The Place of Local Government Under the Constitution," *Russian Review* (London), III, 1914.

MAKLAKOV, B. "Local Justice in Russia," *Russian Review* (London), II, 1913.

————. "The Peasant Question and the Russian Revolution," *Slavonic and East European Review,* II, 1923.

MANNILOV, A. "Agrarian Reform in Russia," *Russian Review* (London), I, 1912.

MEYENDORFF, A. "The Working of the Russian Constitution," *Russian Review* (London), I, 1912.

MILYUKOV, P. N. "Continental Literature: Russia," *Athenaeum,* July, 1889.

————. "The Influence of English Political Thought in Russia," *Slavonic and East European Review,* V, 1926.

————. "The Representative System in Russia," in J. D. DUFF (ed.), *Russian Realities and Problems.*

————. *Russia and Its Crisis.* Chicago, 1905.

————. *Russia To-day and To-morrow.* London: Macmillan & Co., 1922.

————. "The War and Balkan Politics," in J. D. DUFF (ed.), *Russian Realities and Problems.*

————. "The World War and Slavonic Policy," *Slavonic and East European Review,* VI, 1927.

NABOKOV, V., and RODICHEV, F. "Types of Russian Parliamentary Oratory: The Government's Reply to the Address to the Throne of the

First Duma, and Speeches on This Reply by V. Nabokov and F. Rodichev," *Russian Review* (London), II, 1913.

PARES, BERNARD. "Conversations with Mr. Stolypin," *Russian Review* (London), II, 1913.

POBYEDONOSTSEFF, K. P. *Reflections of a Russian Statesman*. Translated by R. C. LONG. London: Richards, 1898.

"Pobyedonostsev and Alexander III," *Slavonic and East European Review*, VII, 1928.

RODICHEV, F. "The Liberal Movement in Russia, 1855–1917," *Slavonic and East European Review*, II, 1923.

————. "The Veteran of Russian Liberalism: Ivan Petrunkevich," *ibid.*, VII, 1929.

RODZYANKO, M. V., *et al.*, "A Symposium on the Third Duma," *Russian Review* (London), I, 1912.

SHIDLOVSKY, S. "The Imperial Duma and Land Settlement," *Russian Review* (London), I, 1912.

SHINGAREV, A. "The Reform of Local Finance in Russia," *Russian Review* (London), I, 1912.

SHIPOV, D. "Correspondence of Count Heyden," *Russian Review* (London), III, 1914.

SHULGIN, V. "The Months Before the Russian Revolution," *Slavonic and East European Review*, I, 1922.

STAKHOVICH, M. "Types of Russian Parliamentary Oratory: Mr. M. Stakhovich on Terrorism, May 17, 1906," *Russian Review* (London), II, 1913.

TIKHOMIROFF, L. *Russia: Political and Social*. Translated from the French by E. AVELING. 2 vols. London: Sonnenschein, 1888.

URUSOV, S. "Types of Russian Parliamentary Oratory: Speech on the Armed Attacks on Jews," *Russian Review* (London), II, 1913.

VINOGRADOFF, P. *The Russian Problem*. London: Constable & Co., 1914.

————. *Self-Government in Russia*.

————. (ed.). *The Reconstruction of Russia*. London: Oxford University Press, 1919.

YARMOLINSKY, AVRAHM (ed. and trans.). *The Memoirs of Count Witte*. London: William Heinemann, 1922.

Studies

AVAKUMOVICH, I. "A Statistical Approach to the Revolutionary Movement in Russia, 1878–1887," *American Slavic and East European Review*, XVIII, 1959.

BECKER, C. "Raznochintsy: The Development of the Word and of the Concept," *American Slavic and East European Review*, XVIII, 1959.

BERLIN, ISAIAH. "Herzen and Bakunin on Individual Liberty," in E. J. SIMMONS (ed.), *Continuity and Change in Russian and Soviet Thought*.

————. "A Marvelous Decade, 1838–48: The Birth of the Russian Intelligentsia," *Encounter*, IV–VI, 1955–56.

————. "Russia and 1848," *Slavonic and East European Review*, XXVI, 1948.

BOWMAN, H. E. "Revolutionary Elitism in Černyshevsky," *American Slavic and East European Review*, XIII, 1954.

————. *Vissarion Belinski: A Study in the Origins of Social Criticism in Russia*. Cambridge, Mass.: Harvard University Press, 1954.

BYRNES, ROBERT F. "Pobedonostsev on the Instruments of Russian Government," in ERNEST J. SIMMONS (ed.), *Continuity and Change in Russian and Soviet Thought*.

————. "Pobedonostsev's Conception of the Good Society: An Analysis of His Thought After 1880," *Review of Politics*, XIII, 1951.

CRISP, O. "The Russian Liberals and the 1905 Anglo-French Loan to Russia," *Slavonic and East European Review*, XXXIX, 1961.

DANIELS, R. V. "Intellectuals and the Russian Revolution," *American Slavic and East European Review*, XX, 1961.

DOROSH, H. *Russian Constitutionalism*. New York, 1944.

FISCHER, GEORGE. *Russian Liberalism: From Gentry to Intelligentsia*. Cambridge, Mass.: Harvard University Press, 1958. (See the review by B. ELKIN in *Slavonic and East European Review*, XXXVIII, 1959.)

FOOTMAN, DAVID. *Red Prelude: The Life of the Russian Terrorist Zhelyabov*. London: Cresset Press, 1944; New Haven, Conn.: Yale University Press, 1945.

HARE, RICHARD. *Pioneers of Russian Social Thought*.

————. *Portraits of Russian Personalities Between Reform and Revolution*.

HECHT, D. *Russian Radicals Look to America, 1825–1894*. Cambridge, Mass.: Harvard University Press; London: Oxford University Press, 1947.

KARPOVICH, MICHAEL. "A Forerunner of Lenin: P. N. Tkachev," *Review of Politics*, VI, 1944.

————. "The Historical Background of Soviet Thought Control," in WALDERMAR GURIAN (ed.), *The Soviet Union: Background, Ideology, Reality*. Notre Dame, Ind.: University of Notre Dame Press, 1951.

————. "Two Types of Russian Liberalism: Maklakov and Miliukov," in ERNEST J. SIMMONS (ed.), *Continuity and Change in Russian and Soviet Thought*.

KIESEWETTER, A. A. "Klyuchevsky and His Course of Russian History," *Slavonic and East European Review*, I, 1923.

KUCHEROV, SAMUEL. *Courts, Lawyers, and Trials Under the Last Three Tsars*. New York: Frederick A. Praeger, 1953.

LAMPERT, E. *Studies in Rebellion*. New York: Frederick A. Praeger; London: Routledge & Kegan Paul, 1957.

LEONTOVITSCH, V. *Geschichte des Liberalismus in Russland*.

LEVIN, ALFRED. "Russian Bureaucratic Opinion in the Wake of the 1905 Revolution," *Jahrbücher zur Geschichte Osteuropas*, Neue Folge, XI, 1963.

MACMAHON, A. W. "Ostrogorsky," *Encyclopaedia of the Social Sciences,* XI. New York, 1933.

MALIA, MARTIN. *Alexander Herzen and the Birth of Russian Socialism, 1812–1835.* Cambridge, Mass.: Harvard University Press, 1961.

MASARYK, T. G. *The Spirit of Russia: Studies in History, Literature, and Philosophy.*

MATHEWSON, R. W., JR., *The Positive Hero in Russian Literature.* New York: Columbia University Press, 1958.

MOSSE, W. E. *Alexander II and the Modernisation of Russia.* London: English Universities Press, 1958.

OWEN, L. A. *The Russian Peasant Movement, 1906–1917.* London: P. S. King, 1937.

PARES, BERNARD. *Russia and Reform.* London: Constable & Co., 1907.

———. "Sir Paul Vinogradoff: The Public Man," *Slavonic and East European Review,* IV, 1926.

RAEFF, MARC. "A Reactionary Liberal: M. N. Katkov," *Russian Review,* XI, 1952.

REEVE, H. S. "Utopian Socialism in Russian Literature: 1840's–1860's," *The American Slavic and East European Review,* XVIII, 1959.

ROBINSON, GERALD T. *Rural Russia Under the Old Regime.* New York: The Macmillan Company, 1932.

SCHAPIRO, LEONARD. "The Pre-Revolutionary Intelligentsia and the Legal Order," in RICHARD PIPES (ed.), *The Russian Intelligentsia.* New York: Columbia University Press, 1961.

SZEFTEL, M. "Personal Inviolability in the Legislation of the Russian Absolute Monarchy," *American Slavic and East European Review,* XVII, 1958.

TIDMARSH, K. "Lev Tikhomirov and a Crisis in Russian Radicalism," *Russian Review,* XX, 1961.

TREADGOLD, DONALD W. *The Great Siberian Migration: Government and Peasant in Resettlement from Emancipation to the First World War.* Princeton, N.J.: Princeton University Press, 1957.

TURIN, S. P. "N. Chernyshevsky and J. S. Mill," *Slavonic and East European Review,* IX, 1930.

UTECHIN, S. V. "Who Taught Lenin?" *Twentieth Century,* July, 1960.

VENTURI, FRANCO. *Roots of Revolution: A History of the Populist and Socialist Movements in Nineteenth-Century Russia.* New York: Alfred A. Knopf, 1960. (Originally published in Italian under the title *Il populismo russo.* 2 vols. Turin, 1952.)

VON LAUE, T. H. "Count Witte and the Russian Revolution of 1905," *American Slavic and East European Review,* XVII, 1958.

———. *Sergei Witte and the Industrialization of Russia.* New York: Columbia University Press, 1963.

YARMOLINSKY, AVRAHM. *Road to Revolution: A Century of Russian Radicalism.* New York: The Macmillan Company, 1959.

Chapter 7: Populism

Sources

BLOK, A. A. "The Collapse of Humanism," in *The Oxford Outlook*. Translated by ISAIAH BERLIN. 1931.

BUNYAN, JAMES, and FISHER, HAROLD H. (eds.). *The Bolshevik Revolution, 1917–1918*. Stanford, Calif., and London, 1934.

CHERNOV, V. *The Great Russian Revolution*. Translated by PHILIP E. MOSELY. New Haven, Conn., 1936.

———. "Lenin," *Foreign Affairs*, 1924.

GOLDER, F. A. (ed.). *Documents of Russian History, 1914–1917*.

KRAVCHINSKY, S. M. *Underground Russia*. New York, 1892. (Contains a Preface by P. L. LAVROV.)

LAVROV, P. L. *Lettres historiques*. Paris, 1903.

———. *La Propagande Socialiste*. Paris, 1898.

McNEAL, ROBERT H. (ed.). *The Russian Revolution: Why Did the Bolsheviks Win?* New York: Rinehart & Company, 1959.

MYAKOTIN, B. "Lenin, 1870–1924," *Slavonic and East European Review*, II, 1924.

Studies

ANWEILER, O. *Die Rätebewegung in Russland, 1905–1921*. ("Studien zur Geschichte Osteuropas," Vol. V.) Leiden, 1958.

AVAKUMOVICH, I. "A Statistical Approach to the Revolutionary Movement in Russia, 1878–1887," *The American Slavic and East European Review*, XVIII, 1959.

BILLINGTON, JAMES H. *Mikhailovsky and Russian Populism*. London and New York: Oxford University Press, 1958.

BLANC, E. T. *Cooperative Movement in Russia*. New York, 1924.

DANIELS, ROBERT V. "Intellectuals and the Russian Revolution," *American Slavic and East European Review*, XX, 1961.

FOOTMAN, DAVID. *Red Prelude: The Life of the Russian Terrorist Zhelyabov*.

HECHT, D. *Russian Radicals Look to America, 1825–1894*. Cambridge, Mass.: Harvard University Press; London: Oxford University Press, 1947.

KAYDEN, E. M., and ANTSIFEROV, A. N. *The Cooperative Movement in Russia During the War*. New Haven, Conn.: 1929.

LAVRIN, J. "Populists and Slavophiles," *Russian Review*, XXI, 1962.

MASARYK, T. G. *The Spirit of Russia: Studies in History, Literature and Philosophy*.

MENDEL, ARTHUR P. *Dilemmas of Progress in Tsarist Russia: Legal Marxism and Legal Populism*. Cambridge, Mass.: Harvard University Press, 1961.

RADKEY, OLIVER H. *The Agrarian Foes of Bolshevism*. New York: Columbia University Press, 1958.

————. "Chernov and Agrarian Socialism Before 1918," in ERNEST J. SIMMONS (ed.), *Continuity and Change in Russian and Soviet Thought.*

————. *The Sickle Under the Hammer: The Russian Socialist Revolutionaries in the Early Months of Soviet Rule.* New York: Columbia University Press, 1963.

SHINN, W. T., JR. "The Law of the Russian Peasant Household," *Slavic Review*, XX, 1961.

TREADGOLD, DONALD W. *Lenin and His Rivals: The Struggle for Russia's Future, 1898–1906.* New York: Frederick A. Praeger, 1955.

VENTURI, FRANCO. *Roots of Revolution: A History of the Populist and Socialist Movements in Nineteenth-Century Russia.*

WALKER, F. A. "The Morality of Revolution in P. L. Lavrov," *Slavonic and East European Review*, XLI, 1962.

WILDMAN, A. K. "The Russian Intelligentsia of the 1890's," *The American Slavic and East European Review*, XIX, 1960.

YARMOLINSKY, AVRAHM. *Road to Revolution: A Century of Russian Radicalism.*

Chapter 8: Regionalism, Anarchism, and Syndicalism
Sources

BUNYAN, JAMES. *Intervention, Civil War, and Communism in Russia, April–December, 1918: Documents and Materials.* Baltimore: The Johns Hopkins Press, 1936.

————, and FISHER, HAROLD H. (eds.). *The Bolshevik Revolution, 1917–1918.* Stanford, Calif., and London, 1934.

KROPOTKIN, P. A. "Anarchism," in *Encyclopaedia Britannica.*

————. *Fields, Factories, and Workshops.* London: Hutchinson & Co., 1899; 1919.

————. *Modern Science and Anarchism.* London: Freedom Press, 1913.

————. *The State: Its Part in History.* 1898; 1943.

MAXIMOFF, G. P. (ed.). *The Political Philosophy of Bakunin: Scientific Anarchism.* Chicago: The Free Press of Glencoe, 1953.

READ, HERBERT (ed.). *Kropotkin: Selections from His Writings.* London, 1942.

Studies

ANWEILER, O. *Die Rätebewegung in Russland, 1905–1921.* ("Studien zur Geschichte Osteuropas," Vol. V.)

FOOTMAN, DAVID. *Civil War in Russia.* New York: Frederick A. Praeger; London: Faber and Faber, 1962.

HARE, RICHARD. *Portraits of Russian Personalities Between Reform and Revolution.*

HECHT, D. *Russian Radicals Look to America, 1825–1894.* Cambridge, Mass.: Harvard University Press; London: Oxford University Press, 1947.

KOLARZ, WALTER. *The Peoples of the Soviet Far East.* New York: Frederick A. Praeger, 1954.

———. *Russia and Her Colonies.* New York: Frederick A. Praeger; London: George Philip & Co., 1952.

LAMPERT, E. *Studies in Rebellion.*

LASERSON, MAX M. *Russia and the Western World: The Place of the Soviet Union in the Comity of Nations.* New York: The Macmillan Company, 1945.

MASARYK, T. G. *The Spirit of Russia: Studies in History, Literature, and Philosophy.*

MAZOUR, ANATOLE G. *Modern Russian Historiography.*

NOMAD, MAX. *Apostles of Revolution.* 1939; rev. ed., New York: Collier Books, 1961.

PIPES, RICHARD. *The Formation of the Soviet Union.* Cambridge, Mass.: Harvard University Press, 1954.

PYZIUR, EUGENE. *The Doctrine of Anarchism of M. A. Bakunin.* Milwaukee, Wis.: The Marquette University Press, 1955.

UTECHIN, S. V. "Bolsheviks and Their Allies After 1917," in SIDNEY HARCAVE (ed.), *Readings in Russian History.*

VENTURI, FRANCO. *Roots of Revolution: A History of the Populist and Socialist Movements in Nineteenth-Century Russia.*

YAROSLAVSKY, E. M. *History of Anarchism in Russia.* London: Lawrence and Wishart, 1937.

Chapter 9: Religious Thinkers of the Late Nineteenth and Early Twentieth Centuries
Sources

KOHN, HANS (ed.). *Documents of Russian History, 1914–1917.* (Chap. xi, "Russia and the West: Solovyev.")

ROZANOV, V. V. *Fallen Leaves.* Translated by S. S. KOLETIANSKY. London: Mandrake Press, 1920.

———. "On the Epochs of Russian History," *Slavonic and East European Review,* VIII, 1929.

———. *Selected Works.* Edited by G. IVASK. New York, 1956.

———. *Solitaria.* Translated by S. S. KOLETIANSKY. London: Wishart & Co., 1927.

SOLOV'ËV, V. S. *The Justification of the Good.* Translated by N. A. DUDDINGTON. London: Constable's Russian Library, 1918.

———. *Lectures on Godmanhood.* Poughkeepsie, 1944; London, 1948.

———. *Russia and the Universal Church.* Translated by H. REES. London: Geoffrey Bles, 1948.

———. *A Solov'ev Anthology.* Edited by S. L. FRANK. 1950.

———. *War, Progress, and the End of History.* Translated by A. BAKSTRY. London: Hodder & Staughton, 1915.

TOLSTOY, LEO. *Works.* Translated by LOUISE and AYLMER MAUDE. 21 vols. London and New York: Oxford University Press, 1928–37.

"Two Letters of L. Tolstoy: 1. On Nonresistance to Evil; 2. To the Slavonic Congress of 1910 in Sofia," *Slavonic and East European Review*, VIII, 1929.

Studies

ALDANOV, M. A. "Some Reflections on Tolstoy and Tolstoyism," *Slavonic and East European Review*, VII, 1929.
BERDYAEV, NICHOLAS. *Leontiev.* Translated by GEORGE REAVEY. London: Geoffrey Bles, 1940.
BERLIN, ISAIAH. *The Hedgehog and the Fox.* New York: Simon and Schuster, 1953.
HARE, RICHARD. *Pioneers of Russian Social Thought.*
————. *Portraits of Russian Personalities Between Reform and Revolution.*
LAVRIN, J. "Vladimir Solovyev (2)," *Slavonic and East European Review*, X, 1921.
LOSSKY, N. *History of Russian Philosophy.* New York: International Universities Press, 1951.
MASARYK, T. G. *The Spirit of Russia: Studies in History, Literature, and Philosophy.* Vol. II.
POGGIOLI, RENATO. *Rozanov.* London, 1957.
STEINER, GEORGE. *Tolstoy or Dostoyevsky: An Essay in Contrast.* New York: Alfred A. Knopf, 1959; London: Faber & Faber, 1960.
UTECHIN, S. V. "Bolsheviks and Their Allies After 1917," in SIDNEY HARCAVE (ed.), *Readings in Russian History.*
ZENKOVSKY, V. V. *A History of Russian Philosophy.* 2 vols. New York: Columbia University Press, 1953.

Chapter 10: Late Nineteenth and Early Twentieth Century Reformist Trends
Sources

BROWDER, ROBERT P., and KERENSKY, ALEXANDER F. (eds.). *The Russian Provisional Government, 1917.*
BULGAKOV, S. N. "At the Feast of the Gods: Contemporary Dialogues," *Slavonic and East European Review*, I, 1922–23.
————. "Heroism and Service: Thoughts on the Religious Character of the Russian Intelligentsia," *Russian Review* (London), III, 1914.
————. "Judas or Saul? Thoughts on the Russian People," *Slavonic and East European Review*, IX, 1931.
————. "The Old and the New: A Study in Russian Religion," *ibid.*, II, 1924.
————. "The Russian Public and Religion," *Russian Review* (London), I, 1912.
————. *Social Teaching in Modern Russian Orthodox Theology.* Evanston, Ill., 1934.

GOLDER, F. A. (ed.). *Documents of Russian History, 1914–1917.*

KERENSKY, ALEXANDER F. *The Catastrophe.* New York, 1927.

STRUVE, P. "The Balkan War and Russia's Task," *Russian Review* (London), II, 1913.

———. "Ivan Aksakov," *Slavonic and East European Review,* II, 1924.

———. "My Contacts and Conflicts with Lenin," *ibid.,* XII and XIII, April and July, 1934.

———. "Past and Present of Russian Economics," in J. D. DUFF (ed.), *Russian Realities and Problems.*

———. "Russia," *Slavonic and East European Review,* I, 1922.

———. *La théorie marxienne de l'évolution sociale: Essai critique.* With an Introduction by RICHARD PIPES. ("Cahiers de l'Institut de Science Economique Appliquée," No. 129.) Paris, 1962. (Originally published in German in *Archiv für soziale Gesetzgebung und Statistik,* Vol. XIV, Berlin, 1899.)

Studies

BLANC, E. T. *Cooperative Movement in Russia.*

FLOROVSKY, G. "Michael Gerschensohn," *Slavonic and East European Review,* V, 1926.

GRANICK, DAVID. *The Red Executive: A Study of the Organization Man in Russian Industry.* Garden City, N.Y.: Doubleday and Company, 1960.

LASERSON, MAX M. *The American Impact on Russia, 1784–1917.* New York: Collier Books.

KAYDEN, E. M., and ANTSIFEROV, A. N. *The Cooperative Movement in Russia During the War.*

MASARYK, T. G. *The Spirit of Russia: Studies in History, Literature, and Philosophy.* Vol. II.

MENDEL, ARTHUR P. *Dilemmas of Progress in Tsarist Russia.* Cambridge, Mass.: Harvard University Press, 1961.

SCHAPIRO, LEONARD. "The Pre-Revolutionary Intelligentsia and the Legal Order," in RICHARD PIPES (ed.), *The Russian Intelligentsia.* New York: Columbia University Press, 1961.

———. "The Vekhi Group and the Mystique of Revolution," *Slavonic and East European Review,* XXXIV, 1955.

TIDMARSH, K. "The Zubatov Idea," *American Slavic and East European Review,* XIX, 1960.

UTECHIN, S. V. "Bolsheviks and Their Allies After 1917," in SIDNEY HARCAVE (ed.), *Readings in Russian History.*

ZAGORSKY, S. O. *State Control of Industry in Russia During the War.* New Haven, Conn.: 1928.

ZENKOVSKY, V. V. *A History of Russian Philosophy.* 2 vols. New York: Columbia University Press, 1953.

Chapter 11: Social Democratism

Sources

BOGDANOV, A. A. *A Short Course of Economic Science*. London: Labour Publishing Co., 1923.

BROWDER, ROBERT P., and KERENSKY, ALEXANDER F. (eds.). *The Russian Provisional Government, 1917*. 3 vols. Stanford, Calif.: Stanford University Press, 1961.

BUNYAN, JAMES, and FISHER, HAROLD H. (eds.). *The Bolshevik Revolution, 1917–1918.*

GOLDER, F. A. (ed.). *Documents of Russian History, 1914–1917.*

GRINEWITSCH, W. *Die Gewerkschaftsbewegung in Russland*. Vol. I. Berlin, 1927.

KHRUSTALYEV-NASAR, G. "The Council of Workmen Deputies," *Russian Review* (London), II, 1913.

LENIN, V. I. "Credo," in *Selected Works*. Vol. I. New York: International Publishers, 1943.

PLEKHANOV, G. V. *Fundamental Problems of Marxism*. New York, 1929.

———. *Introduction à l'Histoire sociale de la Russie*. Paris, 1926.

———. *The Role of the Individual in History*. New York: International Publishers, 1940.

POKROVSKY, M. N. *Brief History of Russia*. 2 vols. London, 1933.

Studies

BARON, S. H. "Between Marx and Lenin: G. Plekhanov," in LEOPOLD LABEDZ (ed.), *Revisionism: Essays on the History of Marxist Ideas*. New York: Frederick A. Praeger; London: Allen & Unwin, 1962.

———. "Plekhanov and the Origins of Russian Marxism," *Russian Review*, XIII, 1954.

BAUER, RAYMOND A. *The New Man in Soviet Psychology*. Cambridge, Mass.: Harvard University Press, 1959.

FÜLÖP-MILLER, RENÉ. *The Mind and Face of Bolshevism*. New York and London: G. P. Putnam's Sons, 1927.

HARE, RICHARD. "M. Gorky and the Bolsheviks," in *Portraits of Russian Personalities Between Reform and Revolution*.

———. *Maxim Gorky: Romantic Realist and Conservative Revolutionary*. London, 1962.

HECKER, J. G. *Moscow Dialogues*. London: Chapman & Hall, 1933.

———. *Russian Sociology*.

KANN, A. "M. Gorky in the Revolution of 1905," *Slavonic and East European Review*, IX, 1930.

KINDERSLEY, R. K. *The First Russian Revisionists: A Study of Legal Marxism in Russia*. London and New York: Oxford University Press, 1962.

MASARYK, T. G. *The Spirit of Russia: Studies in History, Literature, and Philosophy*. Vol. II.

MAZOUR, ANATOLE G. *Modern Russian Historiography.*

MEDALIC, R. J. "The Communist Theory of State," *American Slavic and East European Review,* XVIII, 1959.

MENDEL, ARTHUR P. *Dilemmas of Progress in Tsarist Russia.* Cambridge, Mass.: Harvard University Press, 1961.

ROSTOVTSEV, M. I. *Proletarian Culture.* London, 1919.

SCHAPIRO, LEONARD. *The Communist Party of the Soviet Union.* New York: Random House, 1959.

————. *The Origin of the Communist Autocracy: Political Opposition in the Soviet State, First Period, 1917–1922.* Cambridge, Mass.: Harvard University Press, 1955.

————. "Plechanov als Politiker," *Forschungen zur Osteuropäischen Geschichte,* VIII, 1962.

TREADGOLD, DONALD W. *Lenin and His Rivals.*

ULAM, ADAM B. "Stalin and the Theory of Totalitarianism," in ERNEST J. SIMMONS (ed.), *Continuity and Change in Russian and Soviet Thought.*

UTECHIN, S. V. "Bolsheviks and Their Allies After 1917," in SIDNEY HARCAVE (ed.), *Readings in Russian History.*

————. "Philosophy and Society: Alexander Bogdanov," in LEOPOLD LABEDZ (ed.), *Revisionism: Essays on the History of Marxist Ideas.*

VUCINICH, ALEXANDER. *The Soviet Academy of Sciences.* Stanford, Calif.: Stanford University Press, 1956.

WETTER, GUSTAV A. *Dialectical Materialism.* New York: Frederick A. Praeger; London: Routledge & Kegan Paul, 1958.

WILDMAN, A. K. "The Russian Intelligentsia of the 1890's," *The American Slavic and East European Review,* XIX, 1960.

ZENKOVSKY, V. V. *A History of Russian Philosophy.* Vol. II. New York: Columbia University Press, 1953.

Chapter 12: Communism

Sources

BADAYEV, A. E. *The Bolsheviks in the Tsarist Duma.* New York, 1928.

BUNYAN, JAMES. *Intervention, Civil War and Communism in Russia, April–December, 1918: Documents and Materials.*

————, and FISHER, HAROLD H. (eds.). *The Bolshevik Revolution, 1917–1918.*

BUKHARIN, N. I. *Historical Materialism.* London: Allen & Unwin, 1926.

————. "Imperialism and Communism," *Foreign Affairs,* XIV, July, 1936.

————, and PREOBRAZHENSKY, EVGENI A. *The ABC of Communism.* Translated by EDEN and CEDAR PAUL. London: The Communist Party of Great Britain, 1922.

GOLDER, F. A. (ed.). *Documents of Russian History, 1914–1917.*

HAZARD, JOHN (ed.). *Soviet Legal Philosophy.* Cambridge, Mass.: Harvard University Press, 1961.

————, and SHAPIRO, I. *The Soviet Legal System: Post-Stalin Documentation and Historical Commentary.* Dobbs Ferry, N.Y.: Oceana Publications, 1962.

Khrushchev on Culture. (*Encounter* pamphlet, No. 9.) London, 1963.

KHRUSHCHEV, NIKITA S. "On Peaceful Coexistence," in PHILIP E. MOSELY (ed.), *The Soviet Union, 1922–1962. A Foreign Affairs Reader.* New York and London: Frederick A. Praeger, 1963.

LENIN, V. I. *Collected Works.* 14 vols. Moscow and London, 1960–62.

————. *Selected Works.* 12 vols.

————. *V. I. Lenin's "What Is To Be Done?"* Edited, with an Introduction, by S. V. UTECHIN. Oxford: The Clarendon Press, 1963.

MCNEAL, ROBERT H. (ed.). *The Russian Revolution: Why Did the Bolsheviks Win?* New York: Rinehart & Company, 1959.

PONOMAREV, B., *et al.* (eds.). *The History of the CPSU.* Moscow, 1961.

RITVO, HERBERT. "Twenty-First Party Congress," *The American Slavic and East European Review,* XX, 1961 (Part 1), and *Slavic Review,* XX, 1961 (Part 2).

SCHAPIRO, LEONARD (ed.). *The U.S.S.R. and the Future: An Analysis of the New Program of the CPSU.* New York and London: Frederick A. Praeger, 1963.

SCHWARTZ, HARRY (ed.). *Russia Enters the 1960's.* Philadelphia: J. B. Lippincott Company, 1962.

STALIN, JOSEPH. *Economic Problems of Socialism in the USSR.* New York: International Publishers, 1952.

————. *Foundations of Leninism.* New York, 1939.

————. *Problems of Leninism.* New York: International Publishers, 1928.

TROTSKY, LEON. *The Defence of Terrorism.* 1921.

————. *Draft Programme of the Communist International.* New York: Pioneer Publishers, 1929.

————. *The History of the Russian Revolution.* 3 vols. Translated by MAX EASTMAN. New York: Simon & Schuster, 1936.

————. *Literature and Revolution.* New York: Russell & Russell, 1925.

————. *My Life.* New York: Charles Scribner's Sons, 1930.

————. "Nationalism and Economic Life," *Foreign Affairs,* XII, April, 1934.

————. *Our Revolution.* 1918.

————. *The Revolution Betrayed.* New York: Pioneer Publishers, 1937.

————. *Stalin.* Translated and edited by CHARLES MALAMUTH. New York: Harper & Brothers, 1946.

————. *The Stalin School of Falsification.* Translated by JOHN G. WRIGHT. New York: Pioneer Publishers, 1937.

————. *Trotsky's Diary in Exile: 1935.* Translated by E. ZARUDNAYA. Cambridge, Mass.: Harvard University Press, 1958.

VYSHINSKY, ANDREI Y. *The Law of the Soviet State.* Translated by HUGH W. BABB. New York: The Macmillan Company, 1948.

Studies

ANWEILER, O. *Die Rätebewegung in Russland, 1905–1921.*

ARMSTRONG, JOHN A. *Ideology, Politics, and Government in the Soviet Union: An Introduction.* New York: Frederick A. Praeger, 1962.

————. *The Politics of Totalitarianism: The Communist Party of the Soviet Union from 1934 to the Present.* New York: Random House, 1961.

ASPATURIAN, V. V. *The Union Republics in Soviet Diplomacy: A Study of Soviet Federalism in the Service of Soviet Foreign Policy.* Geneva and Paris, 1960.

BARGHOORN, FREDERICK C. *Soviet Russian Nationalism.* London and New York: Oxford University Press, 1956.

BARTON, PAUL. *L'institution Concentrationnaire en Russie.* Paris: Librairie Plon, 1959.

BASILY, NIKOLAI DE (ed.). *Russia Under Soviet Rule.* London, 1938.

BATSELL, WALTER RUSSELL. *Soviet Rule in Russia.* New York: The Macmillan Company, 1929.

BAUER, RAYMOND A., INKELES, ALEX, and KLUCKHOHN, CLYDE. *How the Soviet System Works: Cultural, Psychological, and Social Themes.* Cambridge, Mass.: Harvard University Press, 1959.

BERGAMINI, J. D. "Stalin and the Collective Farm," in ERNEST J. SIMMONS (ed.), *Continuity and Change in Russian and Soviet Thought.*

BRODERSEN, A. "New Trends in Soviet Social Theory," *The American Slavic and East European Review,* XVII, 1958.

BRUMBERG, ABRAHAM (ed.). *Russia Under Khrushchev.* New York: Frederick A. Praeger; London: Methuen & Co., 1962.

BRZEZINSKI, ZBIGNIEW K. *The Permanent Purge: Politics in Soviet Totalitarianism.* Cambridge, Mass.: Harvard University Press, 1956.

CARR, EDWARD H. *A History of Soviet Russia.* New York: The Macmillan Company, 1951–60.

CONQUEST, ROBERT. *Common Sense About Russia.* New York: The Macmillan Company; London: Victor Gollancz, 1960.

————. *Power and Policy in the U.S.S.R.* New York: St Martin's Press; London: Macmillan & Co., 1961.

CRANKSHAW, EDWARD. *Khrushchev's Russia.* London: Penguin Books, 1959; Gloucester, Mass.: Peter Smith, 1960.

————. *Russia Without Stalin: The Emerging Pattern.* New York: The Viking Press; London: Michael Joseph, 1956.

DANIELS, ROBERT V. *The Conscience of the Revolution: Communist Opposition in Soviet Russia.* Cambridge, Mass.: Harvard University Press, 1960.

————. "Intellectuals and the Russian Revolution," *The American Slavic and East European Review,* XX, 1961.

————. "Lenin and the Russian Revolutionary Tradition," in H. McLEAN (ed.), *Russian Thought and Politics.* The Hague, 1957.

DEUTSCHER, ISAAC. *Prophet Armed: Trotsky, 1879–1921.* London and New York: Oxford University Press, 1954.

———. *Prophet Unarmed: Trotsky, 1921–1929.* London and New York: Oxford University Press, 1959.

———. *Stalin: A Political Biography.* London and New York: Oxford University Press, 1949.

ELLISON, H. J. "The Decision to Collectivize Agriculture," *The American Slavic and East European Review,* XX, 1961.

ERICKSON, JOHN. *The Soviet High Command.* New York: St Martin's Press, 1962.

ERLICH, ALEXANDER. *The Soviet Industrialization Debate, 1924–1928.* Cambridge, Mass.: Harvard University Press, 1960.

———. "Stalin's Views on Soviet Economic Development," in ERNEST J. SIMMONS (ed.), *Continuity and Change in Russian and Soviet Thought.*

FAINSOD, MERLE. *How Russia Is Ruled.* Cambridge, Mass.: Harvard University Press, 1953; rev. ed., 1963.

FOOTMAN, DAVID. *Civil War in Russia.*

FRIEDBERG, MAURICE. "Socialist Realism: Twenty-Five Years Later," *The American Slavic and East European Review,* XIX, 1960.

GEYER, D. *Lenin in der russischen Sozialdemokratie: Die Arbeiterbewegung im Zarenreich als Organisationsproblem der revolutionären Intelligenz, 1890–1903.* Cologne, 1962.

GINSBURGS, GEORGE. "Neutrality and Neutralism and the Tactics of Soviet Diplomacy," *The American Slavic and East European Review,* XIX, 1960.

GRANICK, DAVID. *The Red Executive: A Study of the Organization Man in Russian Industry.*

GSOVSKI, VLADIMIR. *Soviet Civil Law.* 2 vols. Ann Arbor, Mich.: The University of Michigan Press, 1948.

———, and GRZYBOWSKI, KAZIMIERZ (eds). *Government, Law, and Courts in the Soviet Union and Eastern Europe.* 2 vols. New York: Frederick A. Praeger; London: Stevens & Sons, 1959.

HAIMSON, L. H. *The Russian Marxists and the Origins of Bolshevism.* Cambridge, Mass.: Harvard University Press, 1955.

HALPERIN, E. "The Metamorphosis of the New Class," *Problems of Communism,* VIII, 1959.

HAMMOND, T. T. *Lenin on Trade Unions and Revolution, 1893–1917.* New York: Columbia University Press, 1957.

———. "Leninist Authoritarianism Before the Revolution," in ERNEST J. SIMMONS (ed.), *Continuity and Change in Russian and Soviet Thought.*

HAZARD, JOHN. *The Soviet System of Government.* Rev. ed. Chicago: The University of Chicago Press, 1960.

HEITMAN, SIDNEY. *An Annotated Bibliography of N. I. Bukharin's Published Works.* Fort Collins, Colo., 1958.

————. "Between Lenin and Stalin: N. Bukharin," in Leopold Labedz (ed.), *Revisionism: Essays on the History of Marxist Ideas.*

Hunt, Robert N. Carew. *A Guide to Communist Jargon.* New York: The Macmillan Company; London: Geoffrey Bles, 1957.

————. *The Theory and Practice of Communism.* New York: The Macmillan Company, 1956.

Inkeles, Alex. *Public Opinion in Soviet Russia.* Cambridge, Mass.: Harvard University Press, 1950.

————, and Bauer, Raymond A. *The Soviet Citizen: Daily Life in a Totalitarian Society.* Cambridge, Mass.: Harvard University Press; London: Oxford University Press, 1959.

————, and Geiger, Kent. *Soviet Society: A Book of Readings.* Boston: Houghton Mifflin Co., 1961.

Karpovich, Michael. "The Historical Background of Soviet Thought Control," in Waldemar Gurian (ed.), *The Soviet Union: Background Ideology, Reality.*

Kellen, Konrad. *Khrushchev: A Political Portrait.* New York: Frederick A. Praeger; London: Thames and Hudson, 1961.

Kelsen, Hans. *The Communist Theory of Law.* New York: Frederick A. Praeger; London: Stevens & Sons, 1955.

Kolarz, Walter. *Russia and Her Colonies.*

Kucherov, S. "The Communist Party vs. the Peasantry in the Soviet Union," *Political Science Quarterly,* June 1952.

————. "The Future of the Soviet Collective Farm," *The American Slavic and East European Review,* XIX, 1960.

Labedz, Leopold. "The New Soviet Intelligentsia," in Sidney Harcave (ed.), *Readings in Russian History.*

Laird, Roy D. *Collective Farming in Russia: A Political Study of Soviet Kolkhozy.* Lawrence, Kan.: University of Kansas Press, 1958.

Laqueur, Walter A., and Lichtheim, George (eds.). *The Soviet Cultural Scene, 1956–1957.* New York: Frederick A. Praeger; London: Stevens & Sons, 1958.

Leonhard, Wolfgang. *The Kremlin Since Stalin.* New York: Frederick A. Praeger; London: Oxford University Press, 1962.

Lowenthal, Richard. "Totalitarianism Reconsidered," *Commentary,* June, 1960.

Mathewson, R. W. *The Positive Hero in Russian Literature.*

Medalic, R. J. "The Communist Theory of State," *American Slavic and East European Review,* XVIII, 1959.

Mehnert, Klaus. *Soviet Man and His World.* New York: Frederick A. Praeger; London: Weidenfeld & Nicolson, 1962.

————. *Stalin Versus Marx.* London: Allen & Unwin, 1952.

Meyer, Alfred G. *Leninism.* New York: Frederick A. Praeger, 1962.

Moore, Barrington. *Soviet Politics: The Dilemma of Power.* Cambridge, Mass.: Harvard University Press, 1950.

Mosely, Philip E. (ed.). *The Soviet Union, 1922–1962: A Foreign Affairs Reader.* New York and London: Frederick A. Praeger, 1963.

Nove, Alec. *The Soviet Economy: An Introduction.* New York: Frederick A. Praeger; London: Allen & Unwin, 1961.

———. "Was Stalin Really Necessary?" *Encounter,* April, 1962.

Page, Stanley W. *Lenin and the World Revolution.* New York: New York University Press, 1959.

Pistrak, Lazar. *The Grand Tactician: Khrushchev's Rise to Power.* New York: Frederick A. Praeger; London: Thames and Hudson, 1961.

Rush, Myron. *The Rise of Khrushchev.* Washington, D.C.: Public Affairs Press, 1958.

Russell, Bertrand. *The Practice and Theory of Bolshevism.* London, 1920.

Schapiro, Leonard. *The Communist Party of the Soviet Union.* New York: Random House, 1959.

———. "Has Russia Changed?" *Foreign Affairs,* April, 1960.

———. "Judicial Practice and Legal Reform," *Soviet Survey,* No. 29, 1959.

———. *The Origin of the Communist Autocracy: Political Opposition in the Soviet State, First Period, 1917–1922.* Cambridge, Mass.: Harvard University Press, 1955.

———, and Utechin, S. V. (eds.). "Soviet Government Today," *Political Quarterly,* XXXII, 1961.

Schlesinger, Rudolf. *Soviet Legal Theory: Its Social Background and Development.* London and New York: Oxford University Press, 1945.

Schurer, Heinz. "The Permanent Revolution: Lev Trotsky," in Leopold Labedz (ed.), *Revisionism: Essays on the History of Marxist Ideas.*

Scott, Derek J. *Russian Political Institutions.* 2d ed. New York: Frederick A. Praeger; London: Allen & Unwin, 1961.

Selznick, Philip. *The Organizational Weapon.* Chicago: The Free Press of Glencoe, 1959.

Shinn, W. T., Jr. "The Law of the Russian Peasant Household," *Slavic Review,* XX, 1961.

Shteppa, Konstantin F. *Russian Historians and the Soviet State.* New Brunswick, N.J.: Rutgers University Press, 1962.

Shub, David A. *Lenin: A Biography.* Garden City, N.Y.: Doubleday and Company, 1949.

Shulman, Marshall D. *Stalin's Foreign Policy Reappraised.* Cambridge, Mass.: Harvard University Press, 1963.

Somerville, J. *Soviet Philosophy: A Study of Theory and Practice.* New York, 1946.

Souvarine, Boris. *Stalin: A Critical Survey of Bolshevism.* New York: Longmans, Green & Co., 1939.

Swayze, Harold. *Political Control of Literature in the USSR, 1946–1959.* Cambridge, Mass.: Harvard University Press, 1962.

Timasheff, Nicholas S. *The Great Retreat: The Growth and Decline of Communism in Russia.* New York: E. P. Dutton & Company, 1946.

TOWSTER, JULIAN. *Political Power in the USSR, 1917–1947.* London and New York: Oxford University Press, 1948.

————. "Vyshinsky's Concept of Collectivity," in ERNEST J. SIMMONS (ed.), *Continuity and Change in Russian and Soviet Thought.*

TREADGOLD, DONALD W. *Lenin and His Rivals.*

ULAM, ADAM B. *"Stalin and the Theory of Totalitarianism,"* in ERNEST J. SIMMONS (ed.), *Continuity and Change in Russian and Soviet Thought.*

————. *The Unfinished Revolution: An Essay on the Sources of Influence of Marxism and Communism.* New York: Random House, 1960.

UTECHIN, S. V. "Bolsheviks and Their Allies After 1917," in SIDNEY HARCAVE (ed.), *Readings in Russian History.*

————. "New Myths for Old," *Twentieth Century,* January, 1954.

————. Social Stratification and Social Mobility in the U.S.S.R.," in *Transactions of the Second World Congress of Sociology.* Vol. II. London, 1954.

UTIS, O. "Generalissimo Stalin and the Art of Government," *Foreign Affairs,* January, 1952.

WILES, P. J. D. *The Political Economy of Communism.* Cambridge, Mass.: Harvard University Press, 1962.

WILSON, EDMUND. *To the Finland Station: A Study in the Writing and Acting of History.* Garden City, N.Y.: Doubleday and Company, 1953.

WOLFE, BERTRAM D. *Khrushchev and Stalin's Ghost.* New York: Frederick A. Praeger, 1957.

————. "Leon Trotsky as Historian," *Slavic Review,* XX, 1961.

Chapter 13: Post-1917 Reformist Trends
Sources

ABRAMOV, FYODOR. *One Day in the "New Life."* Translated by DAVID FLOYD, with an Introduction by MAX HAYWARD. New York: Frederick A. Praeger; London: Flegon Press, 1963. (Published in England under the title *The Dodgers.*)

BERDYAEV, NICHOLAS. *Christianity and Class War.* 1933.

————. *The Destiny of Man.* Napierville, Ill.: Alec R. Allenson, 1959.

————. *Dostoevsky.* Cleveland and New York: Meridian Books.

————. *The End of Our Time.* 1932.

————. *Freedom and Spirit.* 2 vols. 1935.

————. *The Meaning of History.* Cleveland and New York: Meridian Books.

————. *The Origin of Russian Communism.* Napierville, Ill.: Alec R. Allenson, 1955.

————. *The Russian Idea.* New York: The Macmillan Company, 1947.

————. *Slavery and Freedom.* Napierville, Ill.: Alec R. Allenson, 1944.

————. *Solitude and Society.* Napierville, Ill.: Alec R. Allenson, 1947.

————. *Towards a New Epoch.* 1949.

BLAKE, PATRICIA, and HAYWARD, MAX (eds.). "New Voices in Russian Writing: An Anthology," *Encounter,* No. 115, 1963.

CONQUEST, ROBERT (ed.). *Back to Life.* London: Hutchinson & Co., 1958.

————. *The Pasternak Affair: Courage of Genius.* Philadelphia: J. B. Lippincott Company, 1962.

DUDINTSEV, VLADIMIR. *Not by Bread Alone.* Translated by E. BONE. New York: E. P. Dutton & Company, 1957.

————. "A New Year's Fable," translated by MAX HAYWARD, *Encounter,* June, 1960.

EHRENBURG, ILYA. *The Thaw.* Translated by MANYA HARARI. London: Collins & Harvill, 1955.

KOHN, HANS (ed.). *The Mind of Modern Russia: Historical and Political Thought of Russia's Great Age.* (Chap. xiii, "Communism and Russian History: Berdyaev and Fedotov.")

McLEAN, HUGH, and VICKERY, WALTER N. (eds. and trans.). *The Year of Protest, 1956: An Anthology of Soviet Literary Materials.* New York: Vintage Books, 1961.

MIRSKY, D. S. "The Eurasian Movement," *Slavonic Review,* December, 1927.

NEKRASOV, VICTOR. *Kira Georgievna.* Translated by WALTER N. VICKERY. New York: Pantheon Books, 1962.

PASTERNAK, BORIS. *Doctor Zhivago.* Translated by MAX HAYWARD and MANYA HARARI. New York: Pantheon Books, 1958.

————. *An Essay in Autobiography.* Translated by MANYA HARARI, with an Introduction by EDWARD CRANKSHAW. London: Collins and Harvill, 1959.

POLYAKOV, V. "The Story of a Story, or Fireman Prokhorchuk," in MAX HAYWARD and PATRICIA BLAKE (eds.), *Dissonant Voices.* New York: Pantheon Books, 1963.

SOLZHENITSYN, ALEXANDER. *One Day in the Life of Ivan Denisovich.* Translated by MAX HAYWARD and RONALD HINGLEY, with an Introduction by MAX HAYWARD and LEOPOLD LABEDZ. New York and London: Frederick A. Praeger, 1963.

STILLMAN, EDMUND (ed.). *Bitter Harvest: The Intellectual Revolt behind the Iron Curtain.* New York: Frederick A. Praeger; London: Thames and Hudson, 1959.

YASHIN, ALEXANDER. "The Levers," in EDMUND STILLMAN (ed.), *Bitter Harvest: The Intellectual Revolt behind the Iron Curtain.*

YEVTUSHENKO, YEVGENY. *A Precocious Autobiography.* Translated by ANDREW MacANDREW. New York: E. P. Dutton & Company; London: Collins and Harvill, 1963.

————. *Selected Poems.* Translated and with an Introduction by ROBIN MILNER-GULLAND and PETER LEVI. London and New York, 1962.

Studies

ALEXANDROVA, VERA. "Evgeny Evtushenko," *Russian Review*, XXI, 1962.

BARGHOORN, FREDERICK C. *Soviet Russian Nationalism*. London and New York: Oxford University Press, 1956.

CLARKE, O. F. *Introduction to Berdyaev*. London: Geoffrey Bles, 1950.

FUTRELL, MICHAEL. "Evgeny Evtushenko," *Soviet Survey*, No. 25, 1958.

GIBIAN, GEORGE. *Interval of Freedom: Soviet Literature During the Thaw, 1954–1957*. Minneapolis: The University of Minnesota Press, 1960.

HAYWARD, MAX. "*Doctor Zhivago* and the Soviet Intelligentsia," *Soviet Survey*, April–June, 1958.

———."Soviet Literature in the Doldrums," *Problems of Communism*, VIII, 1959.

———, and BLAKE, PATRICIA. "Soviet Literature, 1917–1961," in *Dissonant Voices*.

HECKER, J. F. *Moscow Dialogues.*

HINGLEY, RONALD. "Leonid Leonov," *Soviet Survey*, No. 25, 1958.

———. "The Soviet Writers' Congress," *ibid.*, No. 29, 1959.

ISHBOLDIN, B. "The Eurasian Movement," *Russian Review*, V, 1946.

LAMPERT, E. *Nicholas Berdyaev and the New Middle Ages*. 1945.

LASERSON, MAX M. *Russia and the Western World: The Place of the Soviet Union in the Comity of Nations.*

LOWRIE, DONALD A. *Rebellious Prophet: A Life of Nicholai Berdyaev*. New York: Harper and Brothers, 1960.

MAZOUR, ANATOLE G. *Modern Russian Historiography.*

MEHNERT, KLAUS. *Stalin Versus Marx.*

MILYUKOV, P. "Eurasianism and Europeanism in Russian History," in SIDNEY HARCAVE (ed.), *Readings in Russian History*. Vol. I.

POLTORATZKY, N. P. "The Russian Idea of Berdyaev," *Russian Review*, XXI, 1962.

SCRIVEN, T. "The 'Literary Opposition,' " *Problems of Communism*, VII, 1958.

SIMMONS, ERNEST J. (ed.). *Russian Fiction and Soviet Ideology*. New York: Columbia University Press, 1958.

"Soviet Literature: The Conspiracy of Silence," *Soviet Survey*, No. 19, 1957.

UTECHIN, S. V. "Bolsheviks and Their Allies After 1917," in SIDNEY HARCAVE (ed.), *Readings in Russian History*.

———. "Patterns of Nonconformity," *Problems of Communism*, VI, 1957.

Chapter 14: Revolutionary Anti-Communism
Sources

BUNYAN, JAMES. *Intervention, Civil War and Communism in Russia, April–December, 1918.*

————, and FISHER, HAROLD H. *The Bolshevik Revolution, 1917–1918.*

Hungary and Russia (The Situation in Russia on the Eve of the Second Anniversary of the Hungarian Revolution as Viewed by the NTS). 1958.

KHOKHLOV, NIKOLAI H. *In the Name of Conscience.* New York: David MacKay Company, 1959.

MCNEAL, ROBERT H. (ed.). *The Russian Revolution: Why Did the Bolsheviks Win?*

NTS Union of Russian Solidarists. Frankfurt/Main, 1961.

ROEDER, BERNHARD. *Katorga: An Aspect of Modern Slavery.* London, 1958. (Originally published in German in 1956.)

Towards Freedom. Proceedings of the Eighth Annual Conference Organized by the Russian Anti-Communist Weekly "Possev." Frankfurt/Main, 1956.

TRUSHNOVICH, Y. A. *The Peaceful Offensive of Freedom and the Free World Public.* Frankfurt/Main, 1960.

VALERIY, I. *The Bluebottle.* London: Collins and Harvill, 1962.

VARNECK, ELENA, and FISHER, HAROLD H. *The Testimony of Kolchak and Other Siberian Materials.* Stanford, Calif.: University of Stanford Press, 1935.

YESENIN-VOLPIN, ALEKSANDR SERGEYEVICH. *A Leaf of Spring.* Translated by GEORGE REAVEY. New York: Frederick A. Praeger; London: Thames and Hudson, 1961.

Studies

CHAMBERLIN, WILLIAM H. *The Russian Revolution, 1917–1924.* 2d ed. Vol. II. New York: The Macmillan Company, 1954.

DALLIN, ALEXANDER. "From the Gallery of Wartime Dissaffection," *Russian Review,* XXI, 1962.

————. *German Rule in Russia, 1941–1945.* New York: St Martin's Press, 1957.

ERLICH, V. "A Testimony and a Challenge: Pasternak's *Doctor Zhivago,*" *Problems of Communism,* November–December, 1958.

FISCHER, GEORGE (ed.). *Russian Emigré Politics.* New York, 1951.

————. *Soviet Opposition to Stalin: A Case Study in World War II.* Cambridge, Mass.: Harvard University Press, 1952.

FOOTMAN, DAVID. *Civil War in Russia.*

PIPES, RICHARD. *The Formation of the Soviet Union: Communism and Nationalism, 1917–1923.* Cambridge, Mass.: Harvard University Press, 1954.

SACK, A. J. *The Birth of Russian Democracy.* New York, 1918.

SCHAPIRO, LEONARD. *The Origin of the Communist Autocracy.* Cambridge, Mass.: Harvard University Press, 1955.

Name Index

Charles I, of England, 65
Chekhov, Anton, 192
Chelintsev, A. N., 138, 139
Chernov, V. M., 141–43, 145
Chernyshevsky, N. G., 113, 122–24, 126, 129, 181, 192, 214, 217
Chicherin, B. N., 104, 105–7, 108, 187, 188
Christ. *See* Jesus Christ
Chuprov, A. I., 110
Cicero, 8, 32, 56, 259
Comte, Auguste, 132, 190
Constant, Benjamin, 107
Constantine the Great, 9, 35
Cromwell, Oliver, 22

Dan, F. I., 203–4
Daniel, Metropolitan, 24, 25
Danilevsky, N. Ya., 86–87, 165, 256, 257
Darwin, Charles, 132
Desnitsky, S. E., 53–56, 63, 93, 148
Dostoevsky, F. M., 87–90, 113, 116, 119, 164, 165, 167, 170, 177, 178, 191, 192, 195, 266, 275
Dragomanov, M. P., 110, 149–51, 152
Dunning, William A., xiii
Dzhugashvili. *See* Stalin, I. V.

Ehrenburg, Il'ya, 254, 255
Elizabeth I, of England, 27
Engels, Friedrich, 198, 211, 217, 250
Esenin, S. A., 146, 277
Evtushenko, Evgeny, 266, 276

Fëdorov, N. F., 164, 177–79, 194, 211, 241
Ferguson, Adam, 56
Feuerbach, Ludwig, 114, 116, 122, 195
Fonvizin, D. I., 43, 66–67
Footman, D. J., 83
Fourier, Charles, 114, 158
Frank, S. L., 262

Galanskov, Yu., 276
Gandhi, Mahatma, 181
Gapon, G. A., 188
Genghis Khan, 151
Gennadius, Archbishop, 22
George, Henry, 180, 187

Gershenzon, M. O., 194
Gide, Charles, 187
Gierke, Otto von, xiii, xiv
Gogol', N. V., 90, 116, 192
Golitsyn, Prince D. M., 46–48, 53, 271
Gol'tsev, V. A., 110
Gorky, Maxim, 179, 213
Gradovsky, A. D., 104, 107–8
Granovsky, T. N., 104, 105, 118
Grekov, B. D., 255
Grigor'ev, A. A., 87–88, 119
Grinevetsky, V. I., 184, 185
Grotius, Hugo, 47, 48, 54, 56
Guchkov, A. I., 109, 111
Guins, G. C., 274

Harari, Manya, 268
Hayward, Max, 268
Hegel, Georg, 84, 190
Heine, Heinrich, 113
Helvetius, C. A., 61, 64
Herder, J. G., 65, 84
Herzen, A. I., 75, 76, 116–19, 120, 123, 124, 128, 129, 131, 150, 190, 192
Hilarion, Metropolitan, 8, 9, 10, 11, 17, 20, 23, 68, 84
Hilferding, Rudolf, 220
Hitler, Adolf, 235, 238, 273
Hobbes, Thomas, 54
Hobson, John, 220
Hume, David, 54, 56

Igor, Prince, 3, 5
Il'ichëv, L. S., 250
Il'in, I. A., 272–74
Ivan III, 19, 20, 21, 22, 26, 27, 28
Ivan IV (the Terrible), 21, 24, 27, 28, 29, 31, 32, 68
Ivanov-Razumnik, R. V., 146

Japhet, 171
Jesus Christ, 6, 8, 35, 49, 89, 167, 168, 175, 180, 267
Joseph of Volok, 22, 23, 24, 25, 27, 32, 66, 68, 73, 74
Justinian, Emperor, 35

Kablits, I. I., 134–35, 181, 201
Kamenev, L. B., 234

Tatishchev, V. N., 43, 48–51, 53
Theodosius, the "Squint," 114
Thomas à Kempis, 95
Tidmarsh, K., 99
Tikhomirov, L. A., 98–100, 167, 169
Tito, Josîp, 239
Tkachëv, P. N., 124–27, 130–31, 150,
    157, 197, 214, 217, 221
Tolstoy, Count A. N., 254, 255
Tolstoy, Count L. N., 164, 178, 180–
    81, 192, 267
Tomasius, C., 47
Totomiants, V. F., 187
Tribonian, 56
Trotsky, Leon, 179, 226–33, 234, 243,
    245
Trubetskoy, Prince N. S., 6, 256–57
Tsederbaum. See Martov, Yu. O.
Turgenev, Ivan, 192
Turgenev, N. I., 117
Tvardovsky, A. T., 265
Tyutchev, Fëdor, 86

Ulyanov. See Lenin, V. I.
Ustryalov, N. V., 253–54
Uvarov, S. S., 72–73, 75

Vladimir Monomakh, 8, 10, 11, 20,
    21, 23

Vlasov, General A. A., 272
Vol'sky, S., 213
Vorontsov, V. P., 136, 138, 197
Voznesensky, A. A., 266
Vyshinsky, A. Y., 231, 239
Vyshnegradsky, I. A., 100

Webb, Beatrice, 206
Webb, Sidney, 206
William of Ockham, 25
Witte, Count S. Yu., 100–102, 109
Wladyslaw, Grand Prince of Poland,
    33
Wrangel, General P. N., 269

Yadrintsev, N. M., 149, 151–52
Yanzhul, I. I., 187, 188
Yesenin-Volpin, A. S., 276–78
Yezhov, N. I., 267

Zaichnevsky, P. G., 126
Zaslavsky, E. O., 160
Zenkovsky, V. V., 105
Zhdanov, A. A., 239, 250, 255
Zhukov, G. K., 243
Zinoviev, G. Y., 230, 231, 234
Zosimas, Metropolitan, 20
Zubatov, S. V., 187–88

Subject Index

Absolutism, 33, 47–48, 51, 81, 84, 93, 101, 104, 106, 142, 175, 193, 196, 199, 259; enlightened, 37–43, 68, 71, 106

Administration, 28–30, 37, 40–41, 45–48, 50, 56, 80, 94, 96, 108, 112, 143, 148, 207, 223–25, 236–37, 244, 251

Agitation, 121, 125, 142, 153, 156, 188, 201, 214, 216, 245. *See also* Propaganda

Agriculture, 54, 66, 100, 103, 113, 137–39, 141–42, 156, 175, 183, 195, 226, 232, 235, 236, 244, 251; collectivization of, 139, 145, 235–37, 244, 246, 251, 267. *See also* Peasantry; Revolution

All-Russian Muslim Union, 151

All-Russian Peasants' Union, 144

America, xii, 59, 63, 97–98, 100, 141, 180–81, 187, 203–4, 220, 229, 239, 251, 274

Anarchism, 31, 42, 58, 112, 115, 125, 148, 150, 152–60, 162, 164, 180–81, 187, 192, 214, 263, 271, 276, 277; Communist, 157–59; individualist, 159. *See also* Bakuninism

Anarcho-syndicalism, 159–60

Anti-Communism, 138, 204–5, 250, 253, 269–78

Anti-Marxism, 138, 277

"Anti-Party group," 243, 248

Anti-Semitism. *See* Jews

Aristocracy, 41, 43–44, 47–49, 51–52, 60, 62, 66, 69, 88, 93, 95, 177, 180, 263. *See also* Nobility

Army, 16, 30, 37, 59, 63, 143, 179, 223; Red, 144, 227, 248, 254; Soviet, 238, 251; White, 269, 271

Asia, xii, 104, 152, 220, 227, 257, 261. *See also* Buddhism; China; Golden Horde; Islam; Mongols; Siberia

Assembly, 27, 53, 60, 74. *See also* Chamber; Citizens' assembly; Constituent Assembly; Council of the

Assembly (*Cont.*)
Land; Representative assembly; Soviets; State Duma

Assembly of Russian Workers, 188

Assimilation. *See* National minorities

Atheism, 71, 156, 193

Austria, 149–50, 153, 221, 229, 256

"Austro-Marxism," 150

Authoritarianism, 72, 131, 210, 212

Autocracy, 18–33, 39, 41, 43–44, 50–51, 57–59, 62, 65, 70–75, 92, 99, 101–2, 122, 150, 166, 168, 192, 199–200, 218, 220, 221, 241, 270

Autonomy: economic, 138, 142; individual, 24, 30, 105, 210; institutional, 107, 169, 189, 208; national-cultural, 94, 110, 150; regional, 15, 69, 148, 151–52

Bakuninism, 140, 153–57, 181, 196–97, 201

Balkans, xii, 10, 85, 149, 194, 223, 256, 272

Bell, The, 118, 120

Belorussia, 40, 188, 225

Berlin Congress of 1878, 165

Bernsteinism, 206–7

Black Hundred, 74, 193

"Black Repartition," 140, 157, 196, 197, 199, 201

Bloc of Rightists and Trotskyites, 231

"Bloody Sunday," 188

Bogdanovism, 207–13, 231, 237, 241, 255, 266

Bolshevism, 75, 111, 138, 144–45, 152, 159, 160, 162–63, 184–85, 190, 196–252 *passim*, 254–55, 261, 269–71, 274. *See also* Bureau of the Majority Committees; Communism; Communist Party

Bourgeoisie, 43, 53, 69, 96, 117, 125, 142, 155–56, 162, 165, 185, 199, 200, 206, 209, 211–12, 216–17, 221, 224, 226, 228–29, 238, 250, 255, 256, 264.